Making Electricity Resilient

Energy risk and security have become topical matters in Western and international policy discussions; ranging from international climate change mitigation to investment in energy infrastructures to support economic growth and more sustainable energy provisions. As such, ensuring the resilience of more sustainable energy infrastructures against disruptions has become a growing concern for high-level policy makers.

Drawing on interviews, participant observation, policy analysis, and survey research, this book unpacks the work of the authorities, electricity companies, and lay persons that keeps energy systems from failing and helps them to recover from disruptions if they occur. The book explores a number of important issues: the historical security policy of energy infrastructures; control rooms where electricity is traded and maintained in real time; and electricity consumers in their homes. Presenting case studies from Finland and Scandinavia, with comparisons to the United States, the United Kingdom, and the European Union at large, *Making Electricity Resilient* offers a detailed and innovative analysis of long-term priorities and short-term dynamics in energy risk and resilience.

This book will be of great interest to students and scholars of energy policy and security, and science and technology studies.

Antti Silvast is a Scottish ClimateXChange Research Fellow on European Energy Policy and Markets at the University of Edinburgh, UK.

Routledge Studies in Energy Policy

Our Energy Future
Socioeconomic implications and policy options for rural America
Edited by Don E. Albrecht

Energy Security and Natural Gas Markets in Europe
Lessons from the EU and the USA
Tim Boersma

International Energy Policy
The emerging contours
Edited by Lakshman Guruswamy

Climate Policy Integration into EU Energy Policy
Progress and prospects
Claire Dupont

Energy Security and Cooperation in Eurasia
Power, profits and politics
Ekaterina Svyatets

Sustainable Urban Energy Policy
Heat and the city
Edited by David Hawkey Janette Webb

Energy, Cities and Sustainability
An historical approach
Harry Margalit

Making Electricity Resilient
Risk and Security in a Liberalized Infrastructure
Antti Silvast

For further details please visit the series page on the Routledge website:
www.routledge.com/books/series/RSIEP/

Making Electricity Resilient

Risk and Security in a
Liberalized Infrastructure

Antti Silvast

First published 2017
by Routledge

2 Park Square, Milton Park, Abingdon, Oxfordshire OX14 4RN
52 Vanderbilt Avenue, New York, NY 10017

Routledge is an imprint of the Taylor & Francis Group, an informa business

First issued in paperback 2018

British Library Cataloguing-in-Publication Data
A catalogue record for this book is available from the British Library

Library of Congress Cataloging-in-Publication Data
Names: Silvast, Antti.
Title: Making electricity resilient : risk and security in a liberalized
   infrastructure / Antti Silvast.
Description: New York, NY : Routledge, 2017. | Includes bibliographical
   references.
Identifiers: LCCN 2016055023 | ISBN 9781138234840 (hb) | ISBN
   9781315306117 (ebook)
Subjects: LCSH: Electric power system stability. | Electric utilities–
   Economic aspects. | Infrastructure (Economics)
Classification: LCC TK1010 .S55 2017 | DDC 621.31—dc23
LC record available at https://lccn.loc.gov/2016055023

ISBN: 978-1-138-23484-0 (hbk)
ISBN: 978-0-367-17923-6 (pbk)

Typeset in Goudy
by Apex CoVantage, LLC

Contents

PART V
Conclusions 147

Figures

Tables

Acknowledgements

This book began as a doctoral dissertation for the University of Helsinki, Faculty of Social Sciences, sociology. The dissertation was formally supervised by a panel including Turo-Kimmo Lehtonen, Janne Hukkinen, Marja Häyrinen-Alestalo, Mika Pantzar, and Veli-Pekka Nurmi. I am grateful to all the panel members for their creative and critical discussions both as a panel and individually. The dissertation's three examiners – Robin Williams, Paul N. Edwards, and Jane Summerton – were particularly important for the development of this work. Each has helped advance the ideas behind this book considerably and I acknowledge their help with many thanks.

I started to update this book as a postdoctoral research associate in Princeton University's Global Systemic Risk Research Community, Princeton Institute for International and Regional Studies (PIIRS). These provided a lively academic community that motivated me and provided me with many relevant new directions in my work. I would especially like to thank Miguel A. Centeno and Thayer S. Patterson for their support and interest in my work and both of them for our many interesting discussions. I also would like to thank Rosemary Taylor and Magaly Sanchez from this period for our contacts. I finalized the manuscript while working in another fellowship for the University of Edinburgh, Science, Technology and Innovation Studies, funded by the Scottish ClimateXChange, and focused on European energy policy and markets. In Edinburgh, Robin Williams, Dominic Berry, James Mittra, Jake Ansell, Mark Winskel, Ronan Bolton, Steve Yearley, and Janette Webb have all discussed a number of interesting points that figure in this research and commented on my ideas or manuscript in great detail and I thank them for all their help.

The various people who have helped me with my research over the past years are too numerous to name here. However, I would particularly like to thank Nina Blom Andersen, Nikos Petropoulos, Stephen Collier, Sampsa Hyysalo, Salla Sariola, Mikko J. Virtanen, Mikko Jalas, Jenny Rinkinen, Vincent Ialenti, Onur Özgöde, Peter Lutz, Maarit Pedak, Salli Hakala, Veijo Kauppinen, and Björn Wallsten for their input and ongoing contact that have reshaped many ideas in this book.

From Routledge, Annabelle Harris prompted me to pursue this book and I thank her for our contacts, as well as Margaret Farrelly for seeing the book to its production in a timely fashion. Kerry Boettcher offered important help when managing the project in its copyediting. I also acknowledge with thanks the input of two anonymous referees who provided very helpful feedback to the book proposal and an earlier version of the manuscript.

Finally, I am deeply indebted to Molla Vanhatupa, Tiina Vanhatupa, Seija Silvast, Pekka Silvast, Anna Selin, and Arttu Silvast as well their families for all their support. Molla brightened each stage of writing this book.

In part the same empirical materials have appeared under a different argument in articles in the journal of the Finnish Society for the History of Technology, *Tekniikan Waiheita* (2014, Vol. 32, No. 1; and 2007, Vol. 25, No. 1); *Science & Technology Studies* (2014, Vol. 27, No. 2, with Mikko J. Virtanen); the Finnish journal of sociology, *Sosiologia* (2013, Vol. 50, No. 4, with Mikko J. Virtanen); *STS Encounters* (2011, Vol. 4, No. 2); and *Tiede & Edistys* (Science & Progress) (2008, Vol. 39, No. 1, with Mikko J. Virtanen).

In Edinburgh, November 2016
Antti Silvast

Part I

Overview

1 Infrastructure, risk, and resilience

System transition and infrastructure fragilities

Large infrastructures – including electricity supply, heating, transportation, computer networks, and telecommunications – are widely believed to be vital and critical for the functioning of societies. This means that infrastructures ensure, for the most part, smoothly functioning political decision-making at all levels, including military defence, products and services, security, health, the movement of people, a functioning economy, and the welfare of populations (Graham & Marvin 2001; Collier & Lakoff 2008; Larkin 2013). Historical scholarship has highlighted the societal embeddedness of these infrastructure networks, coupling technologies, organizations, legislation, research efforts, and raw resources within the same structure (Hughes 1983; van der Vleuten 2004). Framed as an infrastructure, energy, too, can be characterized through its indispensability for contemporary forms of life. Not merely closed supplies or systems that support society, infrastructures rather sit at the centre of collective life (Edwards 2003, 2010).

These considerations in their turn almost immediately suggest issues about risk. On the one hand, large infrastructures are used to mitigate risks, increase collective security, and create conditions for economic activities. Hence, when infrastructures fail, this is on the other hand a risk to the economy, government, and the population – as major electric power failures and their aftermath, such as India in 2012, Continental Europe in 2006, and North America in 2003, have sharply demonstrated.

In this book, I contribute to knowledge about electricity infrastructures and interruptions by utilizing and contributing to social science perspectives on infrastructures and systems, risk, and resilience. The key overarching question is: *how are interruptions to the electricity infrastructure anticipated, how are they managed as risks, and how do people and organizations bounce back from these interruptions?* A growing community of social scientists is involved in the study of complex and socio-technical issues associated with energy systems. However, this discussion has tended to centre analyses on particular actors, settings, and viewpoints, such as technology policies, energy experts, or energy users only (see Silvast, Hänninen & Hyysalo 2013).

In contrast to the single-site studies, this book explores a number of special sites within the energy supply chain. The first case examines how national security experts mitigate electricity interruptions as risks to the population, government, and economy. In the second case, I turn to the management of interruptions as risks in the open electric power markets – a topical focus considering that energy infrastructures have been liberalized and opened to market competition all over the world for the past number of decades. The third case moves to energy consumers in their homes, which directly relates to the vitality of electricity networks for sustaining everyday life. This last empirical part of the book explores how lay people reconstruct electric power interruptions and their effects as risks in households. The impact of the detailed multi-sited work in this book is multi-faceted: it recognizes long-term priorities and short-term dynamics in energy risk and also systematically interrelates policy, maintenance, and end-use perspectives on these risks.

The book sits among growing concerns in not only academic research, but also industry reports, policy papers, public statements, and other grey literature on electricity interruptions, risks, and resilience. Outages of electric power are now raised as a national security problem by a large number of governments, including the United States and more than 20 other advanced industrial countries and developing states such as Finland, the United Kingdom, Australia, Canada, Germany, New Zealand, Switzerland, Indonesia, and India (Brunner & Suter 2009, 530–531). For the US Department of Homeland Security (2013), for example, resilience is one in five core national priorities and the protection of US critical infrastructures, including energy, a major concern in that context (Sims 2011). In the United Kingdom, the risk of looming winter power blackouts makes national news (e.g. Davies 2016a) and the worry on national electricity capacity has reshaped the energy infrastructure's components: diesel power firms have established specific diesel farms to stay on standby for situations where energy supplies may fall short (Davies 2016b). The European Commission (2004, 2005) and the European Council (2008), too, consider energy supply to be, along with transport, one of the two most important critical infrastructures in Europe. Recently, the European Commission (2015) summarized this concern in its strategy for an European-wide integrated energy system that is to withstand energy supply disruptions outwith Europe; that is, a "Resilient Energy Union with a Forward-Looking Climate Change Policy".

Meanwhile, energy suppliers and their customers are also to be prepared for the power failing. The northeast US electricity grid operator National Grid US (2016), among many power companies, has issued guidelines on electric outage preparation and safety to its customers. Concentrating on large storms, its instructions span preparedness activities (such as stockpiling emergency kits), proactive crisis management (such as having a standby generator), and practices after the power comes back on (such as replacement and repair). In industrial policy, the European electricity company association EURELECTRIC (2014) seeks new ways to combine functioning energy markets with security of electricity supply, amid growing renewable energy resources in European power supplies.

Advocating market solutions in particular, the association takes on the now familiar policy problem of *intermittency* in renewable generation – "with wind farms only able to generate when it is windy and solar power proportional to the amount of sunlight" as the United Kingdom's recently appointed National Infrastructure Commission (2016, 19) explains this problem.

It is this great number of contemporary problematizations (Collier, Lakoff & Rabinow 2004) about energy interruption risk that suggest the relevance of this theme. However, the gap in knowledge in these contemporary debates is two-fold. The first shortcoming is conceptual: key security concepts such as infrastructure, risk, or resilience are occasionally defined, but rarely discussed or analysed in any greater depth. Understandably, this is perhaps part of their appeal: what the concepts lack in substance and depth they gain in flexibility, allowing the concepts to problematize a wide variety of contemporary events and issues. Infrastructure, risk management, and resilience indeed all denote positive capacities of systems, people, and communities and very few would perhaps question the pursuit of these capacities as such.

Nevertheless, more than three decades of research in the social sciences have scrutinized the concept of risk, large technological system, infrastructure, and resilience. In this book, I draw from this social science literature to add to the debates on alleged infrastructural fragilities in electricity supplies. Drawing from emerging research on risk governance, I argue that risk management is a process that encompasses a range of tools or *techniques* (O'Malley 2004) that has different uses, conceptual definitions, and hence effects across the energy supply chain. Furthermore, I do not understand the word *infrastructure* to point to any supportive or enabling structures in general, but as an object to be studied in its own right. Similarly, the concept of *resilience* is not seen just as an overall virtue, but is directed to the empirical interrogation of those practices through which people and organizations have bounced back from infrastructure disruptions. While such observations are commonplace in the social sciences and especially science and technology studies (STS), anthropological, and organizational studies literature, as I show below, they continue to be overlooked in contemporary debates around infrastructure risk and resilience.

My premises for the study of infrastructure risk and resilience lead to the second issue of concern: the relative lack of empirical observations on how infrastructures work and get used by people (cf. Star 1999). With a few exceptions, concerns over infrastructure fragilities are rooted in visions about future systems and sometimes rather loose assumptions about controllability, its lack, adaptations, and flexibility in power generation technologies and infrastructures – and increasingly also among energy consumers.

Policy reports all over the world once again suggest this point. Calls for more transnational, leaner, and flexible electric power infrastructures are imbued by worries over integrating variable renewable energy into energy supplies (see also Verbong & Geels 2007). From Finland (Finnish Roadmap 2015) and the European Commission (2015) to the United Kingdom (UK National Infrastructure Commission 2016), European industrial associations (EURELECTRIC 2014), and the United Nations Environment Programme (REN21 2016), many envision that more flexibility in the power system and in energy demands will solve this intermittency problem and produce the necessary malleability. This much is clear: if energy resources become variable, then the supply system, energy exports, or consumers will need to meet them by adaptive actions. However, these assumptions also suggest a rather strict division: some experts now talk directly to "non-controllable" renewable energies (Finnish Roadmap 2015), but fewer have explained how controllable incumbent energy generation was in the first place (cf. Silvast & Kelman 2013).

Yet, if infrastructures sit at the middle of collective life, we need to gain further and more systematic evidence about their functioning and effects in terms of risk and resilience. Adopting the well-honed tradition of infrastructure studies and STS, in this book I focus on this aim by "inverting" the electricity infrastructure. This means I will attend to the infrastructure itself, its history and context, and the real work that makes it come to life on an everyday basis (Karasti et al 2016; Parmiggiani & Monteiro 2016). To do so, my constitutive method follows the actors in this field, including security experts, network operators, and lay persons, and the ways in which they themselves attend to the power infrastructure and invert its structures in so doing, in their own ways and contexts – whether thinking about national security, infrastructure maintenance, or during a power failure. Building on interviews, participant observation, historical research, survey study, and policy analysis, the book unpacks the work of the authorities, planners, electricity companies, and lay persons that keeps energy systems from failing and helps them to recover from interruptions if they occur (see the Appendix for a detailed description of the materials). A review of the terms critical infrastructure, risk, and resilience explains how I build on the existing work, expanding on these themes and taking them into new directions.

Vital electricity infrastructure

Security discussions in the context of infrastructure, such as electricity, have changed in the past few decades. Concerns over *security of supply* in electrical power systems have existed for a number of years (e.g. EURELECTRIC 2006; European Parliament & Council 2009) and the close association of *energy security* with fuel import dependency dates back at least to the aftermath of the 1970s oil crises (Farrell, Zerriffi & Dowlatabi 2004). More recently, however, the discussion has adopted a number of rationales, concepts, and concrete tools from long-standing discussions within the military. Influential national and international policies have started to designate electricity as a *critical infrastructure*, which, as researchers see it, brings a specific national security issue to the fore (Collier & Lakoff 2008). This security issue concerns the protection of critical infrastructures from threats such as "natural" disasters, major technological failures, or terrorist attacks. Considering what then is such a critical infrastructure, historian Paul N. Edwards (2003, 187) cites a version of the following policy term definition of an infrastructure from the United States:

The framework of interdependent networks and systems comprising identifiable industries, institutions (including people and procedures), and distribution capabilities that provide a reliable flow of products and services essential to the defense and economic security of the United States, the smooth functioning of government at all levels, and society as a whole.

(US Department of Homeland Security 2013, 37)

These networks and systems become *critical* US infrastructures when their "incapacity or destruction . . . would have a debilitating impact on security, national economic security, national public health or safety, or any combination of those matters" (US Department of Homeland Security 2013, 29). The European Council and the Finnish government define a critical infrastructure or just an *infrastructure* as follows:

An asset, system or part thereof located in Member States which is essential for the maintenance of vital societal functions, health, safety, security, economic or social well-being of people, and the disruption or destruction of which would have a significant impact in a Member State as a result of the failure to maintain those functions.

(European Council 2008, Article 2(a))

The technical structures and organisations which are necessary for the population's livelihood and for the functioning of society.

(SSS 2010, 36)

The definitions are clearly very different. For instance, the US definition views the flow of products and services as "critical", while the EU and Finnish definitions designate infrastructure systems themselves as "critical". And whereas the US definition mentions society as a whole and includes national public health, it lacks explicit consideration of social well-being and livelihood which are visible in the other definitions. Finally, in the US and Finnish cases, organizations and institutions are defined as part of an infrastructure, but they are not directly referred to in the European Union's definition. Nonetheless, in one way or the other, all three texts designate infrastructures as those vital provisions without which the society as a whole could not operate (Edwards 2003, 187). In national and international policies, these provisions typically include electricity and energy, water supply, transportation and logistics, telecommunication and information and communication technologies, banking and finance, the central government, emergency and rescue services, and health services (Brunner & Suter 2009, 529).

The question of why infrastructures became such a significant security problem has also received scrutiny among academics. Some note the immediate impact of information technologies in the 1990s: policy concerns over security and risk in information and communication technologies became influential in the 1990s and have expanded to a host of other infrastructural provisions such as energy (Dunn Cavelty 2008). Histories in their turn highlight longer-term path dependencies – the vulnerability of current systems is elevated by their increasing complexity and growing energy demands, whose roots stem from a number of decades ago (Hughes 1983; Nye 2010; van der Vleuten & Lagendijk 2010). But anthropologists Stephen Collier and Andrew Lakoff (2008) point to a different and more frequently overlooked factor: historical security discourse and practice in military and civil security. Building on American security debates from the last 100 years, Collier and Lakoff (2008, 24) find clear continuities between contemporary worries over infrastructures and earlier problematizations, such as strategic bombing theories of the early 20th century or post-WWII anxieties over the impacts of a Soviet nuclear strike on the United States' critical systems (Collier 2008). Understanding this history better is crucial as security discourse that is shaped by its earlier formulations can, at the same time, frame what infrastructure risk is all about in present policies (Kristensen 2008).

This book's first case, in Part II, builds upon the work by Collier and Lakoff (2008) to shed new light on the traits of infrastructural security discourse and practice in Finland. The research question of this first case is: *how do national security experts in Finland mitigate electricity outages as risks and attempt to enhance the resilience of society's infrastructures to disruptions?* The case divides two chapters. In Chapter 2, I visit the early origins of what was called economic military defence in Finland and examine how experts understood society's vital resources as a "machinery" that needs to be made prepared for looming national emergencies. In Chapter 3, starting from the 1970s oil crises, I explain how the situation changed and turned toward securing networked provisions in society rather than mere stockpiling of resources that had been the key security practice before. The material of the study comprises objects gathered during a period of fieldwork: histories about technology and organizations, interviews with Finnish infrastructure and energy experts, and participation in Finnish infrastructure security seminars. My analysis of this data centres on the kind of terminology, rationales, and techniques that are manifested in the studied risk discourses. Motivated by initial findings and earlier studies, I pay particular attention to the ways in which the risk management of Finnish national energy provisions has been problematized (Collier, Lakoff & Rabinow 2004; Berglund 2009) at different times, often motivated by experiences of pivotal national disasters and critical events such as wars, shortages, and energy price crises.

The concern of the first empirical study is hence with the indispensable status of national infrastructures and the protection of these large structures by the state. The study looks at cases where the state and its security experts intervene in infrastructure provision and develop ways to manage the uncertainties caused by national and global disasters and fluctuations of international markets. It distinguishes markets and national security or welfare and, at least implicitly, suggests that markets and public welfare must be on another's opposites. The study hence directly links risk management with public policy, following many studies on risk governance (e.g. Klinke & Renn 2016).

However, the concept of risk in the social sciences now deserves greater scrutiny, as not all studies fix risk to a particular political rationale such as market liberalism, public control, or "neoliberalism" (O'Malley 2004). The social science discussions about risk are considerably more flexible and extensive. In sum, these discussions draw on risk to open up a relevant debate concerning security norms, risk knowledge, and even the whole society in terms of how it understands and mitigates risk.

Risk, society, and risk governance

Risk, according to its common everyday meaning, is more or less a synonym for any unfortunate event, hazard, danger, or harm (Lupton 1999). For experts in safety (in, for example, the fields of insurance, health, engineering, or infrastructure protection), risk management is something more systematic: it is a way for anticipating future threats and mitigating their effects before they have occurred. When researcher and infrastructure security expert Myriam Dunn (2006) discusses critical infrastructure protection, she also begins with the notion of risk to conceptualize infrastructure protection practices. This is also the choice in many recent infrastructure protection policies, where risk analysis and risk management frameworks appear as the key security practice (e.g. European Council 2008; US Department of Homeland Security 2013).

This book also considers risk as its key concepts. I have chosen to study risk because the term opens up the social science discussion, which, I argue, also throws new light on problems associated with electricity infrastructure. Let me summarize these debates briefly before tailoring them somewhat and returning to the topic of infrastructures.

For Dunn (2006, 48), risk in the context of critical infrastructure protection has the following meaning: "a function of the likelihood that a given threat source will attempt to exploit a given vulnerability and the magnitude of the impact, should a threat source successfully exploit the vulnerability", In this case, while the definition is certainly somewhat more developed than I suggest, risk essentially is a combination of a quantitative chance and measured consequences of a threat event (Warner 1992, 4). These definitions understand the essence of risk in statistical analysis and probabilistic calculation (Burgess 2016). This technical formulation of risk is also relatively simple and has been a matter of much debate in social science research.

The key critique here has been that the technical risk concept may overlook wider issues in at least two ways. For many social science researchers, first of all, discussions about risk should be expanded considerably to understand the society and its relation with security and insecurity (Beck 1992; Giddens 1994; Furedi 2006). For the sociologist Ulrich Beck (1992), for example, the incalculable and hence both uncontrollable and uninsurable *modernization risks* have included the effects of genetic engineering and nuclear accidents, but also financial crises, terrorism, global climate change, and much else besides (see O'Malley 2004; Collier 2008). Such hazards, in their turn, motivate new more reflective and political risk responses in public debates, by scientific experts, in the family, within working life, by individuals in their personal lives, and in other fields (Beck 1992).

A topical example of this societal dynamic is the emergence of risks amid globalization. Princeton sociologist Miguel A. Centeno and his colleagues (2015) argue that as societies become increasingly interdependent – through information, services, goods, and capital, and including the flow of people – that also produces new global-scale systemic instabilities and fragilities. In Beck's (1992) terminology, the very success of modern interconnectedness produces more complexity which then needs to be addressed as a risk. Critical infrastructures pose a highly relevant example: growingly dependent on each other and global information technologies in particular, functioning in a universal just-in-time logic to save costs, "tightly coupled and interdependent infrastructure networks may be vulnerable in ways that cannot be predicted on the basis of the properties of the constituent networks themselves" (Centeno et al 2015, 75). In other words, global systemic infrastructure risks may be unpredictable and hence incalculable and provoke new, more imaginative ways of thinking about infrastructure risks and mitigating their impacts, according to Centeno and colleagues (2015). This observation comes very close to how Finnish expert circles think about infrastructure risk and outline its problems, as my book shows. However, the extent to which such risks are near catastrophic, and the extent to which they are manageable by organizations and their staff even if they may be, is a slightly different matter that I will also discuss (see Roe & Schulman 2008).

Secondly, social science scholars have also drawn more attention to people and institutions that deal with risk or *perceive* it. Specifically, people, groups, and institutions do not manage risks merely by calculating them (Douglas & Wildavsky 1982; Klinke & Renn 2002; Lupton 1999). Instead, it is claimed that subjective and cultural risk perceptions – starting with a fundamental question, namely why are some risks seen as more important than others – are shaped by such factors as cultural background, worldviews, social membership, status, and meaning-making.

These are the two main criticisms against the technical risk formula in the social sciences. Over the past decade, however, a third approach to the topic of risk has emerged. In studies about risk governance, its rationalities, and its concrete techniques (Collier, Lakoff & Rabinow 2004; O'Malley 2004; Ialenti 2014), the concern has not primarily been with broad societal transformations, with the multiple societal effects of new hazards, or with the cultural and social perceptions of risks. Certainly these issues remain relevant, but the research objective is more specific. This objective is to study those rationales and technologies which are applied when enacting hazards as objects for thought and action.

A key object of this risk studies research is *risk techniques*. This term highlights those tools – such as statistical calculations, social and private insurance, and and actuarialism – that operationalize the aspirations of risk management; or *risk governance*, as it is often called to stress the collective nature and public policy implications of many risks (Andreeva, Ansell & Harrison 2014; Klinke & Renn 2016). Technique also means a particular way of doing something. Risk, specifically, enacts threats in a particular way by uncovering their probability and impact and signifying them as harms to be acted upon (Ewald 1993; Helén 2004, 32–33). In use, hence, risk management techniques are linked to different *styles of reasoning* (Hacking 2002), such as statistical analysis and the construction of models, that have their own "systemicity, specificity, and rigour" and provide "frameworks [. . .] for choice" (Collier 2008, 230). These explanations are highly relevant for identifying what counts as risk management in the book's first case, in Part II – as for much of its earlier time span, the concept of risk did not exist in Finnish.

Risk techniques and styles of reasoning furthermore have a close connection with practical deployment: they are not separate from the instances where they are manifested (Hacking 2002; O'Malley 2004). For instance, risk management preconfigures specific ex-ante anticipatory actions and problems are then mitigated through such performative actions (Luhmann 1993). Focusing on practices, research of risk hence also relates to norms and *habits*: in sociological terms, people's common sense about those actions that have already worked before on several occasions (Kilpinen 1998, 2000; also Giddens 1994; Rabinow 2008). In the first case study, for example, threats against infrastructures were often managed in a similar way for a prolonged time before something disrupted the risk norm, replaced by another way of thinking about security.

Researchers Jane Summerton and Boel Berner have summarized these various research interests as follows:

> Our approach [. . .] involves analyzing the dynamic intertwining of knowledge, politics, and authority through which interpretations of risks are negotiated, contested, and become stabilized at specific sites.
>
> (Summerton & Berner 2003, 19)

The key here is that risk and its interpretation is produced and negotiated at specific sites, rather than being a given probability or harm. In a socio-technical infrastructure, one part of this knowledge, politics, and authority clearly exists on the national scale and its descriptions of critical infrastructures. However, in the same spirit of layered infrastructures, the issue of risk stabilization does not stop at these policy sites. Infrastructures, power failures, and their effects also have to be managed all the time and continuously by staff in electricity companies. While some programmes on critical infrastructure protection do acknowledge organizations and organizational structures (e.g. US Department of Homeland Security 2013), this issue of organizations is rather multifaceted and now needs more scrutiny. I turn to literature and a case study that opens up these themes next.

Infrastructure risk and organization

Massive electric power failures are often used as evidence in support of different notions of risk (Bennett 2005; Graham 2009). For example, the major blackouts of Italy in 2003 and continental Europe in 2006 were associated with lacking prevention and preparation measures, insufficient interorganizational coordination, inactive Europe-wide market regulation of the electricity sector, and even more specifically in 2006, the increasing competition among electricity providers (CRE & AEEG 2004; UCTE 2004, 2007; CEER 2006; see Silvast & Kaplinsky

2007). Considering that infrastructures such as electricity are public common goods more than mere commodities to their users (Gramlich 1994), these problematics about private vices are not entirely intuitive. However, the once almost ubiquitous monopolistic model of infrastructure provision began to be critiqued already in the 1960s. Led by the poor condition of networks then and a positive faith in free enterprising, economists and policy makers developed the practices of "liberalizing" and "unbundling" infrastructure networks (Graham & Marvin 2001, 141–142). This means splitting infrastructures into a provision that can compete on the market with other providers, such as energy generation, and other segments that remain a monopoly, such as local electricity networks.

In industrialized countries, infrastructures and their risks are now increasingly expected to be governed by market mechanisms (Jalas, Rinkinen & Silvast 2016). Clearly, the critics above question the credibility of unbundled market-based organizations that provide electricity (Ullberg 2005). Blaming market competition for the failures of infrastructures is also sustained by comparison: arguably, the earlier monopolistic system had prioritized preventive maintenance, power reserves, and diversity of supplies and had energy excess (Berglund 2009). But the critics also have an inherent problem. They assume that one can reduce risky behaviour to its one cause such as competition, regulation, or poor coordination, but few complex organizational accidents are triggered merely by a single factor, as sociological research has shown (Perrow 1999).

Associating markets with new risks also turns away from an opposite aspect of this relationship: how market competition is supposed to increase security by producing more flexible, real-time, and efficient infrastructure services. One may rightly want to question such free market sloganism, but the popularity of market-based governing of infrastructures was unquestionable at the time of my study, as I show. Thus, this attention on how the energy markets continuously work in risk and security terms shapes my interest in this book in the third part (see also Breslau 2013). Recently, a number of organizational and urban researchers have started to show an interest in similar questions in infrastructure *control rooms* – a site where technological systems are monitored and different organizations communicate (Heath & Luff 2000; Suchman 2011; Luque-Ayala & Marvin 2016). Urban scholars Andrés Luque-Ayala and Simon Marvin characterize these key nodes for infrastructures and their vital functions as follows:

> Thanks to their continuous work in preventing breakdown, responding to disruption, and overcoming interruption, control rooms play a key role in the achievement of infrastructural "black boxing", and through this, "the continuation of what has become normal" (Gordon et al 2014, 10). . . . The literature on control rooms identifies two broad types: those established for normal operations – for the management of the everyday – and those, usually temporal, established for exceptional operations – for the management of the emergency.
> (Luque-Ayala & Marvin 2016, 196)

As the electricity infrastructure both sustains everyday life and is a critical infrastructure whose failure may pose emergencies, arguably electricity control rooms combine the two functions above. A particularly interesting research focus, considering these wide aims in infrastructure management, has been in organizational studies on reliability, the effects of market liberalization, and control room operators, their skills, and their habitual activities (de Bruijne & van Eeten 2007; Roe & Schulman 2008).

Motivated by these themes, I visited two electricity control rooms of a Finnish electricity company in 2007 and 2008. My research here owes a great deal to my contact with the managers and operators of the utility, who let me access these normally restricted sites. The book reports on my field study, which centres on the way in which electricity control room operators trade energy on the common Nordic energy market, Nord Pool, and maintain an electricity grid continuously and in real time. The research question of this case is: *how are electricity interruptions managed as risks in the liberalized electricity market in Finland and Scandinavia and what do these practices imply for the resilience of the electricity infrastructure?*

Reported in Part III, the case comprises three chapters. I begin by introducing the history, design, and public regulation of the Nordic and Finnish energy markets in Chapter 4. I also discuss the generic operation of Finnish electricity and its market on the level of national electricity transmission in this same chapter. In the chapters that follow, more attention is paid to the manner in which markets and public welfare figure in the concrete management of electricity markets (Chapter 5) and electricity networks on the local distribution level (Chapter 6). This division follows from the power company having divided two control rooms that handled markets and networks, respectively, enacting the policies of unbundling infrastructure in this fashion.

Considering management of market-based electricity, energy market scholar Daniel Breslau (2013, 2) summarizes a similar focus as mine when he argues that "[c]orrespondences between economic theory and economic reality are not discovered but built". Likewise, my attention will be fixed on the activities and tools that manifest competition and security in the control rooms. This includes international energy markets and their daily routines with different temporal rhythms, the disciplining calculative instruments such as marketplace bids, the physical and spatial arrangements (e.g. walling off different parts of an organization), and the figuration of markets tools – computer screens and their effects in particular – in the everyday working practices (see also Heath & Luff 2000; Suchman 2000, 2011; Özden-Schilling 2016). Rather than viewing risk as merely a danger or a threat, such a focal point outlines those assemblages of people, habits, monitors, numbers, and market mechanisms that continuously work together to mitigate risks and maintain the reliable flows of energy from producers to consumers (Silvast 2011). These practices happen all the time and not merely when interruptions to electricity supplies are anticipated by actors.

Resilient infrastructure as an empirical problem

With its various rich meanings and contexts of use, it is worth stressing the limitations of risk thinking. To a large extent, risk management is an anticipatory strategy that suggests ex-ante actions, prudence, and foresight to mitigate threats. Yet, it says considerably less about those threats that were not anticipated by risk analysis – naming them rather as *uncertainty* (O'Malley 2004) – nor about those threats that cannot be decided upon as risks – named as mere *dangers* (Luhmann 1993). The increasingly common concept of *resilience* sits with this temporal problem by addressing what happens after a threat has already occurred (Berglund 2009).

The popularity of resilience in energy and infrastructure policies seems to have developed in tandem with the raising commonality of the concept in policy reports more generally (e.g. UNISDR 2005; US National Infrastructure Council 2009; US Department of Homeland Security 2013; European Union 2016). The concept is not easy to define according to many academics (e.g. Manyena 2006; Furedi 2008; Krieger 2016), but several influential attempts exist nevertheless. For instance, in its integrated emergency management programme, the United Kingdom's Cabinet Office (2011, 14) understands by *infrastructure resilience* "the ability of assets, networks, and systems to anticipate, absorb, adapt to, and/or rapidly recover from a disruptive event". Resistance of hazards, reliability of components, redundancy through backup installations, and fast response and recovery sum into this vital capability (cf. Stirling 2014). A related explanation of *energy system resilience* is given by the United Kingdom's network of academics, UK Energy Research Centre (UKERC), adding considerations on consumers and energy services:

> Resilience is the capacity of an energy system to tolerate disturbance and to continue to deliver affordable energy services to consumers. A resilient energy system can speedily recover from shocks and can provide alternative means of satisfying energy service needs in the event of changed external circumstances.
>
> (UKERC 2011, 7)

Psychologists also advanced the concept of *individual resilience* from the 1940s onwards (Krieger 2016) and systems ecology drew on the concept in the 1970s (Lindseth 2011). Literatures on risk assessment and risk perception have separated *anticipation* of potential but known threats from *resilience* to recover from both expected and unexpected threats for a number of decades (Douglas & Wildavsky 1982; Hood et al 1992) – although the two strategies are often blurred in policy term definitions (e.g. US National Infrastructure Council 2009, 8; UK Cabinet Office 2011, 14).

This research tradition insists that resilience opens up a relevant debate even if the term is often contested, but first it is useful to ask what the problem of resilience concerns more exactly. On one level, resilience points to capabilities of whole states and societies (European Union 2016). I will be exploring how security experts attempted to build such generic capabilities in the protection of the state from infrastructure failures in Part II of the book. Later in the book, other layers of resilience become more insightful: including personal resilience and the resilience of institutions and large technological systems as they are continuously maintained (Healy & Mesman 2014). This lines up with discussion of a critical infrastructure breakdown by disaster scholarship: accordingly, rather than mere prior preparedness plans, the adaptive behaviour of citizens, front-line workers, and middle managers will determine effective disaster response once an infrastructure fails (Boin & McConnell 2007; see also Tierney 2003). Similar actors will also be in my focus in the ethnographic and interview parts of the book that concern the management of the electricity infrastructure and its use.

But implicitly, does this focus on resilience also assume vulnerability as a fact of life? This is what some such as critical sociologist Frank Furedi (2008) suggests in his study of official usage and academic literature of the concept. For him, resilience is merely subordinate to vulnerability: "the official rhetoric of promoting resilience . . . assumes that vulnerability is the defining condition of social life" (Furedi 2008, 645). However important this concern may be, the view needs more attention on how people manage and use electricity in everyday life and how its disruptions may impact people from that premise.

Power outages at home

I have now considered national worries over society's welfare infrastructures in the introduction of the first case study. The previous section then drew attention to the various mechanisms that try to economize infrastructure security: to act upon electricity and its risks economically. However, in both of these cases, the starting point is similar: a power cut is an exceptional accident. According to the known technological system accidents scholar, Charles Perrow (1999, 63–64), an *accident* by definition damages people or objects, is unintended, and disrupts the organizing actions of people. All the previous sections' considerations have framed power interruptions similarly; as damaging, unintended, and disrupting events whose effects should be regulated and mitigated by the government and private companies. It seems that when a blackout is assigned a cost – however high that cost is – what follows is that compensations are paid and a transgression has happened when the power fails.

However, Perrow's perspective does not concern just accidents, but *system* accidents. This qualifier is because according to Perrow (1999, 63–64), the traits of an accident – the degree of damages, unintendedness, and disruptiveness – can only be measured against some systematic whole. A failure of an individual system component or unit is merely an incident that can often be quite easily isolated to use another one of Perrow's distinctions. On the other hand, what is more severe is a systemic accident that concerns the whole system or its subsystems and initiates more wide-ranging and uncertain consequences.

Perrow (1999) considered different industries in his study and will be followed in Part III of the book considering electricity control rooms, but also poses a useful comparison to people's electric energy use. It is clear that the most relevant "system" in everyday life is not just the power grid. As many social scientists have said over the past decades, electricity provision or "energy services" (Southerton, van Vlie & Chappells 2004; Silvast, Hänninen & Hyysalo 2013) should be rather understood through the everyday practices that they sustain: ranging from heating and air conditioning to lighting, cleaning, personal hygiene, the storing and preparing of food, and the use of media technologies, alarm systems, and computers (Shove 2003, 2010; Hyysalo, Jensen & Oudshoorn 2016).

From this premise, if a light dims or a single appliance fails to work, it may often be replaced or the end users might decide to use something else that does not require that particular technology. These are just *incidents* rather than *accidents* to draw on Perrow's distinction. More serious though is a power cut that disrupts a whole systemic chain of mundane actions: such as writing a job application with a computer and sending it electronically or preparing breakfast and sending children to school (Silvast & Virtanen 2014).

If electricity is understood as a societal infrastructure vital for people's well-being, then the ways in which lay persons bounce back from its failures is an important topic. The premise of my third case study, in Part IV, Chapter 7, is that power failures – albeit their many potentially disastrous impacts for the national state and industries – are also events of everyday life. It analyses the systemic effects of blackouts for energy users by asking the following research question: *how do lay people reconstruct blackouts and their effects as risks in households and bounce back from these disruptions?*

This question is not motivated by just some general interest in everyday life. Rather, infrastructure experts often assume a particular rationality for lay people: that of a prepared individual who constantly reflects on financial harms and compensations for a power cut (Graham & Marvin 2001, 208–209). Such a starting point pays virtually no attention to more habitual forms of thinking or to whether people are interested and able, or even willing, to do such calculations in everyday life (Silvast & Virtanen 2014). The habitual forms of thinking are in turn my interest in the third case study.

A partiality of a different sort also figures in some disaster mitigation activities. Anthropologists Julien Langumier and Sandrine Revet (2010; Revet 2013) approach catastrophes anthropologically and one thing they note is that sources such as the media, disaster relief, and simulated crisis exercises often portray people merely as passive victims of a disaster. Similarly, difficult Finnish power failures have caused commentary on how anxious and helpless people are during a long blackout, how little they have prepared in practice, and how they unnecessarily phone the emergency services and overload them (Tennberg & Vola 2014).

To address everyday reasoning about risk, the term lay people, though also used here for brevity's sake, is indeed somewhat inappropriate. The term indicates some lay sphere of a population or victims that is completely separate from the sphere of experts. Yet, as Revet (2013, 43) points out, local people tend to be intrinsically involved with disasters and many experts know this: a "natural" disaster, for example, creates novel interactions among rescue workers and residents. After Hurricane Sandy in 2012, for example, similar interactions were formalized in the official rebuild process, presuming an "active public" that would attend workshops, town hall meetings, task forces, and public consultations in co-designing more resilient infrastructures for New York City (Collier, Cox & Grove 2016). Whether people will in fact take these kinds of actions is an empirical problem. With this issue in mind, I want to pay attention to some ways in which Finnish people reconstruct blackout events and try to resume their habitual actions when the power fails (Kilpinen 2000). I shall also talk about the interactions that blackouts motivate – or could motivate – between homes, electricity experts, and authorities. The material in the third case study consists of interviews and a questionnaire on Finnish homes.

A note on geographical scale

The topics of risk, resilience, and critical infrastructure are clearly international, widespread in the United States, the United Kingdom, and Western Europe. Having said that, the materials in this book centre on particular situations in the Finnish electricity supply chains, markets, and consumers, themselves part of the Scandinavian power markets. The focus of the case studies might suggest that I am generating knowledge on energy risk merely in the Finnish history, society, and culture, and I would like to clarify an important point here. Studying the energy infrastructure as *Finnish* is not the main objective, even if I hope to advance some understanding of Finnishness, too, in this book. Rather, my point is more pragmatic: geographical scale is as it happens in particular ways in the situations that I study (Levin 2016). At some points, this scale will be the Scandinavian power market. At others, it is a Finnish city or a household, at yet others Finnish relations with its neighbouring countries or the European Union. The very point with infrastructures is that as technologies they transgress particular time and space (Star 1999). Consequently, infrastructure experts, and arguably also users, have to be able to move among different scales and their problem domains when they use and maintain them. The ways in which this happens, documented in what follows, could be of interest to any university, institution, and policy maker with an interest in risk, security, infrastructure, and resilience.

   To be clear, I do not claim that infrastructure, risk, and resilience are global concepts that will always be the same regardless of the location or time. But the opposite error, which anthropologist Paul Rabinow flags (in Rabinow et al 2008, 109), is assuming that global phenomena can only be understood in their local situated conditions. Neither the "local" nor the "global" can be taken as an ex-ante scale here. Rather, the production of scale is an empirical problem that needs to be pursued by description of situations where people and organizations manage risk and maintain resilience. This premise underpins the book's research into the Finnish and Scandinavian power supplies and markets, their anticipated risks, resilience, and shifting character as critical infrastructures.

Structure of the book

The structure of this book is as follows.

   Chapter 2 traces the history of vital infrastructures such as energy from the point of view of ensuring their protection from different kind of threats, initially of the military kind. Previous studies have examined this problem in the United States, but the focus in this section concerns applying their approach to Finland.

Contemporary worries over dependence on infrastructures and electricity in particular and public-private partnership in infrastructure protection have clear analogies in these early modern military protections, as I show.

Chapter 3 assesses how economic military defence became problematic in the face of unpredictable, cross-cutting threats, after the 1970s oil crises in particular, and shifted from merely stockpiling vital resources to a focus on networked systems that the society depends upon. I also show that in this critical infrastructure protection, emergency planning becomes increasingly focused on non-calculable catastrophic risks or risks with high consequences, but low probabilities and what new risk techniques are deployed to deal with such problems.

The open energy markets posit another scale where global uncertainties are anticipated and managed as risks of energy provisions. Starting from recent decades' priorities of liberalizing infrastructures, Chapter 4 explains the history and policy work of materializing infrastructure markets in Finland and the Nordic countries that became the Nordic power stock exchange, Nord Pool. Public efforts in regulating energy market risk are also introduced for comparison and I end by explaining how the free power markets are supposed to work by a separation of commercial and non-commercial energy flows, which results in a specific understanding of security.

Chapter 5 focuses ethnographically on market-making in a Finnish control room where electricity is traded on Nord Pool. The chapter discusses how economic understandings of energy risk and resilience infuse into this everyday work through material arrangements and working habits, including new professional roles, organization restructurings, spatial arrangements, and computer software. My ethnography also demonstrates the major relevance of operator skills and local knowledge in making trades instead of automation of this control room work.

Chapter 6 shows how, next to the market control room, another control room is managing the real-time distribution of electricity and its security through ongoing monitoring and maintenance. I ask how this separation influences the professions and expertise of the control room and show how it originated in international, national, and municipal policies of "unbundling" infrastructure markets from public monopolies. The different working habits in the two control rooms are highly effective in keeping these two infrastructural worlds apart just as recent energy policy programmes have foreseen.

In both national security initiatives and on the free energy markets, households are increasingly expected to be prepared for power failures or pay for a certain level of security. Chapter 7 contrasts this rational and economic view of energy users to long-standing research on the richer practices and cultures of energy use. Working from these perspectives and using household interviews, I explain how lay people enact blackouts as relaxing breaks or difficult harms, as well as how that separation is drawn by people to assign blame for electricity risk. The gender, age, and regional dynamics of these findings are explored further with results from a focused survey of Finnish households.

Chapter 8 ties the different field sites and their findings together and argues that their examination motivates further theorization of the concepts of risk and resilience. Here, I argue that risk management and its techniques emerged from a specific history, but it is also important to understand how the knowledge and practices of risk are deployed in local situations, their anticipatory actions, and foresight as well as resilient actions. I conclude by asking how the topics of risk and resilience may take social studies of energy into new directions, particularly discussing the difference between the concepts of *system* and *infrastructure* in understanding energy.

References

Andreeva, Galina; Ansell, Jake & Harrison, Tina (2014). Governance and Accountability of Public Risk. *Financial Accountability & Management* 30 (3): 342–361.

Beck, Ulrich (1992). *Risk Society: Towards a New Modernity*. London: Sage (German original 1986).

Bennett, Jane (2005). The Agency of Assemblages and the North American Blackout. *Public Culture* 17 (3): 445–465.

Berglund, Björn (2009). *Svarta svanar och högspänningsledningar – om försörjningstryggheten i det svenska elsystemet ur ett teknikhistoriskt perspektiv* ("Black Swans in the Power Grid – How Critical Events Has Affected the Security of Electricity Supply"). Dissertation, Uppsala University, Disciplinary Domain of Science and Technology. Link accessed 24 November 2016: www.utn.uu.se/sts/cms/filarea/0901_Berglund.pdf

Boin, Arjen & McConnell, Allan (2007). Preparing for Critical Infrastructure Breakdowns: The Limits of Crisis Management and the Need for Resilience. *Journal of Contingencies and Crisis Management* 15 (1): 50–59.

Breslau, Daniel (2013). Designing a Market-Like Entity: Economics in the Politics of Market Formation. *Social Studies of Science* 43 (6): 829–851.

Brunner, Elgin & Suter, Manuel (2009). *International CIIP Handbook 2008/2009: An Inventory of 25 National and 7 International Critical Information Infrastructure Protection Policies*. Zürich: Center for Security Studies. Link accessed 24 November 2016: www.css. ethz.ch/publications/pdfs/CIIP-HB-08–09.pdf

Burgess, Adam (2016). Introduction. In Burgess, Adam; Alemanno, Alberto & Zinn, Jens (eds) *Routledge Handbook of Risk Studies*. London: Routledge, 1–14.

CEER (Council of European Energy Regulators) (2006). European Energy Regulators Investigate Blackout in Europe. Press release 7 November 2006. Link accessed 24 November 2016: www.cre.fr/documents/presse/communiques-de-presse/les-regulateurs-europeens-de-l-energie-lancent-une-enquete-sur-la-panne-d-electricite-qui-a-touche-l-europe2/consulter-le-communique-de-presse-version-uk

Centeno, Miguel; Nag, Manish; Patterson, Thayer; Shaver, Andrew & Windawi, Jason (2015). The Emergence of Global Systemic Risk. *Annual Review of Sociology* 41: 65–85.

Collier, Stephen (2008). Enacting Catastrophe: Preparedness, Insurance, Budgetary Rationalization. *Economy and Society* 37 (2): 224–250.

Collier, Stephen & Lakoff, Andrew (2008). The Vulnerability of Vital Systems: How Critical Infrastructures Became a Security Problem. In Dunn Cavelty, Myriam & Kristensen, Kristian Søby (eds) *Securing 'the Homeland': Critical Infrastructure, Risk and (In) security*. London: Routledge, 17–39.

Collier, Stephen; Lakoff, Andrew & Rabinow, Paul (2004). Biosecurity: Proposal for an Anthropology of the Contemporary. *Anthropology Today* 20 (5): 3–7. Collier, Stephen; Cox, Savannah & Grove, Kevin (2016). Rebuilding by Design in

Post-Sandy New York. *Limn* 5 (7). Link accessed 14 November 2016: http://limn.it/rebuilding-by-design-in-post-sandy-new-york/

CRE (Commission de Regulation de l'Energie) & AEEG (Autorita per l'Energia Elettrica e il Gas) (2004). Report on the Events of September 28th, 2003 Culminating in the Separation of the Italian Power System from the other UCTE Networks. Allegato A - delibera n. 61/04. Link accessed 24 November 2016: www.autorita.energia.it/allegati/docs/04/061-04all.pdf

Davies, Rob (2016a). Winter Electricity Blackouts Risk Recedes, says National Grid. *The Guardian* 14 October 2016. Link accessed 9 November 2016: www.theguardian.com/environment/2016/oct/14/winter-electricity-blackouts-risk-recedes-says-national-grid

Davies, Rob (2016b). Diesel Farms Set to Win Lucrative Contracts to Back Up National Grid. *The Guardian* 17 October 2016: www.theguardian.com/business/2016/oct/17/diesel-farms-set-win-lucrative-contracts-back-up-national-grid

de Bruijne, Mark & van Eeten, Michel (2007). Systems that Should Have Failed: Critical Infrastructure Protection in an Institutionally Fragmented Environment. *Journal of Contingencies and Crisis Management* 15 (1): 18–29.

Douglas, Mary & Wildavsky, Aaron (1982). *Risk and Culture: An Essay on the Selection of Technological and Environmental Dangers*. Berkeley: University of California Press.

Dunn Cavelty, Myriam (2006). Understanding Critical Information Infrastructures: An Elusive Quest. In Dunn, Myriam & Mauer, Victor (eds) *International CIIP Handbook 2006 Vol. II: Analyzing Issues, Challenges and Prospects*. Zürich: Center for Security Studies, 27–54. Link accessed 24 November 2016: http://e-collection.library.ethz.ch/eserv/eth:31123/eth-31123-04.pdf

Dunn Cavelty, Myriam (2008). Like a Phoenix from the Ashes: The Reinvention of Critical Infrastructure Protection as Distributed Security. In Dunn Cavelty, Myriam & Kristensen, Kristian Søby (eds) *Securing 'the Homeland': Critical Infrastructure, Risk and (In)security*. London: Routledge, 40–62.

Edwards, Paul (2003). Infrastructure and Modernity: Force, Time and Social Organization in the History of Sociotechnical systems. In Misa, Thomas; Brey, Philip & Feenberg, Andrew (eds) *Modernity and Technology*. Cambridge, MA: MIT Press, 185–225.

Edwards, Paul (2010). *A Vast Machine: Computer Models, Climate Data, and the Politics of Global Warming*. Cambridge, MA: MIT Press.

EURELECTRIC (2006). *Security of Electricity Supply: Roles, Responsibilities and Experiences within the EU*. Working Group on Security of Electricity Supply. Brussels: Union of the Electricity Industry EURELECTRIC. Link accessed 24 November 2016: www.eurelectric.org/Download/Download.aspx?DocumentID=19253

EURELECTRIC (2014). *Renewable Energy and Security of Supply: Finding Market Solutions*. Brussels: Union of the Electricity Industry EURELECTRIC. Link accessed 24 November 2016: www.eurelectric.org/media/154655/res_report_140919_lr-2014-030-0569-01-e.pdf

European Commission (2004). Communication from the Commission to the Council and the European Parliament – Critical Infrastructure Protection in the Fight against Terrorism. COM/2004/0702 final. Link accessed 24 November 2016: http://eur-lex.europa.eu/LexUriServ/LexUriServ.do?uri=CELEX:52004DC0702:EN:NOT

European Commission (2005). Green Paper on a European Programme for Critical Infrastructure Protection. COM/2005/576 final. Link accessed 24 November 2016: http://eur-lex.europa.eu/ LexUriServ/LexUriServ.do?uri=CELEX:52005DC0576:EN:NOT

European Commission (2015). A Framework Strategy for a Resilient Energy Union with a Forward-Looking Climate Change Policy. COM/2015/080 final. Link accessed 10 October 2016: http://eur-lex.europa.eu/legal-content/EN/TXT/?uri=COM:2015:80:FIN

European Council (2008). On the Identification and Designation of European Critical Infrastructures and the Assessment of the Need to Improve Their Protection. Directive 2008/114/EC. Link accessed 24 November 2016: http://eur-lex.europa.eu/LexUriServ/LexUriServ.do?uri=CELEX:32008L0114:EN:NOT

European Parliament & Council (2009). Concerning Common Rules for the Internal Market in Electricity and Repealing Directive 2003/54/EC. Directive 2009/72/EC. Link accessed 24 November 2016: http://eur-lex.europa.eu/LexUriServ/LexUriServ.do?uri=CELEX:32009L0072:en:NOT

European Union (2016). Shared Vision, Common Action: A Stronger Europe. A Global Strategy for the European Union's Foreign and Security Policy. Link accessed 10 October 2016: https://eeas.europa.eu/top_stories/pdf/eugs_review_web.pdf

Ewald, François (1993). *Der Vorsorgestaat.* Berlin: Suhrkamp (French original 1986).

Farrell, Alexander; Zerriffi, Hisham & Dowlatabadi, Hadi (2004). Energy Infrastructure and Security. *Annual Review of Environmental Resources* 29: 421–469.

Finnish Roadmap (2015). Roadmap 2025: Sähkömarkkina- ja verkkovisio 2035 & Roadmap 2025 ("Roadmap 2025: Visionary Electricity Markets and Networks 2035 & Roadmap 2025"). University of Vaasa – Merinova – Lappeenranta University of Technology – Tampere University of Technology. Link accessed 10 October 2016: http://vaasanseutu.fi/app/uploads/sites/7/2015/02/Loppuraportti.pdf

Furedi, Frank (2006). *Culture of Fear Revisited.* London – New York: Continuum.

Furedi, Frank (2008). Fear and Security: A Vulnerability-led Policy Response. *Social Policy & Administration* 42 (6): 645–661.

Giddens, Anthony (1994). *Modernity and Self-Identity: Self and Society in the Late Modern Age.* Palo Alto, CA: Stanford University Press.

Gordon, Rachel; Anderson, Ben; Crang, Mike & Marvin, Simon (2014). Controlling Networks: Modes of Governing Infrastructural Assemblages. Working paper. Durham: Durham University.

Graham, Stephen (2009). When Infrastructures Fail. In Graham, Stephen (ed.) *Disrupted Cities: When Infrastructure Fails.* London: Routledge, 1–26.

Graham, Stephen & Marvin, Simon (2001). *Splintering Urbanism: Networked Infrastructures, Technological Mobilities and the Urban Condition.* London: Routledge.

Gramlich, Edward (1994). Infrastructure Investment: A Review Essay. *Journal of Economic Literature* 32 (3): 1176–1196.

Hacking, Ian (2002). *Historical Ontology.* Cambridge, MA: Harvard University Press.

Healey, Stephen & Mesman, Jessica (2014). Resilience: Contingency, Complexity, and Practice. In Hommels, Anique; Mesman, Jessica & Bijker, Wiebe (eds) *Vulnerability in Technological Cultures: New Directions in Research and Governance.* Cambridge, MA: MIT Press, 155–178.

Heath, Christian & Luff, Paul (2000). *Technology in Action.* Cambridge, UK: Cambridge University Press.

Helén, Ilpo (2004). Technics Over Life: Risk, Ethics and the Existential Condition in High-Tech Antenatal Care. *Economy and Society* 33 (1): 28–51.

Hood, C. C.; Jones, D. K. C.; Pidgeon, N. F.; Turner, B. A. & Gibson, R. (1992). Risk Management. In Royal Society Study Group (eds) *Risk: Analysis, Perception and Management.* London: The Royal Society, 135–191.

Hughes, Thomas (1983). *Networks of Power: Electrification in Western Society, 1880–1930.* Baltimore, MD: Johns Hopkins University Press.

Hyysalo, Sampsa; Jensen, Torben Eelgard & Oudshoorn, Nelly (2016, eds). *The New Production of Users: Changing Innovation Collectives and Involvement Strategies.* London: Routledge.

Ialenti, Vincent (2014). Adjudicating Deep Time: Revisiting the United States' High-Level Nuclear Waste Repository Project at Yucca Mountain. *Science & Technology Studies* 28 (2): 27–48.

Jalas, Mikko; Rinkinen, Jenny & Silvast, Antti (2016). The Rhythms of Infrastructure. *Anthropology Today* 32 (4): 17–20.

Karasti, Helena; Millerand, Florence; Hine, Christine & Bowker, Geoffrey (2016). Knowledge Infrastructures: Part I. *Science & Technology Studies* 29 (1): 2–12.

Kilpinen, Erkki (1998). Creativity Is Coming. *Acta Sociologica* 41 (2): 173–179.

Kilpinen, Erkki (2000). *The Enormous Fly-Wheel of Society: Pragmatism's Habitual Conception of Action and Social Theory*. Doctoral thesis, University of Helsinki, Department of Sociology. Helsinki: Department of Sociology Research Reports, No. 235.

Klinke, Andreas & Renn, Ortwinn (2002). A New Approach to Risk Evaluation and Management: Risk-Based, Precaution-Based and Discourse-Based Strategies. *Risk Analysis* 22 (7): 1071–1094.

Klinke, Andreas & Renn, Ortwinn (2016). Risk Governance: Concept and Application to Technological Risk. In Burgess, Adam; Alemanno, Alberto & Zinn, Jens (eds) *Routledge Handbook of Risk Studies*. London: Routledge, 204–215.

Krieger, Kristian (2016). Resilience and Risk Studies. In Burgess, Adam; Alemanno, Alberto & Zinn, Jens (eds) *Routledge Handbook of Risk Studies*. London: Routledge, 335–343.

Kristensen, Kristian Søby (2008). 'The Absolute Protection of our Citizens': Critical Infrastructure Protection and the Practice of Security. In Dunn Cavelty, Myriam & Kristensen, Kristian Søby (eds) *Securing 'the Homeland': Critical Infrastructure, Risk and (In)security*. London: Routledge, 63–83.

Langumier, Julien & Revet, Sandrine (2010). Disasters and Risks: From Empiricism to Criticism, Paris, France. *E-Newsletter of the Disaster and Social Crisis Research Network* 11 (41): 5–7.

Larkin, Brian (2013). The Politics and Poetics of Infrastructure. *Annual Review of Anthropology* 42: 327–343.

Levine, Amy (2016). *South Korean Civil Movement Organisations: Hope, Crisis, and Pragmatism in Democratic Transition*. Oxford, UK: Oxford University Press.

Lindseth, Brian (2011). The Pre-History of Resilience in Ecological Research. *Limn* 1 (1). Link accessed 24 November 2016: http://limn.it/the-pre-history-of-resilience-in-ecological-research/

Luhmann, Niklas (1993). *Risk: A Sociological Theory*. Berlin–New York: Walter de Gruyter (German original 1991).

Lupton, Deborah (1999). *Risk*. London: Routledge.

Luque-Ayala, Andrés & Marvin, Simon (2016). The Maintenance of Urban Circulation: An Operational Logic of Infrastructural Control. *Environment and Planning D* 34 (2): 191–208.

Manyena, Siambabala Bernard (2006). The Concept of Resilience Revisited. *Disasters* 30 (4): 434–450.

National Grid US (2016). *Before, During and after the Storm: Your Guide to Electric Outage Preparation and Safety*. Warwick: National Grid plc. Link accessed 10 October 2016: www9.nationalgridus.com/non_html/stormpreparedness.pdf

Nye, David (2010). *When the Lights Went Out: A History of Blackouts in America*. Cambridge, MA: MIT Press.

O'Malley, Pat (2004). *Risk, Uncertainty and Government*. London – Sydney – Portland: Glasshouse Press.

Özden-Schilling, Canay (2016). The Infrastructure of Markets: From Electric Power to Electronic Data. *Economic Anthropology* 3 (1): 68–80.

Parmiggiani, Elena & Monteiro, Eric (2016). A Measure of 'Environmental Happiness': Infrastructuring Environmental Risk in Oil and Gas Off Shore Operations. *Science & Technology Studies* 29 (1): 30–51.

Perrow, Charles (1999). *Normal Accidents: Living with High-Risk Technologies*. Princeton, NJ: Princeton University Press, updated edition (original 1984).

Rabinow, Paul (2008). *Marking Time: On the Anthropology of the Contemporary*. Princeton, NJ: Princeton University Press.

Rabinow, Paul; Marcus, George; Faubion, James & Rees, Tobias (2008). *Designs for an Anthropology of the Contemporary*. Durham: Duke University Press.

REN21 (Renewable Energy Policy Network for the 21st Century) (2016). *Renewables 2016: Status Report*. Paris: REN21. Link accessed 10 October 2016: www.ren21.net/wp-content/uploads/2016/06/GSR_2016_KeyFindings1.pdf

Revet, Sandrine (2013). 'A Small World': Ethnography of a Natural Disaster Simulation in Lima, Peru. *Social Anthropology* 21 (1): 38–53.

Roe, Emery & Schulman, Paul (2008). *High Reliability Management: Operating on the Edge*. Stanford, CA: Stanford Business Books.

Shove, Elizabeth (2003). Converging Conventions of Comfort, Cleanliness and Convenience. *Journal of Consumer Policy* 26 (4): 395–418.

Shove, Elizabeth (2010). Beyond the ABC: Climate Change Policy and Theories of Social Change. *Environment and Planning A* 42 (6): 1273–1286.

Silvast, Antti (2011). Monitor Screens of Market Risks: Managing Electricity in a Finnish Control Room. *STS Encounters* 4 (2): 145–174.

Silvast, Antti; Hänninen, Hannu & Hyysalo, Sampsa (2013). Energy in Society: Energy Systems and Infrastructures in Society. *Science & Technology Studies* 26 (3): 3–13.

Silvast, Antti & Kaplinsky, Joe (2007). White Paper on Security of European Electricity Distribution. Project Understand, European Commission, Leonardo da Vinci programme.

Silvast, Antti & Kelman, Ilan (2013). Is the Normal Accidents Perspective Falsifiable? *Disaster Prevention and Management* 22 (1): 7–16.

Silvast, Antti & Virtanen, Mikko (2014). Keeping Systems at Work: Electricity Infrastructure from Control Rooms to Household Practices. *Science & Technology Studies* 28 (2): 93–114.

Sims, Benjamin (2011). Resilience and Homeland Security: Patriotism, Anxiety, and Complex System Dynamics. *Limn* 1 (1). Link accessed 24 November 2016: http://limn.it/resilience-and-homeland-security-patriotism-anxiety-and-complex-system-dynamics/

Southerton, Dale; van Vlie, Bas & Chappells, Heather (2004). Introduction: Consumption, Infrastructure, and Environmental Sustainability. In Southerton, Dale; Chappells, Heather & van Vliet, Bas (eds) *Sustainable Consumption: The Implications of Changing Infrastructures of Provision*. Cheltenham, UK – Northampton, MA: Edward Elgar, 1–14.

SSS (2010). *Security Strategy for Society: A Finnish Government Resolution 16 December 2010*. Authored by the Security and Defence Committee of the Finnish Ministry of Defence. Helsinki: Ministry of Defence. Link accessed 24 November 2016: www.yhteiskunnanturvallisuus.fi/en/materials/doc_download/26-security-strategy-for-society

Star, Susan Leigh (1999). The Ethnography of Infrastructure. *American Behavioral Scientist* 43 (3): 377–391.

Stirling, Andrew (2014). From Sustainability to Transformation: Dynamics and Diversity in Reflexive Governance of Vulnerability. In Hommels, Anique; Mesman, Jessica &

Bijker, Wiebe (eds) *Vulnerability in Technological Cultures: New Directions in Research and Governance*. Cambridge, MA: MIT Press, 305–332.

Suchman, Lucy (2000). Embodied Practices of Engineering Work. *Mind, Culture & Activity* 7 (1/2): 4–18.

Suchman, Lucy (2011). Practice and Its Overflows: Reflections on Order and Mess. *Tecnoscienza* 2 (1): 21–30.

Summerton, Jane & Berner, Boel (2003). Constructing Risk and Safety in Technological Practice: An Introduction. In Summerton, Jane & Berner, Boel (eds) *Constructing Risk and Safety in Technological Practice*. London: Routledge, 1–24.

Tennberg, Monica & Vola, Joonas (2014). Myrskyjä ei voi hallita: Haavoittuvuuden poliittinen talous ("Storms Cannot Be Controlled: The Political Economy of Vulnerability"). *Alue ja Ympäristö* 43 (1): 73–84.

Tierney, Kathleen (2003). Conceptualizing and Measuring Organizational and Community Resilience: Lessons from the Emergency Response Following the September 11, 2001 Attack on the World Trade Center. Preliminary paper. Newark, DE: University of Delaware Disaster Research Center. Link accessed 24 November 2016: http://udspace.udel.edu/bitstream/handle/19716/735/PP329.pdf

UCTE (Union for the Co-ordination of Transmission of Electricity) (2004). Final Report of the Investigation Committee on the 28 September 2003 Blackout in Italy. UCTE Report April 2004. Brussels: UCTE.

UCTE (Union for the Co-ordination of Transmission of Electricity) (2007). Final Report: System Disturbance on 4 November 2006. Brussels: UCTE. Link accessed 24 November 2016: www.entsoe.eu/fileadmin/user_upload/_library/publications/ce/otherreports/Final-Report-20070130.pdf

UK Cabinet Office (2011). *Keeping the Country Running: Natural Hazards and Infrastructure: A Guide to Improving the Resilience of Critical Infrastructure and Essential Services.* London: Cabinet Office. Link accessed 9 November 2016: www.gov.uk/government/uploads/system/uploads/attachment_data/file/61342/natural-hazards-infrastructure.pdf

UK National Infrastructure Commission (2016). Smart Power: A National Infrastructure Commission Report. Link accessed 10 October 2016: www.gov.uk/government/uploads/system/uploads/attachment_data/file/505218/IC_Energy_Report_web.pdf

UKERC (UK Energy Research Centre) (2011). Building a Resilient UK Energy System. Written by Modassar Chaudry, Paul Ekins, Kannan Ramachandran, Anser Shakoor, Jim Skea, Goran Strbac, Xinxin Wang, and Jeanette Whitaker. London: UKERC. Link accessed 10 October 2016: http://nora.nerc.ac.uk/16648/1/UKERC_energy_2050_resilience_Res_Report_2011.pdf

Ullberg, Susann (2005). *The Buenos Aires Blackout: Argentine Crisis Management across the Public-Private Divide*. Stockholm: CM Europe Volume Series. Link accessed 24 November 2016: www.fhs.se/Documents/Externwebben/forskning/centrumbildningar/Crismart/Publikationer/Publikationsserier/VOLUME_28.PDF

UNISDR (United Nations Office for Disaster Risk Reduction) (2005). Hyogo Framework for Action 2005–2015: Building the Resilience of Nations and Communities to Disasters. Link accessed 10 October 2016: www.unisdr.org/we/inform/publications/1037

US Department of Homeland Security (2013). *National Infrastructure Protection Plan 2013: Partnering for Critical Infrastructure Security and Resilience*. Washington: Department of Homeland Security. Link accessed 10 October 2016: www.dhs.gov/sites/default/files/publications/National-Infrastructure-Protection-Plan-2013-508.pdf

US National Infrastructure Council (2009). *Critical Infrastructure Resilience Final Report and Recommendations*. Washington: Department of Homeland Security. Link accessed

10 October 2016: www.dhs.gov/xlibrary/assets/niac/niac_critical_infrastructure_resil
ience.pdf

van der Vleuten, Erik (2004). Infrastructures and Societal Change: A View from the Large
Technical Systems Field. *Technology Analysis & Strategic Management* 16 (3): 395–414.

van der Vleuten, Erik & Lagendijk, Vincent (2010). Interpreting Transnational Infrastructure Vulnerability: European Blackout and the Historical Dynamics of Transnational Electricity Governance. *Energy Policy* 38 (4): 2053–2062.

Verbong, Geert & Geels, Frank (2007). The Ongoing Energy Transition: Lessons from a
Socio-Technical, Multi-Level Analysis of the Dutch Electricity System (1960–2004).
Energy Policy 35 (2): 1025–1037.

Warner, Frederick (1992). Introduction. In Royal Society Study Group (eds) *Risk: Analysis, Perception and Management.* London: The Royal Society, 1–12.

Part II

Things we need

The emergence of infrastructural crisis preparedness

2 Emerging infrastructures in economic military defence

Basics of preparedness

Each experience of an electrical power failure emphasizes those technologies that do not work without electricity, ranging from lights and refrigerators to elevators, desktop computers, and Internet connections. At the same time, concerns for functioning electricity figure much more broadly than just in everyday life. Today it is common for governments and international institutions to view electricity as part of society's critical infrastructure. Critical infrastructures are those services, sites, and technical networks which governments regard as indispensable (Edwards 2003) and which are therefore to be protected from disruptions (Collier & Lakoff 2008). Energy and electricity are considered society's *critical sectors* in more than 20 countries (Brunner & Suter 2009) as well as the Council of the European Union's definition of *European critical infrastructure* (European Council 2008).

A number of considerations on electricity as a vital societal infrastructure emerged in Finnish security debates in the early 2000s. In 2003, the Finnish government published *The Strategy for Securing the Functions Vital to Society* (YETTS 2003). The strategy's purpose was threefold: to identify those national *vital functions* that are indispensable for national sovereignty, citizen's livelihood, and security; to describe what may compromise these functions according to specific *threat scenarios*; and to assign responsibilities to actors such as governmental ministries to mitigate the probability of such anticipated threats and their effects if they occurred.

The initial threat scenarios from 2003 emphasized what might be called *nation-state security* and *population security* (Collier & Lakoff 2006): most of the time, the subject of security was collective risks to the Finnish nation state and the population, such as public health problems, international conflicts, serious crime, major accidents, or military pressures. The next version of the strategy (SSFVS 2006), however, had changed as it prominently featured technological threats. The strategy outlines an increasing dependence on technology, especially on electric energy, and deems that the government should pay a great deal of attention to this dependence. According to the strategy, a major urban electricity blackout, for example, may lead to a "virtual paralysis" of the society (SSFVS 2006, 49).

Similar threat scenarios continued into the subsequent version of the strategy, *The Security Strategy for Society* (SSS 2010), and the dangers of blackouts were also assessed in a number of other contemporary official documents (Kauppa- ja teollisuusministeriö 2006; Puolustustaloudellinen suunnittelukunta 2006; Puolustusministeriö 2009; Turvallisuuskomitea 2015).

Especially noticeable regarding the topicality of international debates on critical electricity infrastructures was an official risk communication of the effects of long electricity blackouts, called *Long Blackout and Securing the Functions Vital to Society*, published by the Finnish Ministry of Defence, and contracted from two professional journalists. The document's introduction, by a communication manager in the Ministry of Defence and a Finnish infrastructure security expert, notes various shifts in technology and society and outlines their impacts on the notion of societal crisis preparedness:

> The basics of the preparedness of Finnish society have changed markedly due to technological development and globalization in the last ten years. The most significant trend is the networking of the society and increasing dependence on different technical systems. The dependence on electricity has become especially notable.
>
> (Puolustusministeriö 2009, 3)

Preparedness is hence now basically different from before. Finnish society is particularly dependent on electricity, which the document demonstrates through outlining a series of knock-on effects of blackouts on other infrastructures (e.g. sewage, transport, heating). When this document was updated in 2015, its title became simply *Electricity Dependence in a Modern Society* (Turvallisuuskomitea 2015). That such issues interest the publisher, the Ministry of Defence, certainly suggests that the documents were placed in a broader context of the demilitarization of national security. During these years, several other Finnish policy documents had also outlined non-military threats and discussed shifts in the environment of national security (Finnish Security and Defence Policy Report 2004; Gaia Group & Net Effect 2005).

The concerns, summarized above, about complex infrastructural interdependencies, diverse non-military national security threats, and technological disasters that affect the society's various sectors are clearly relevant. The respective documents have been handled in the mainstream national media even in years without major electricity outages (e.g. HS 29 May 2009, 16 October 2011). The same materials were also used in an information campaign on blackout preparedness (Puolustusministeriö 2008; see Chapter 7 in this book) and electricity companies issue similar instructions to their customers (e.g. National Grid US 2016), which they are required to do by law in Finland since 2013.

Power failure statistics and probabilistic thinking may cause further concerns about looming power failures and their risk levels. American researcher of control, dynamical systems, and electrical engineering John Doyle stated in 2004 that "[t]hese kinds of outages [like the major 2003 electrical power failure in the US -AS] are consistent with historical statistics and they'll keep happening" (quoted in Fairley 2004). Elsewhere, Doyle has calculated that a major catastrophic blackout occurs every 35 years statistically (see Nye 2010, 167) and Scandinavian scholars have found corresponding alarming risk levels. A report to the Nordic Council of Ministers on the vulnerability of the Nordic electric power system concluded that the entire system is in a "medium risk state" both concerning a breakdown leading to a major electricity blackout and an energy shortage (that could cause power failures of its own). In practice, "large blackouts in Southern Scandinavia cannot be completely ruled out" and "the probability of a situation like the 2002/03 winter [a hydro energy shortage initiated by low levels of precipitation -AS] or considerably worse is once every ten years" (Doorman et al 2004, 3).

Table 2.1 compiles power failure statistics at the European scale from 1999 to 2013. There are clear gaps in the data of some countries and one should be wary of comparing different national electricity networks with one another: national geographical and climate conditions, for example, vary and can affect power failure levels. But the existing statistics still suggest that Finland belongs to a particular group of European countries: high overall reliability of electricity supplies is met with difficult years when the duration of power failures spikes, such as 2001, 2011, and 2013. Similar countries include Sweden (especially before 2010) and the Baltic states. This somewhat unpredictable trendline also differentiates Finland from a number of other European countries – including Central European states and the United Kingdom, where reliability levels stay consistently high, and countries such as Portugal, Spain, Ireland, Poland, and Hungary, where the initially high level of power failures in the early 2000s have constantly lowered.

Many have envisioned that variable renewables such as wind and solar will challenge electricity security of supply (e.g. UCTE 2007; EURELECTRIC 2014; UK National Infrastructure Commission 2016), but there may be no direct link between Finnish power failures and the country's electricity generation sources. Finnish industry statistics (Energiateollisuus 2016) show that the majority of power supply faults lie in the local electricity distribution networks and are caused by acts of nature such as storms. Wind and solar power could not exert an influence on the large scale: of the Finnish electricity consumption, just 1.3% was covered by wind in 2014 and solar installations are even lower relatively (Haukkala 2015; STY 2016). While 39% of electricity in the Finnish electricity mix is renewable, more than 90% of that is hydropower, wood industry waste products, and wood fuels; Finland also relies on nuclear power, coal, and electricity imports to a much greater extent than wind and solar (Official Statistics Finland 2015a,b).

Nevertheless, when the perception of the society's shift towards energy dependence is combined with these kinds of numbers on the frequency of power failures, the generic conclusion would be that Western societies have become increasingly vulnerable to electricity outages whose occurrence is furthermore almost unavoidable in countries such as Finland. In epochal and urgent discussions such as these, the historical traits of security discourse often have only limited visibility. Yet, at

Table 2.1 Average national annual times of electrical power interruptions (minutes), 1999–2013

Country	1999	2000	2001	2002	2003	2004	2005	2006	2007	2008	2009	2010	2011	2012	2013
Austria				83.08	38.44	30.34	39.41	48.07	72.33	85.68	38.18	31.77	27.85	44.51	39.64
Belgium													36.18	39.45	34.75
Croatia								669.5	375.4	330.9	296.3	307	250.6	372.5	306
Cyprus														148	
Czech Republic										185.5	210.9	135.9	114.1	125.2	195.1
Denmark										16.48	15.29	15.18	17.04	14.75	15.86
Estonia								243.5	185.8	405.3	186.7	406	346	170.9	378.5
Finland	198	130	468	284	212	105	87	64	53	59	41	170	225	68	138
France	55	46	59	42	69.3	57.1	55.9	86.3	61.6	74.1	173.8	95.1	53.9	62.9	83.6
Germany								23.25	35.67	16.96	15.29	20.01	17.25	17.37	32.75
Greece												163	166	150	133
Hungary	411	241.2	250.2	196.8	155.4	137.4	121.8	127.8	141	111	125	132.6	85.12	76.89	138.5
Ireland	273.6	257.9	199.3	230.2	171.9	162.8	163.6	148.3	129.7	108.9	100.4	110			
Italy	191.8	187.4	149.1	114.7	546.1	90.53	79.86	60.55	57.89	89.64	78.67	88.84	108	132.7	105.4
Latvia									269	236	424	1073	708	371	341
Lithuania							373.6	168.7	301.7	155.7	161.3	260	302.6	287.7	153.9
Luxembourg													12	10	10
Malta	25.3		381.5	523.8	567	486.8	398.8	304.4	409	186.6	687.9	620.6	191	286.2	360
The Netherlands		27	31	28	30	24	27.4	35.6	33.1	22.1	26.5	33.7	23.4	27	23
Norway							93	113	96	104	84	66	216	66	144
Poland									410	354.5	408.6	385.5	325.8	263.2	281.8
Portugal			530.7	468	406.2	217.8	198.7	243.2	136	162.7	280	276	131.4	94.15	258.8
Romania										696	682				
Slovak Republic															
Slovenia										116	133	81	76	169	187.1
Spain	156.4	145.4	179.7	142.6	141.9	123.6	117	112.8	103.9	86.82	133.9	140.9	58.2	89.01	109
Sweden	165.8	89.2	162.9	101.8	148.1	78.1	912.6	100	321.9	110.8	73.3	92.3	186.5		154.3
Switzerland												14	16	22	15
United Kingdom				83.69	110.4	81.11	94.29	69.16	100.1	81.94	75.69	81.42	70.02	68.05	61.02

Source: CEER 2015, 26

the same time, research suggests that concerns about infrastructural dependencies and interdependencies have not become relevant merely recently. It is true, at least in the United States, that concerns for critical infrastructure protection originate most directly from information security considerations in the 1990s, as Myriam Dunn Cavelty (2008) has shown. However, in their historical study of the security of US infrastructures, anthropologists Stephen Collier and Andrew Lakoff (2008) found that the current worries over society's critical systems, their vulnerabilities and threats, and the mitigation of system vulnerabilities also have clear analogies to the earlier worries by national security experts – whether these worries have concerned military air raids, nuclear strikes, or the effects of "natural" disasters in particular. If more contemporary policies are influenced by such origins, then it is important to know how, as so many policies have often tried to fix what national security is all about. For example, researcher Kristian Søby Kristensen (2008, 66) has argued that national security policy discourse always generates "certain conditions of possibility for what security is, how it is conceptualized, and what security strategies can and cannot be applied".

In this chapter and the following one, I build upon the research by Collier and Lakoff (2008) to focus on similar issues: the changing meaning of systems without which the Finnish society cannot function; the understanding of national security threats against such systems; and risk techniques such as calculations, classification schemes, and illustrations that take threats into account and sensitize actors such as the government and the industry to minimize their harms. The research question is: *how do national security experts in Finland mitigate electricity outages as risks and attempt to enhance the resilience of society's infrastructures to disruptions?*

Based on my interviews with Finnish infrastructure experts and on reading historical studies (Seppinen 1996; Voimatalouspooli 50 vuotta 2006), two particularly pivotal periods emerged as the focus. The first period extends from the 1920s to the 1950s and concerns the origins of Finnish economic military defence, later the key basis for critical infrastructure protection in Finland. However, this policy evolution was not all that smooth and continuous and the second historical period I discuss spans from the late 1960s to the early 1980s, when one particular rational approach to Finnish national security, namely the storing of raw resources against military crises, became a target of criticism. These critiques wanted to redeploy economic national security in order to secure a continuous provision of food, energy, and various other infrastructural services. The security of these societal services rose on the agenda particularly due to two critical events: the 1973 energy crisis and a concurrent realization of dependence on computer systems and electricity. These issues highlighted that the understanding of the "things we need" had to be shifted away from raw resources that only last a certain amount of time in a trade blockage – in practice, always a military strike – and towards a sufficient level of supply with regard to the needs of the civil society.

The overall claim in this part of the book is that the tension between the older security practice – which the Finnish experts called *storage security* – and its critique – called *security of supply* – is still prominent in the more recent debates about security of infrastructures. First of all, the premise of the security debates is similar: to identify society's critical provisions or systems. Indeed, as I will show, the recent Finnish lists of society's critical sectors or vital functions are only extended versions of a 1984 list of society's *basic supply systems*. Such systems can fail in "normal" conditions and should be protected from diverse threats and not merely from military attacks. While the worry is topical today, it also has parallels with the contemporary response to the 1973 energy crisis. At the same time, the concern with diverse non-military threats also has its roots in the tension between securing a storage and securing a supply. Finnish storage security was exclusively concerned with military threats, while the new practice of security of supply helped diversify the notion of crisis. These powerful and influential ideas are now redeployed in the context of more contemporary infrastructure issues.

I raise historical emergence of ideas in this chapter and the following one, but do not suggest that nothing has changed in the security field. Rather, historical origins of ideas should be acknowledged so one can better identify and explain those shifts that have taken place. As I will claim in what follows, these shifts concern two things in particular. Firstly, the intensity of the security debate has grown: according to security experts, the number of critical systems has increased and the crises are even more diverse than before. Secondly, the studied security practice displays important new developments in non-calculative risk assessment methods. The new strategies concerning vital functions are not so innovative just because they are concerned with complex infrastructural risks, but because for the first time, the mitigation of threats on infrastructures and the increasing of their resilience relies on imaginative scenario work rather than just mathematical calculations (see Collier 2008).

Early modern economic military defences

While their balance has tilted both ways, civil protection of infrastructures intertwines with respective military practices (Collier 2008; Collier & Lakoff 2008). Consequently, at least some key information about this topic is classified and public historical records remain limited. National-scale practices such as stockpiling vital emergency supplies (e.g. oil) and preparedness for infrastructure failures (e.g. outages) are not always apparent to the general public. Finnish experts seem to be aware of this: it is not a coincidence that the Finnish Ministry of Defence contracted journalists to author their risk communications on national threats from electricity blackouts (Puolustusministeriö 2008, 2009; Turvallisuuskomitea 2015).

Yet, a longer history of such efforts exists and became visible in my research. When I talked to infrastructure experts in Finland, they drew my attention to a markedly strong local security tradition. Many emphasized that infrastructure protection in Finland is a peculiarly Finnish problem and practice to begin with. This protection has its roots and origins that according to the experts needed to be acknowledged. One of my informants then suggested a book, a history of an organization that deals with different indispensable supplies and their protection from national emergencies, *national emergency supply* (Seppinen 1996). I decided to concentrate on such materials to investigate traditional security concepts, debates, and problematizations that Finnish governmental and industry experts themselves have found significant over the last 100 years or so. Subsequently, I began to supplement this history from other sources to deepen the attention to infrastructures: including histories of technology, academic military history, and publications by an economic military association.

The historical studies of Finnish emergency supplies (Seppinen 1996; Voimatalouspooli 50 vuotta 2006) concur on the origin of infrastructure protection in Finland. This origin is not the 1973 energy crisis and not the 1910s shortage of paraffin for burning (Myllyntaus 1991, 78; 132–134), but the food shortage of 1917, which occurred in the same year as the Finnish independence from Russia. Often attributed as an acute cause for the Finnish Civil War in 1918 (Myllyntaus 1991, 78), experience from the 1917 food shortage and depression from 1917 to 1919 raised discussions about the need for planning for national emergencies in Finland.

Aside from these national critical events, another definite influence was the emergence of military defence itself in the newly independent country. The Russian army vacated the country in 1917, but left behind what became Finland's early war materials such as guns and cannons. National military preparedness also initiated more systematic policy work around these years. By the mid-1920s, several parliamentary committees were planning national defence in Finland from different perspectives – including both military and economic preparedness. For the first area, a *Defence Revision* operated from 1923 and 1926 in order to estimate the expenditure for the Finnish defence forces and its need of soldiers and equipment. The leader of this body was Eirik Hornborg, a Finnish historian and philosopher, teacher, Member of Parliament, and a voluntary military activist. The revision also helped found a Defence Council, working alongside the president, to pursue defence matters in the country (Sotatieteen laitos 1991, 238).

On the second area, a high-level *economic defence committee* worked since 1924, led by Senator Kaarlo Castrén, a former Prime Minister and Finance Minister of Finland. This body was established to determine "what activities we must pursue so that our nation could withstand the possible perils and difficulties of a war with as few difficulties and losses as possible" (quoted in Sotatieteen laitos 1991, 238). Yet another economic defence committee was coordinated by Bernard Wuolle, also a pioneering Finnish electrical engineer – who once remarked elsewhere that "the degree of electrification measures a nation's level of civilization" (Herranen 1996, 11). While all of these bodies were mainly advisory, the two economic committees concurred on an important outcome: Finland would need to found an office for the military mobilization of the economy, an *Economic Defence Council*.

In 1929, the Finnish Parliament accepted the proposal for the Economic Defence Council. Although stressing military matters already in its name, the concerns regarding this office were actually more wide ranging, as historian Ilkka Seppinen (1996, 21) notes. According to the government proposal for establishing the council, the underlying aim was ambitious: to "mitigate and reduce the effects that an emergency period has on the society's machinery". The aim comprised broad responsibilities for the state as well as for industry. In particular, the anticipation of emergencies was a matter of

> the defence preparedness of the whole industry, the maintaining of agricultural activities and food production, the rationing of the consumption of food, fuel, clothes etc, the organization of many kinds of relief efforts etc. social actions and the arrangement of monetary and credit conditions.
>
> (Finnish Government Proposal 14 for allocating a budget to organize economic defence preparedness, 1 February 1929; quoted in Seppinen 1996, 21)

It is hence stressed here that an advanced society becomes dependent upon the functioning of its industry, food production, consumption of fuel and clothes, and, one notes, even the liquidity of banks. These large-scale provisions are depicted as the "machinery" of the society that is vulnerable to emergencies.

The terminology differs, but in the light of the recent worries over critical infrastructures, the view still seems topical and apt. For example, in resemblance to critical infrastructure sectors (e.g. Brunner & Suter 2009), the Economic Defence Council also divided between departments – for agriculture, industry, transportation, discipline, monetary matters, and public nutrition. Talk of public-private partnerships abounds in critical infrastructure protection (e.g. US Department of Homeland Security 2013), so it is also worth noting the various representatives in the Economic Defence Council, including the Finnish Ministry of Trade and Industry, Ministry of Social Affairs, Ministry of Defence, Bank of Finland, and building associations for railroads, postal services, and telegraphs. Dependence on electricity is a common theme in recent programmes on critical infrastructures, as was shown above; yet, already one of the many tasks of the Finnish historical defence council was securing electric power supply during wartime (Sotatieteen laitos 1991, 239).

Its worries concerning dependence on metaphorical "society's machinery" were also probably not an altogether common account for its time. Several histories outline how modern novelties such as telephone and electricity created a "frenzy" (Myllyntaus 1991, 37; Kaijser 1994; Graham & Marvin 2001, 45–47) when they were introduced in the late 19th and early 20th centuries. For instance, for the Finnish government in 1921, cheap electricity brought new industrial opportunities, increasing international competitiveness, and economic welfare (Myllyntaus 1991, 82). Such grand aspirations possibly never concerned all electricity users. In practice, the printing industry and metallurgical and engineering sectors became the only notable initial electricity users in Finland (Myllyntaus 1991, 49); as late as 1939, many Finnish towns were only partly electrified (Myllyntaus 1991, 95) and rural electricity grids remained unreliable (Myllyntaus 1991, 248–249). Compared to other Nordic countries, Finland remained for a long time a "backward" country concerning its electrification (Kaijser 1995, 50; Thue 1995, 22).

Nonetheless, aspirations about opportunities, competitiveness, and welfare due to electricity clearly existed in Finland and drew on what resembles what Graham and Marvin (2001) call the *modern infrastructural ideal* or what van der Vleuten (2004, 395) similarly names the *ideology of circulation*: "'ideology of circulation' connects infrastructural integration of peoples with economic and ideological exchanges in the service of joint progress, democracy, and peace." In other words, societal and economic progress and control of the natural environment would ensue due to expanding electricity provision (Edwards 2003). This trajectory was also supported by numbers: national projections highlighted a significant growth of the Finnish electricity need (Jahkola 1993, 63). In 1920, MSc Viljo Ylöstalo estimated a growth of 6.5% per year in 1916–1930, which can be related to the Finnish total energy consumption actually lowering during most years from 2003–2011 (Official Statistics Finland 2012). Large-scale electricity provision was also partly the result of the First World War and its troubles in supplying coal-produced gas (Jahkola 1993, 63). Hence, while bottlenecks or even collective crises could have emerged with one energy source, it was widely believed it could be replaced with another infrastructural provision. A very different conclusion emerges in the 1929 Finnish government proposal for economic defence that regards the inherent vulnerability of a society that is dependent on the large-scale provisions of its "machinery".

Total national defence

The initial meaning of war economy, prompted by the Economic Defence Council, encompassed both military and civil matters extensively. It included preparations for the actual wartime economy, which relates to the Finnish defence forces, and economic defence preparedness also during peacetime that has fallen under the Ministry of Trade and Industry since the 1950s (Merjola 1987, 7). However, this style of reasoning about military and civil crises in the wider meaning would not take effect in Finland until many decades later. An Economic Defence Council was founded in 1929, but its tasks were soon narrowed down and the board was later terminated. The reason for this was political defence: with the Second World War looming, the Finnish government was much more concerned with war preparations than with crisis preparedness in the civil life (Seppinen 1996, 22). In 1936, the Finnish Ministry of Defence founded a new War Economy Department whose tasks included developing economic defence preparedness, mobilizing the business world, and stockpiling necessary goods for the defence forces (Merjola 1987, 9). The department was led by Colonel Leonard Grandell – key figure in economic defence and active in the military at the time, later the CEO of the state-owned flight company Aero, today's Finnair.

It is well known that national crises such as wars affect infrastructure provisions including electricity on an intense basis. Often, a national crisis has called for practical solutions, new technologies, and the solving of bottlenecks in infrastructures (Hughes 1983, 286; Kaijser 1994, 159). In Europe, the First World War already drew attention to the rationalization of electricity organizations and their public regulation through price caps, export limits, subsidies, and, in some cases, even state ownership (Lagendijk 2008, 51–57). On the other hand, the Second World War showed the vulnerability of electricity infrastructures to sabotage and strategic bombing as prolonged blackouts emerged in countries such as France (Lagendijk 2008, 118–119).

During the Second World War in Finland, the threat of Soviet air raids raised the advantages of having redundancy in the electric power system, such as preparing more than one power plant that could deliver electricity to war-material factories (Myllyntaus 1991, 99–100; see also Collier & Lakoff 2008). The wartime economy, with its loss of almost all foreign energy imports and one third of the Finnish water generation power, also happened to concur with several unusually dry years (Jahkola 1993, 65). This helped initiate a centrally controlled energy system managed by a public Energy Office.

A few years later after the war, Finnish policy makers began considering the nationalization of the electricity industry, corresponding with what France and Britain had done between 1946 and 1948 (Myllyntaus 1991, 110). The Finnish Parliament voted on the nationalization in 1952, but the bill was rejected by 96 votes to 89. In contrast, for example, Finnish metal factories had been reorganized as a state corporation, Valmet, in 1946 (Merjola 1987, 14). It is likely that these proposals for nationalization and socialization supported cooperation between private electricity companies and the state that would also affect the emerging forms of infrastructural crisis management (see Kaijser 1994, 43–46).

As Finland had lost the war to the Soviet Union, the private sector could not mobilize any war efforts for about a decade. The Finnish defence forces themselves purchased nearly no basic supplies between 1945 and 1955 (Merjola 1987, 14–15). The predisposition to think about civil preparedness through relying on military techniques had, however, not likely disappeared. In the Finnish machine shop culture, for example, as late as the 1960s "the industry had fresh memories of wartime production and the war reparations, which were familiar to many employees. Therefore, national defence attitudes and procedures existed and it was convenient to build upon them" (Kauppinen 2009, 50).

After about 1955, the concerns for Finnish infrastructural crisis preparedness found new support, especially within the security environment of the Cold War, as the security experts themselves thought (Seppinen 1996, 31). The support was accordingly also partly motivated from the "Westernization" of Finland: the country had joined the United Nations and the Nordic Council in 1955 (Voimatalouspooli 50 vuotta 2006, 13). The *Economic Defence Planning Authority* was established in 1955–1956 in place of the Economic Defence Council in order to "develop the country's economic defence preparedness and to protect the population's livelihood and the economic life during crises" (Haukilahti 1973a, 104). This new authority marked also the formal separation of preparedness in defence forces themselves and among the civil industries, which economic defence planning would concern (Merjola 1987, 7).

In 1956, the Industrial and Power Economy Sector (later the Power Economy Pool) of this authority held their first meeting. The functions of the Power

Economy Pool, which still exists, are closely connected with various kinds of emergencies. According to a former manager of the Finnish National Emergency Supply Agency that deals with the country's indispensable supplies and their security, Mika Purhonen (2006, 6), these functions involve the preparedness planning of all "societally vital" electric energy as well as district heating provisions. Private companies did and continue to participate in this emergency planning through voluntary contracts. In other countries, such collaborations are often enforced or then the private sector is not present within civil protection; hence, Purhonen (2006, 6) names this specific arrangement as the *Finnish model*, although it has recognizable parallels both with Switzerland and Sweden (Seppinen 1996, 31).

The concern of this national security collaboration was with "total national defence". This meant defence which involved both political and economic as well as military aspects (hence the term "total") (Seppinen 1996, 37). In spite of such broader considerations, the experts still tended to always equate crisis with war during the 1950s and many decades later. The security concerns that figured in this period stemmed from experiences of foreign trade crises, shortages, rationing, poverty, and depression (Voimatalouspooli 50 vuotta 2006, 11). There was therefore an overarching concern about the duration of raw resources and the maintenance of national production capabilities. If these capabilities lacked in the face of a crisis, national security experts widely believed then this gap could be filled by stockpiling nationally important resources (Haukilahti 1973b, 113).

Preparedness by storage security

Storage security was a slow-onset practice in Finland. When the Second World War broke in Finland in 1939, the country had no national stockpiles – the law on stockpiling fuels and wheat had been enacted then, but too late to gather materials to the national storages (Merjola 1987, 11). Figure 2.1 is another rather rudimentary example of a Finnish stockpile during the Second World War. It shows firewood being stored in a marketplace. Here a stockpile is a concrete storage where materials are kept and managed. A couple of decades later, the approach to national risks in storage security had become markedly more systematic. Figure 2.2, from 1972, displays the consumption (thousand tonne) and stockpile (duration in months) of various Finnish goods. The goods include crops, sugar, coffee, cigarettes, cattle feed, vegetable oil, butter, fertilizers, chemicals, different kinds of coal, oil and gasoline, textiles, rubber and tyres, and various types of metal and steel. One can see that the storage of coal, for example, lasts for over seven months, while coffee runs out in three months. There are two kinds of bars in the figure, one for "commercial centre storages" (diagonal filling) and other for "state security storages" (cross filling). While most goods are stored by private entrepreneurs, particularly lead and tin are stockpiled by the state.

The visuals of the image are basic, especially by today's standards. Yet, this storing already conveys a rather calculative technique of risk governance. That is, once one knew the duration of raw resources by calculating it, one could then

Figure 2.1 Wood is stockpiled in a marketplace in Helsinki (Kasarmitori) during the continuation war, 1943

Source: Pietinen 22 July 1943, Finland's National Board of Antiquities/Museovirasto

assign responsibilities of stockpiling both to the state and private companies. Thus, what is also at stake once again is cooperation by both public and private stakeholders.

A national infrastructure security expert and researcher I talked to highlighted how systematic stockpiling has always been and will continue to be relevant:

> The ancient rural societies had stockpiles for wheat. These practices con-
> tinue to live on, there will be new methods, the old ones become less signifi-
> cant, but they do not disappear altogether and there will be new methods
> and new problems. Look at oil stockpiles, they are still a significant part of
> our preparedness.

But in spite of its systemicity and continued relevance in societies that depend on goods, this style of reasoning also has limitations. Most particularly, as already indicated, classic storage security only dealt with the threat of war. In 1956, the Chair of The Economic Defence Planning Authority, General K. A. Tapola, had proposed a *crisis typology*, which consisted of five kinds of crises (see Table 2.2)

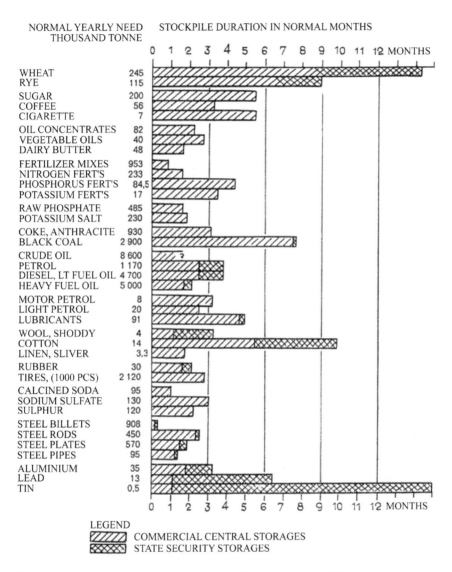

Figure 2.2 The duration (in months) of various Finnish goods in 1972

Source: Translated from Haukilahti 1973b, 118–119

ranging from regular conditions to various kinds of disturbances. Such considerations of crises were not altogether unusual in the 1950s: early American studies of disasters had also proposed that disasters are not merely military attacks, but all those incidents that prevent the maintenance of essential societal functions

Table 2.2 A Finnish crisis typology in economic
defence planning, proposed in 1956
but not implemented

Code	Type of crisis
A1	State of war
A2	Threat of war
B1	Worldwide disorder
B2	Nationwide disorder
C	Regular conditions

Source: Adapted from Seppinen 1996, 32

and disrupt social order (Perry 2007, 6). Also Tapola's inspiration for defence economic organization was international: according to Seppinen (1996, 31), however, it mainly stemmed from his knowledge of civil protection arrangements in Switzerland and in Sweden particularly.

In Finland, it would nonetheless actually take several decades before Tapola's diverse crisis typology was implemented. The underlying problem seems to have been the status of the persons responsible for national crisis management, the so-called *commanders of state*, who were nominated by the President, whose power was comparable to a minister, and whose organization and roles had been rather directly influenced by Second World War thinking. These commanders of electricity, industry, agriculture, finance, and other domains had such extensive rights that it was felt that they could not have been assigned during anything less than an actual state of war (Myllyntaus 1991, 99). For almost 20 years, the concerns for national security remained preoccupied with military threats and with a notion of crisis that is rather straightforward: a crisis was equated with military pressure and most particularly with the rapid onset of the actual state of war.

References

Brunner, Elgin & Suter, Manuel (2009). *International CIIP Handbook 2008/2009: An Inventory of 25 National and 7 International Critical Information Infrastructure Protection Policies*. Zürich: Center for Security Studies. Link accessed 25 November 2016: www.css.ethz.ch/publications/pdfs/CIIP-HB-08-09.pdf

CEER (Council of European Energy Regulators) (2015). *CEER Benchmarking Report 5.2 on the Continuity of Electricity Supply*. Data update. Brussels: Council of European Energy Regulators ASBL. Link accessed 19 October 2016: www.ceer.eu/portal/page/portal/EER_HOME/EER_PUBLICATIONS/CEER_PAPERS/Electricity/Tab4/C14-EQS-62-03_BMR-5-2_Continuity%20of%20Supply_20150127.pdf

Collier, Stephen (2008). Enacting Catastrophe: Preparedness, Insurance, Budgetary Rationalization. *Economy and Society* 37 (2): 224–250.

Collier, Stephen & Lakoff, Andrew (2006). Vital Systems Security: Anthropology of the Contemporary Research Collaboratory Working Paper no. 2. Link accessed 25 November 2016: http://anthropos-lab.net/wp/publications/2007/08/workingpaperno2.pdf

Collier, Stephen & Lakoff, Andrew (2008). The Vulnerability of Vital Systems: How Critical Infrastructures Became a Security Problem. In Dunn Cavelty, Myriam & Kristensen, Kristian Søby (eds) *Securing 'the Homeland': Critical Infrastructure, Risk and (In) security*. London: Routledge, 17–39.

Doorman, Gerard; Kjølle, Gerd; Uhlen, Kjetil; Huse, Einar Ståle & Flatabø, Nils (2004). *Vulnerability of the Nordic Power System: Report to the Nordic Council of Ministers*. Trondheim: SINTEF Energy Research.

Dunn Cavelty, Myriam (2008). Like a Phoenix from the Ashes: The Reinvention of Critical Infrastructure Protection as Distributed Security. In Dunn Cavelty, Myriam & Kristensen, Kristian Søby (eds) *Securing 'the Homeland': Critical Infrastructure, Risk and (In) security*. London: Routledge, 40–62.

Edwards, Paul (2003). Infrastructure and Modernity: Force, Time and Social Organization in the History of Sociotechnical Systems. In Misa, Thomas; Brey, Philip & Feenberg, Andrew (eds) *Modernity and Technology*. Cambridge, MA: MIT Press, 185–225.

Energiateollisuus (Finnish Energy Industries) (2016). *Sähkön keskeytystilastot* ("Electricity Interruption Statistics"). Helsinki: Energiateollisuus. Link accessed 27 October 2016: http://energia.fi/tilastot-ja-julkaisut/sahkotilastot/sahkon-keskeytystilastot

EURELECTRIC (2014). *Renewable Energy and Security of Supply: Finding Market Solutions*. Brussels: EURELECTRIC. Link accessed 10 October 2016: www.eurelectric.org/media/154655/res_report_140919_lr-2014-030-0569-01-e.pdf

European Council (2008). On the Identification and Designation of European Critical Infrastructures and the Assessment of the Need to Improve Their Protection. Directive 2008/114/EC. Link accessed 25 November 2016: http://eur-lex.europa.eu/LexUriServ/LexUriServ.do?uri=CELEX:32008L0114:EN:NOT

Fairley, Peter (2004). The Unruly Power Grid: Advanced Mathematical Modeling Suggests that Big Blackouts are Inevitable. *IEEE Spectrum* 2 August 2004. Link accessed 25 November 2016: http://spectrum.ieee.org/energy/the-smarter-grid/the-unruly-power-grid

Finnish Security and Defence Policy Report (2004). Prime Minister's Office: Publications 18/2004. Link accessed 25 November 2016: www.defmin.fi/files/311/2574_2160_English_White_paper_2004_1_.pdf

Gaia Group & Net Effect (2005). Yhteiskunnan elintärkeiden toimintojen turvaamisen strategian arviointi ("Evaluation of the Strategy for Securing Functions Vital to Society.") Link accessed 25 November 2016: www.defmin.fi/files/249/2769_Yhteiskunnan_elintArkeiden_toimintojen_turvaamisen_strategian_arviointi.pdf

Graham, Stephen & Marvin, Simon (2001). *Splintering Urbanism: Networked Infrastructures, Technological Mobilities and the Urban Condition*. London: Routledge.

Haukilahti, Väinö (1973a). Säännöstelytalouden valmistelu ja sen organisatorinen valmistelu kriisiaikana ("Preparing the Rationing Economy and Its Organisation During Crisis"). In Haukilahti, Väinö; Hyvärinen, Erkki; Korhonen, Keijo; Korte, Olavi; Löyttyniemi, Veikko; Savolainen, Aapo; Öhman, Gunnar; Valtanen, Jaakko & Makkonen, Lauri (eds) *Tietoja maanpuolustuksesta: Maanpuolustus turvallisuuspolitiikan osana* ("Information about National Defence: National Defence as Part of Security Policy"). Helsinki: Pääesikunnan koulutusosasto (Finnish Defence Force's Defence Command Training Department), 105–112.

Haukilahti, Väinö (1973b). Taloudelliset voimavaramme ja niiden kehittäminen ("Our Economic Resources and Their Development"). In Haukilahti, Väinö; Hyvärinen, Erkki; Korhonen, Keijo; Korte, Olavi; Löyttyniemi, Veikko; Savolainen, Aapo; Öhman, Gunnar; Valtanen, Jaakko & Makkonen, Lauri (eds) *Tietoja maanpuolustuksesta:*

Maanpuolustus turvallisuuspolitiikan osana ("Information about National Defence: National Defence as part of Security Policy"). Helsinki: Pääesikunnan koulutusosasto (Finnish Defence Force's Defence Command Training Department), 113–120.

Haukkala, Teresa (2015). Solar Energy and Finland – Do They Match? *PV Magazine* 29 January 2015. Link accessed 19 October 2016: www.pv-magazine.com/opinion-analysis/ blogdetails/beitrag/solar-energy-and-finland – do-they-match_100017982/

Herranen, Timo (1996). *Valtakunnan sähköistyskysymys: strategiat, siirtojärjestelmät sekä alueellinen sähköistys vuoteen 1940* ("The Question of Electrifying a Nation: Strategies, Distribution Systems and Regional Electrification Until 1940"). Helsinki: Suomen historiallinen seura (Finnish Historical Society).

HS (Helsingin Sanomat) (29 May 2009). Sähkökatko vaarantaisi apua tarvitsevat ("An Electricity Blackout Would Endanger Those in Need of Help"). Written by Sanna Jokila, A7.

HS (Helsingin Sanomat) (16 October 2011). Jokainen kriisi on poliittinen ("Every Crisis Is Political"). Written by Anna-Stina Nykänen, D1–D2.

Hughes, Thomas (1983). *Networks of Power: Electrification in Western Society, 1880–1930*. Baltimore, MD: Johns Hopkins University Press.

Jahkola, Antero (1993). Energian tarpeen kehitys ja siitä laaditut ennusteet ("The Development of Energy Need and the Forecasts that Concern It"). In Keskinen, Risto (ed.) *Suomen energiatekniikan historia: teknis-historiallinen tutkimus energian tuottamisesta ja käytöstä Suomessa 1840–1980* ("The History of Finnish Energy Technology: A Technological-Historical Investigation of Energy Production and Use in Finland 1840–1980"). Tampere: Tampere University of Technology Publications, 115.

Kaijser, Arne (1994). *I fädrens spår: den svenska infrastrukturens historiska utveckling och framtida utmaning* ("In the Tracks of the Fathers: The Historical Development and the Future Challenges of the Swedish Infrastructure"). Stockholm: Carlsson.

Kaijser, Arne (1995). Controlling the Grid: The Development of High-tension Power Lines in the Nordic Countries. In Kaijser, Arne & Hedin, Marika (eds) *Nordic Energy Systems: Historical Perspectives and Current Issues*. Canton: Science History Publications, 31–54.

Kauppa- ja teollisuusministeriö (Finnish Ministry of Trade and Industry) (2006). *Sähkönjakelun toimitusvarmuuden kehittäminen: Sähkön jakeluhäiriöiden ehkäisemistä ja jakelun toiminnallisia tavoitteita selvittäneen työryhmän raportti* ("Developing the Supply Security of Electricity Distribution: The Report by the Working Group that Explored the Prevention of Electricity Supply Failures and the Practical Targets for the Supply"). Helsinki: Kauppa- ja teollisuusministeriö.

Kauppinen, Veijo (2009). *Konepajateknisiä pohdintoja: Suomalaisen konepajakulttuurin muutoksia 1960-luvulta 2000-luvulle* ("Deliberations over the Most Significant Changes within the Finnish Machine Shop Culture from the End of the 20th Century to the Beginning of the 21st Century"). Espoo: Teknillinen korkeakoulu, Koneenrakennustekniikan laitos (Helsinki University of Technology, Department of Engineering Design and Production).

Kristensen, Kristian Søby (2008). 'The Absolute Protection of our Citizens': Critical Infrastructure Protection and the Practice of Security. In Dunn Cavelty, Myriam & Kristensen, Kristian Søby (eds) *Securing 'the Homeland': Critical Infrastructure, Risk and (In)security*. London: Routledge, 63–83.

Lagendijk, Vincent (2008). *Electrifying Europe: The Power of Europe in the Construction of Electricity Networks*. Doctoral thesis, Eindhoven University of Technology. Amsterdam: Aksant Academic Publishers. Link accessed 25 November 2016: http://alexandria. tue. nl/extra2/200811526.pdf

Merjola, Timo (1987). Sotatalousesikunta täytti 50 vuotta ("The War Economy Staff Turned 50 Years"). In Väyrynen, Pertti (ed.) *Sotataloustietoutta* ("War Economy Information"). Helsinki: Sotatalousseura (War Economy Association), 7–22.

Myllyntaus, Timo (1991). *Electrifying Finland: The Transfer of a New Technology into a Late Industrialising Economy.* Helsinki: ETLA.

National Grid US (2016). *Before, During and after the Storm: Your Guide to Electric Outage Preparation and Safety.* Warwick: National Grid plc. Link accessed 10 October 2016: www9.nationalgridus.com/non_html/stormpreparedness.pdf

Nye, David (2010). *When the Lights Went Out: A History of Blackouts in America.* Cambridge, MA: MIT Press.

Official Statistics Finland (2012). *Energy Supply and Consumption, 4th Quarter 2012, Appendix Figure 8, Total Energy Consumption 1975–2012.* Helsinki: Statistics Finland. Link accessed 25 November 2016: www.stat.fi/til/ehk/2012/04/ehk_2012_04_2013-03-22_kuv_008_en.html

Official Statistics Finland (2015a). *Electricity Generation by Energy Source 2014.* Helsinki: Statistics Finland. Link accessed 19 October 2016: www.stat.fi/til/salatuo/2014/salatuo_2014_2015–2010–2029_kuv_001_en.html

Official Statistics Finland (2015b). *Electricity Generation with Renewables 2014.* Helsinki: Statistics Finland. Link accessed 19 October 2016: www.stat.fi/til/salatuo/2014/salatuo_2014_2015-10-29_kuv_002_en.html

Perry, Ronald (2007). What Is a Disaster? In Rodrígues, Havidan; Quarantelli, Enrico & Dynes, Russell (eds) *Handbook of Disaster Research.* New York: Springer, 1–15.

Puolustusministeriö (Finnish Ministry of Defence) (2008). Pahasti poikki: Näin selviät pitkästä sähkökatkosta ("Severely Cut: How to Survive a Long Blackout"). Text written by Jaana Laitinen and Suvi Vainio. Link accessed 25 November 2016: www.defmin.fi/files/1275/Pahasti_poikki_nettiversio.pdf

Puolustusministeriö (Finnish Ministry of Defence) (2009). Pitkä sähkökatko ja yhteiskunnan elintärkeiden toimintojen turvaaminen ("Long Blackout and Securing the Functions Vital to Society"). Text written by Jaana Laitinen and Suvi Vainio. Link accessed 25 November 2016: www.defmin.fi/files/1436/pitka_sahkokatko_ja_yett.pdf

Puolustustaloudellinen suunnittelukunta (Finnish Economic Defence Planning Authority) (2006). Viestintä- ja sähkönjakeluverkkojen keskinäiset riippuvuudet ("The Mutual Interdependencies between Telecommunications Networks and Electricity Distribution Networks"). PTS Tietoyhteiskuntasektori 1/2006. Link accessed 25 November 2016: www.huoltovarmuus.fi/static/pdf/231.pdf

Purhonen, Mika (2006). Toimintaympäristön muutoksista huolimatta energia-alan huoltovarmuus on edelleen hyvä ("In Spite of the Shifting Working Environment, the Security of Supply of the Energy Sector is Still Good"). In *Voimatalouspooli 50 vuotta.* A history whose working group included Heikki Hartikainen, Eino Hälikkä, Leni Lustre-Pere, Timo Ristokankare, Maria Hallila, and Tuija Sorsa. Helsinki: Puolustustaloudellinen suunnittelukunta (Finnish Economic Defence Planning Authority) and Voimatalouspooli (Power Economy Pool), 6–7.

Seppinen, Ilkka (1996). *Ahdinkoajan varalle: Taloudellinen puolustusneuvosto ja puolustustaloudellinen suunnittelukunta huoltovarmuuden kehittäjänä 1929–1955–1995* ("For Times of Distress: The Economic Defence Council and the Economic Defence Planning Authority as Developers of Security of Provision 1929–1955–1995"). Helsinki: Puolustustaloudellinen suunnittelukunta (Finnish Economic Defence Planning Authority).

Sotatieteen laitos (Department of War Studies) (1991). *Talvisodan historia, osa 4* ("History of Winter War, Part 4"). Finnish National Defence University. Helsinki: WSOY.

SSFVS (2006). *The Strategy for Securing the Functions Vital to Society: A Finnish Government Resolution 23 November 2006.* Authored by the Security and Defence Committee of the Finnish Ministry of Defence. Helsinki: Ministry of Defence. Link accessed 25 November 2016: www.defmin.fi/files/858/06_12_12_YETTS__in_english.pdf

SSS (2010). *Security Strategy for Society: A Finnish Government Resolution 16 December 2010.* Authored by the Security and Defence Committee of the Finnish Ministry of Defence. Helsinki: Ministry of Defence. Link accessed 24 November 2016: www. yhteiskunnanturvallisuus.fi/en/materials/doc_download/26-security-strategy-for-society

STY (Finnish Wind Power Association) (2016). Tuulivoima Suomessa ("Wind Power in Finland"). Website. Link accessed 19 October 2016: www.tuulivoimayhdistys. fi/tietoa-tuulivoimasta/tietoa-tuulivoimasta/tuulivoima-suomessa-ja-maailmalla/ tuulivoima-suomessa

Thue, Lars (1995). Electricity Rules: The Formation and Development of the Nordic Electricity Regimes. In Kaijser, Arne & Hedin, Marika (eds) *Nordic Energy Systems: Historical Perspectives and Current Issues.* Canton: Science History Publications, 11–30.

Turvallisuuskomitea (Finnish Security Committee) (2015). *Sähköriippuvuus modernissa yhteiskunnassa* ("Electricity Dependence in a Modern Society"). Jaana Laitinen (ed.). Helsinki: Turvallisuuskomitea (Finnish Security Committee). Link accessed 19 October 2016: www.defmin.fi/files/3070/sahkoriippuvuus_modernissa_yhteiskunnassa_verk kojulkaisu.pdf

UCTE (Union for the Co-ordination of Transmission of Electricity) (2007). Final Report: System Disturbance on 4 November 2006. Brussels: UCTE. Link accessed 25 November 2016: www.entsoe.eu/fileadmin/user_upload/_library/publications/ce/otherreports/ Final-Report-20070130.pdf

UK National Infrastructure Commission (2016). Smart power: A National Infrastructure Commission Report. Link accessed 10 October 2016: www.gov.uk/government/uploads/ system/uploads/attachment_data/file/505218/IC_Energy_Report_web.pdf

US Department of Homeland Security (2013). *National Infrastructure Protection Plan 2013: Partnering for Critical Infrastructure Security and Resilience.* Washington: Department of Homeland Security. Link accessed 10 October 2016: www.dhs.gov/sites/default/ files/publications/National-Infrastructure-Protection-Plan-2013-508.pdf

van Der Vleuten, Erik (2004). Infrastructures and Societal Change: A View from the Large Technical Systems Field. *Technology Analysis & Strategic Management* 16 (3): 395–414.

Voimatalouspooli 50 vuotta (The Power Economy Pool 50 Years) (2006). *Voimahuollon varautumisen vaiheita 1956–2006* ("The Phases of Preparedness in Power Supply 1956–2006"). A history whose working group included Heikki Hartikainen, Eino Hälikkä, Leni Lustre-Pere, Timo Ristokankare, Maria Hallila, and Tuija Sorsa. Helsinki: Puolustustaloudellinen suunnittelukunta (Finnish Economic Defence Planning Authority) and Voimatalouspooli (Power Economy Pool).

YETTS (2003). Yhteiskunnan elintärkeiden toimintojen turvaamisen strategia ("The Strategy for Securing the Functions Vital to Society"). A Finnish government resolution 27 November 2003. Authored by the Security and Defence Committee of the Finnish Ministry of Defence. Helsinki: Ministry of Defence. Link accessed 25 November 2016: www.defmin.fi/files/248/2515_1687_Yhteiskunnan_elintArkeiden_toiminto jen_turvaamisen_strategia_1_.pdf

3 Towards critical infrastructure and vital systems protection

New security problems and security of supply

Considering the Finnish electricity infrastructure and its security of supply, concerns over the duration of raw resources and stockpiling may have been justified in the context of the war and the post-war shortage of electricity (Myllyntaus 1991, 102–108). Over the next few decades, however, the prices of fossil fuel prices lowered, Finland established a number of new water power plants, energy imports were initiated first from Sweden in 1959 and then from the Soviet Union in 1961, and in 1969 there was a decision to build a Finnish nuclear power plant which became operational in 1977 (Jahkola 1993, 67). In summary, it would seem that the Finnish electricity infrastructure was becoming more resilient due to new cheaper energy generation and energy imports. However, it was a perceived collective energy crisis that helped the style of reasoning about infrastructure crisis management expand to address newly found infrastructural problems in Finland. But this did not take place before the key threat scenarios and vocabularies of this reasoning had shifted considerably.

By the late 1960s and early 1970s, a number of events had challenged Finnish national security. Perhaps the most dramatic was the 1973 energy crisis, which happened to concur with a marked decrease in Finland's energy self-reliance. An illustration of the crisis from a historical study shows three trend lines (Seppinen 1996, 81). The price of crude oil displays in 1973 a sudden shock. There were, however, two more creeping developments: the Finnish society had slowly become a larger consumer of energy and was less self-sufficient energy-wise. These two trends can be seen as a gradual development that led to vulnerability to the oil price shock. As a contemporary comment noted, what had emerged was a "decisive dependence of Finnish energy supply on the import and storing of foreign fuels" (Haukilahti 1973, 116). Another Finnish military expert on energy reflected on this in his study, titled *Energy Supply Crisis Preparedness*: "considering self-sufficiency, the future prospects of our energy supply are not particularly encouraging" (Auer 1973, 139).

The oil crisis was widely debated in the Nordic countries at the time (Myllyntaus 1991; Kaijser 1994; Ruostetsaari 1998) and historian Timo Myllyntaus (1991, 132) argues that the oil crisis even "led to a reformulation of the objectives of Finnish energy policy". These reimagined policy aims included rational energy consumption, increasing the share of indigenous energy sources, and improvements to the efficiency of the management and planning in the national energy economy. The government hence increased its influence in energy decision-making and the promotion of energy saving (Jahkola 1993, 68) and also started to tax electricity consumption for the first time (Myllyntaus 1991, 132). While it is not clear whether such energy policy reforms gave more prominence to the national infrastructure security experts, the oil crisis was still a crucial national security event that led to challenging existing styles of thinking and proposing new forms of problem-solving.

At the same time, it was also becoming more apparent that perhaps not all "indispensable" economic activities had been identified within the mainstream national security practice and thinking. As I discussed in the previous chapter, it was a tradition to prepare for crises by stockpiling goods such as oil, fuel, and food. By the late 1960s, technologies had arrived, however, which required more than just a storage to function reliably. Indeed, these technologies needed to be operational all the time. This was true for the computer systems that were already used extensively in the 1970s finance and industrial processes, while it was also apparent that 1970s convenience stores with their lighting and cooling systems were entirely dependent on electric energy supplies (Seppinen 1996, 89).

Ilkka Kananen, the director of the Finnish National Emergency Supply Agency, describes the historical difference between 1980s production technologies and earlier vital goods as follows:

> As production technology develops and becomes more complex, this emphasizes the security of supply of components, spare parts, and semi-finished products as well the requirement for knowhow. To maintain production one should also take care of energy, water, and waste supplies, transport and distribution systems, communications, computing, and the functioning of the public administration's information systems.
>
> (Kananen 2011, 5)

In other words, while still requiring raw resources in components and parts, the complex production technologies that he described had created seemingly higher demands on maintaining their reliable infrastructures. Electricity-related incidents such as the famous New York blackout in 1977 or the strike of Finnish power plant personnel in the same year no doubt also highlighted interdependencies between energy and society, but were not the only cause for concern (cf. Myllyntaus 1991, 144; 348).

The Economic Defence Planning Authority and its Power Economy Pool were engaged in what is reported to have been strong internal disputes. The central disagreement was about whether these organizations had comprehended up-to-date hazards and threats such as the above (Voimatalouspooli 50 vuotta 2006, 25). Along with other disparate events, the oil crisis, growing complexity of production technologies, and dependence on electricity all showed that a crisis develops over a long period, not through rapid onset like a military attack. A catastrophe may arise or even loom in the midst of "normal" civil conditions; not merely in the context of a state of war (Seppinen 1996, 81–83).

With these issues in mind, security thinking and practice was problematized by critical national security experts. In 1977, K. H. Pentti, the then-vice CEO of the state petrol company Neste and soon-to-become planning director of the Economic Defence Planning Authority, intervened in security debates by suggesting the term *security of supply* (huoltovarmuus). It was meant to replace the previously established term *storage security* (varastovarmuus). It is not known whether Pentti invented the concept of "huoltovarmuus" and it is true that the authority dealing with this issue, the *National Emergency Supply Agency* (Huoltovarmuuskeskus), was only founded in 1992. But the meaning given to this concept by experts and its emerging importance is of considerable interest and what concerns me here.

These terms cannot carry all of their connotations in English translation. The official translation of *huoltovarmuus* has either been *security of supply* or *emergency supply*. In English, *supply* means a provision or a resource, which might actually also be a storage. The word huolto has these meanings as well, nonetheless its most literal translation might be *maintenance*: the process of keeping something in good condition. While nowadays having quite a specialized technical and military meaning in Finnish, *huolto* is an old word that stems from the late 18th century and is derived from the word *huoli* (Häkkinen 2004). *Huoli* literally means a *concern* and acquired the form *huolehtia*, meaning "to take care of", in the mid-19th century. All of this indicates not just a supply of resources, but that huoltovarmuus is a broader process of taking care of people's living conditions.

For Pentti, the new term was characteristic of the security situation in many ways:

> The old question had been: "How long do raw resources last with normal consumption?" Now the question has become: "Which level of supply is satisfactory with regards to the need of raw material and fuel in different kinds of crises?"
>
> (Quoted in Seppinen 1996, 91)

Security thinking rarely changes altogether, as the infrastructure researcher and expert pointed out in the previous chapter. As the quote here also shows, the problem is still about foreseeing and mitigating national security threats by means of calculation. But the objective of the calculation has changed: from determining the duration of raw resources to finding a level of supply. A more significant change is visible in the end, which notes that there are "different kinds of crises". Hence, in other words, there is more to national security than just military crises.

New kinds of accidents and other emergencies were indeed soon raised on the agenda, including disasters that had effect in everyday life and took on a life of their own rather than being merely short-lived military events. Such crises also required a new typology, which was deployed in 1978 (Table 3.1). This was actually very close to K. A. Tapola's proposal from 1956 (Table 2.2).

Table 3.1 A Finnish crisis typology in security of supply, first implemented in 1978

Type of crisis	Preliminary stage	Crisis	Recovery
Economic crisis	0.5–1 months	12 months	3 months
Threat of war	0.5–1 months	12 months	3 months
Military attack (including 6 months of total blockage of foreign trade)	0.5–1 months	3 months	3 months

Source: Adapted from Seppinen 1996, 90

The classifications are similar to Tapola's, from an economic crisis to threat of war and military attack (a major accident was proposed as the fourth category by the Finnish Defence Council, but not implemented in the policy). In addition, the crises were also given durations. Each crisis had three phases: firstly, a preliminary stage; secondly, the actual crisis; and finally, recovery. Military attack also included a six-month blockage of foreign trade. Crises were hence diversified on many parameters: not only by their type, but also by the time they typically took to escalate, develop, and eventually finish. Summing up, crises act like processes: there is a period of stability, followed by disruption and adjustment, and subsequently new disruptions, which follow a similar cycle. This Finnish multi-scale typology of disasters was sophisticated for its time internationally: similar considerations had begun to be developed in the American academic literature on disaster studies in the 1960s (Perry 2007, 8).

According to the official history of the organization that is responsible for Finnish security of supply, national security had now opened up to the needs of civil society (Seppinen 1996, 94). Preparedness practice used to be highly secretive: according to one infrastructure and electricity expert I interviewed, it was strongly suggested that preparedness plans by electricity utilities be kept in a safe because a crisis was an event that might always escalate to a war. Many of the ways in which electricity utilities, the industries, telecommunications, and other civil sectors prepare for military defence remains classified of course. The new security practice presented here, however, concerned more than such a military preparedness. As another researcher and infrastructure expert explained, it might be best characterized as continuity planning: "this simply means that different situations have been thought about, regarding how we act if this or that happens, if the majority of your personnel get flu, then how will you act, and how do you keep the wheel turning."

Continuity is a marked concern of businesses in all conditions. Influenza and other such occurrences can happen all the time, not merely when a military power strikes. These are civil and not military problems. But it is important to add that the crisis management techniques themselves were not "demilitarized". Rather, the critical security experts took risk techniques from military security and redeployed them in the civil crisis management context. Closely parallel events may also be seen in the United States: techniques such as evacuation planning and training emergency responders stem from the military, although they may be applied to "natural" disasters, energy shortages, infrastructure failures, and humanitarian emergencies (Collier & Lakoff 2006, 20–27).

This represented one picture, although I would argue it is a contested one concerning what risk in the context of the electricity infrastructure is all about. In 1982, professor, geographer, and former Finnish Minister of Trade and Industry Ilmari Hustich (1982, 12) stated: "In industrial countries over these years, there has emerged a widely spread fear by citizens of where large-scale development of technology and energy is headed. A fear of an ecological catastrophe has been born." One worry in this context concerned the exhaustion of raw resources, another was about nuclear power. While Finland had been an enthusiastic adopter of nuclear power in the 1960s and early 1970s, by 1982, the majority of the Finnish population was against new nuclear power plants, influenced in part by the Three Mile Island accident in 1979 and the referendum against nuclear energy in Sweden in 1980 (Myllyntaus 1991, 143; 348). However, the national security experts in my study were probably not arguing against large technological provisions in themselves even if it was widely acknowledged that they may have an inherent tendency to fail catastrophically (see also Perrow 1999). Their concern was more with identifying threats – ecological threats could also have been included – finding systemic vulnerabilities, protecting systems, and mitigating accidents if something went wrong. Knowing this helps understand the possibilities and the aims – as well as the limitations – of contemporary forms of infrastructure protection in Finland.

Catalogues of national security infrastructures

As a purely practical matter, the systems and provisions which are part of society's security of supply cannot be safeguarded before they are defined. Dated to 1984 but developed a few years earlier, Finland's first catalogue of basic supply systems went as follows (Seppinen 1996, 100):

Systems necessary for securing the living conditions of citizens:

- Food supply
- Clothing supply
- Dwelling and community services
- Health care

Systems necessary for maintaining national independence:

- Different sectors of national defence
- Public administration and finance
- Communications and publicity

Secondary support systems:

- Transportation
- Energy supply
- Imports and exports

This list repeated in an unpublished government resolution for aims of national security of supply, later the basis for founding the Finnish National Emergency Supply Agency in 1992 (Kananen 2011, 3–6). The Agency became responsible for securing "indispensable" economic activities such as the above. Storage security was also designated as one part of emergency supply, as the first Security of Supply Act (1992) incorporated the previous Legislation on State Security Storages (1958). Since then, the Finnish government has produced four binding decisions on security of supply aims (1995, 2002, 2008, and 2013). Today, both terms "security of supply" and "storage security" are rather eclectic and rarely used in everyday language. But I would claim that their underlying ideas and tensions have remained influential when we start to consider more recent developments in infrastructure security.

Supply, *huolto*, figured for one thing in the ways that energy experts in my study talked about what kind of service they produce. For many, electricity appeared more than a technology or a purely technical supply system. One expert in electrical engineering and communications said:

> I have taken electricity as a natural trait of modern society. Electricity is very much a factor in ensuring that society even stays together. It's a little like the education system or health care, energy belongs structurally to society.

Even though rarely expressed in everyday thinking, the likening of electricity to education and health is understandable considering its history: this is how the style of reasoning about society's basic supplies, outlined above, works. A number of the experts I interviewed did also imply that electric energy is a basic supply, not merely any market commodity. In 2013, Mauri Pekkarinen, the former Finnish Minister of Trade and Industry, raised this same viewpoint and the concept of "huoltovarmuus" when worrying about the effect of the sales of a major Finnish electricity network to outside investors (Yle 7 February 2013).

Over the recent years, however, it has become more common to talk about the security and protection of infrastructures than about supply or storage (e.g. Dunn Cavelty 2008; European Council 2008; Brunner & Suter 2009; US Department of Homeland Security 2013). The Finnish 2002 catalogue of societal basic technical structures was translated by experts to "critical infrastructure sectors" for an international policy survey (Abele-Wigert & Dunn 2006, 84) – even if these terms were not yet used in Finnish expressions of the time.

- Energy networks and supply
- Telecommunication networks
- Information systems and ICT maintenance
- Electronic and print media
- Financing services
- Payment systems and currency supply
- Water supply and other municipal utilities
- Transportation, storage, and distribution systems

- Food supply
- Social services and public health
- Defence-related industry and system maintenance

Viewed alongside the list of Finnish basic supply systems, it is clear that the lists have similarities. More than half of the sectors in the 2002 list have counterparts in the 1984 list. The most notable change is terminological. The newer list draws on the words *networks* and *systems*: for example, the list includes energy networks (rather than just energy supply); telecommunication networks (rather than just communications); and payment systems (rather than just finance). While not talking about infrastructures before 2008, the Finnish government's decisions on security of supply display the same development: critical infrastructures in this are less a supply, more a networked technological system. In academic literature, a very similar difference exists between *large technological systems* – sometimes understood as more-or-less closed supplies – and more networked, open, and reconfigurable *infrastructures* (Edwards 2010, 11–12).

It could be hence that the notion of a technological infrastructure is finding more support and expanding. This would correspond with the analyses of the US infrastructure protection policy (Dunn Cavelty 2008). Yet, it is also clear that the expansion has a different character in Finland. It is not a matter of first being concerned with information and communication technologies and then extending the worry to other infrastructures. Rather, the list of provisions is extensive to begin with and is only subsequently added to with newer networked technical systems.

How far does this readjustment of the 1984 list of basic supplies continue? As mentioned in the beginning of this part of the book, there is also a second policy area that figures in the Finnish efforts to protect systems such as electricity: the protection of society's vital systems. It is more recent than security of supply and the first official document relating to it was released in 2003. As the name implies, vital functions security thinking is about various functions that are deemed vital. According to a security policy document (Finnish Security and Defence Policy Report 2004, 145), its origins can be found in the Finnish security and defence policy concerns for "structural changes in society", "internationalization", and "threats associated with international developments" in the early 2000s. The strategies on vital functions are resolutions and have no direct legislative effects. But their evolution closely follows the binding catalogues of security of supply, and arguably, they are also a more extensive source: resolutions are a type of discussion papers or preparatory decisions, and may offer more detailed insights than mere legislation into what the government was anticipating regarding societal security at the time of their publication (Silvast 2014).

The first official document that considered these provisions that are needed for the "functioning of society" was released in Finland in 2003. The document was called *The Strategy for Securing Functions Vital to Society* and these functions were defined as those measures "whose protection is necessary for helping to maintain national sovereignty and the citizen's livelihood and security" (YETTS 2003, 22).

Curiously, although in line with the idea that risk-based reasoning and discourse are often redeployed rather than completely reinvented, the definition is not very far from the definition of security of supply in legislation: "the economic functions and related technical systems which are indispensable for securing the livelihood of the population, the country's economy, and national defence in case of serious emergencies" (Laki huoltovarmuuden turvaamisesta 2016, Section 1). The YETTS (2003, 22) definition does not mention emergencies nor the economy, but otherwise both texts contain almost the same elements.

A look at these "vital functions" shows again marked similarities to the 1984 list of basic supply systems. Indeed, as we can observe, only one of the 1984 "systems", namely clothing supply, was dropped from the 2003 list of "vital functions".

- Management of government affairs
- International activity
- National military defence
- Internal security
- The functioning of the economy and society
- The population's income security and capability to function
- Psychological crisis tolerance

This strategy was first revised in 2006 and then in 2010, with the next update expected in 2017. Most of the vital functions remained unaltered in 2006; however, one of the 2003 vital functions "functioning of the economy and *society*" was changed to "functioning of the economy and *infrastructure*". Furthermore, infrastructures received a formal definition which they lacked in the 2003 strategy. This was "the technical structures and organizations which are necessary to provide a livelihood for the population and for the functioning of society" (SSFVS 2006, 16) – an understandable inclusion given that technological threats had to receive ample attention starting from the 2006 strategy based on contemporary defence policy documents (Finnish Security and Defence Policy Report 2004, 151–152) and the former strategy's official evaluation (Gaia Group & Net Effect 2005). In 2010, the name of the strategy was changed to the Security Strategy for Society, but the list of the vital functions remained the same as in 2006, although some terms were changed, in particular "national military defence" became "Finland's defence capability" while "psychological crisis *tolerance*" was now "psychological *resilience* to crisis".

Table 3.2 is a comparison of three catalogues of the most vital societal systems in Finland. Eight provisions are visible in all of the lists: dwelling and municipal utilities, electricity and energy, finance and payment, food supply, media and communication, national defence, public health, and transportation. Public administration and international trade are in the 1984 list, but not in the 2002 list; however, they reappear starting from 2003. The 2002 list of critical infrastructures for its part adds two technical infrastructure systems: information and communication devices and water supply. Social services are also part of the 2002 list, later adding labour force, education, research, internal security, and the population's

Table 3.2 Three different Finnish classifications of basic societal supplies

	Basic supply systems (1984)	Critical infrastructure sectors (2002)	Vital societal functions (2003, 2006, 2010)
Clothing	X		
Dwelling and municipal utilities	X	X	X
Electricity and energy	X	X	X
Finance and payments	X	X	X
Food supply	X	X	X
Media and communication	X	X	X
National defence	X	X	X
Public health	X	X	X
Transportation	X	X	X
International trade and cooperation	X		X
Public administration	X		X
Information systems		X	X
Telecommunications		X	X
Water supply		X	X
Social services		X	X
Education and research			X
Insurance			X
Internal security			X
Labour force			X
Psychological crisis resilience			X

psychological crisis tolerance starting from 2003. Clothing appears in the 1984 list but is not repeated after that. A final notable addition since 2003 is insurance, since when it has been apparently noticed that securing society's vital functions "requires a functioning insurance system in all conditions" (YETTS 2003, 31).

Summing up, the list of society's vital functions has expanded, yet the idea that there are basic provisions in society that can be identified is not new as such. The same also seems to apply to many of the points made by the new Finnish strategies on vital functions and societal security. For example, these strategies often start from the observation that disasters can occur in everyday conditions. In 2003, the strategy notes the effects of an electricity blackout:

> Computer systems depend on an electricity supply. There are blackouts also in normal conditions. In serious disturbances and exceptional situations, electricity production, electricity transmission and distribution can be disturbed even for a long time.
>
> (YETTS 2003, 7)

Without knowing the history of the debates in Finland, this excerpt is slightly dubious. Why mention normal conditions at all? The explanation comes clearer when looking at the 1970s debate on national security and military threats. The point seems to be that an electricity blackout is not simply an emergency condition "in which the authorities are no longer able to control the situation by regular powers or resources" (SSFVS 2006, 66). Rather, an electricity blackout, even a long one, might occur in everyday situations, exactly like the 1973 energy crisis did earlier.

The new strategies also problematize complex infrastructural interdependencies, especially starting from the 2006 strategy. Particular attention is paid to the reliance on electricity, as in this passage from 2006: "A new focus area, exemplifying the growing dependency on technology, is the security of energy supply. It is a fundamental prerequisite for the systems to function in the information society" (SSFVS 2006, 45). Yet, it is rather easy to see parallels with the 1970s considerations for computerization and electricity dependence here – 1970s banking, industrial processes, and daily commerce already depended on automation, electric lighting, and cooling to function reliably. As Table 3.2 shows, many of these more general systems were themselves considered society's basic "supplies".

Let us situate one final theme which is pervasive in the new Finnish strategies. This is the notion that threats and crises can be diverse. Each strategy outlines different threat scenarios regarding society's vital functions – there were 10 scenarios in 2003, 9 scenarios in 2006, and 13 scenarios in 2010 – ranging from disturbances in the electricity grid to "natural" disasters and the use of military force. The strategy from 2006 also highlights the diversity with image in Figure 3.1. The image displays the interrelationship between a risk and threat analysis and the resources of the actors that are concerned with the risks and threats. The strategy is represented with the symbol in the middle,

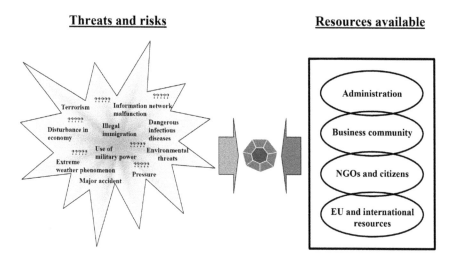

Figure 3.1 A Finnish analysis of threats and risks from a national security strategy

Source: SSFVS 2006, 22

mediating between the resources and what seems like a very diverse notion of threats and risks indeed. Inside the explosion on the left, there are various threats, such as "illegal immigration", "information network malfunction", and (with no further specification) "pressure". Even more visible, however, are the multiple question marks. It is apparent here that the national security threats have become so diverse that even experts do not know what kind of events might pose a future harm.

Yet, these are not an entirely novel or original security concern. The notion of diverse crises can be traced back as far as the 1950s, starting from the origins of US disaster sociology, K.A. Tapola's unconventional crisis typology and its deployment in 1978 in developing security of supply practices in Finland. Even then, the idea was that national risks are different and comprise not merely states of war, but also civil contingencies such as economic crises. The strategies from the 2000s add even more to the diversity, especially by admitting that the national security threat might well be unknown (Furedi 2007), but they are still drawing on ideas and techniques which are old and already established.

Similar charting of national risks is also more widespread than to just Finland. For example, the UK government has published National Risk Registers since 2008 and outlined those high-consequence risks that face the United Kingdom, ranging from coastal flooding to widespread electricity failure, pandemic influenza, and attacks on infrastructures (Figure 3.2). There are just a few main differences between the UK picture and the Finnish picture. Firstly, the UK figure orders risks by likelihoods and impacts, while the Finnish figure has no magnitudes at all, not even schematic ones, and the Finnish strategy also has question marks which are missing from the UK figure. Secondly, the current UK risk registers separate terrorist risks from all "other risks", but the Finnish strategies combine all known risks and even beyond into one figure.

The electricity managers I interviewed were clearly influenced by such ways of thinking about uncertain security problems. Many emphasized that disturbances to electricity supply come as a surprise to them, that electricity blackouts are inevitable, and that there are threats whose impacts are even unknown: as a manager of an electricity network told me, "if many large energy plants become disconnected from the network due to an error, no-one knows if we can manage it or not." When prompted about a major electricity failure in Finland, he continued "everything is possible. I'd rather use the term it is not very probable." Hence even major failures could occur even if they are improbable. This is why another manager, a CEO of a company, was sceptical about methods that measure how much blackouts "cost" to energy customers and redistribute risks from this premise. His concern was not with impacts measured in monetary terms, but with something much more serious: "Major blackouts are rare, but still possible and if they occur, lacking preparedness and anticipation could mean that we shall really have fatalities." While termed in temporality of prior preparedness, his aim was something more extensive: improving society's resilience to major electricity outages was all about safeguarding human vitality and national health.

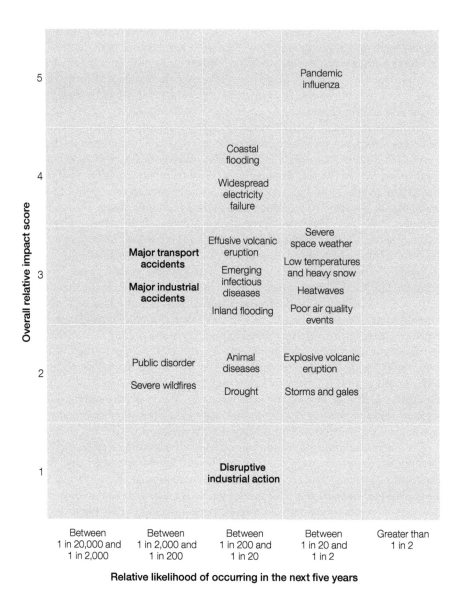

Figure 3.2 The UK National Risk Register on "other risks", excluding "terrorist risks"
Source: UK Cabinet Office 2015, 13 © Crown Copyright 2015

A periodization of Finnish infrastructural crisis preparedness

These two chapters studied the security of Finnish electricity infrastructures, especially by looking at the longer history of security of supply and interventions against emergencies by the Finnish state. A model, outlined by Collier and

Lakoff (2008), was used in the analysis to focus on key issues for infrastructure protection and its history. While their case is about the United States, it would seem that similar considerations figured in Finland and fit into what Collier and Lakoff identify as elements of infrastructural lines of security reasoning. Most likely, the relatively similar risk techniques of these two regions contribute to this applicability. It has been suggested above that Finnish national security experts knew about developments in disaster studies in the United States. The link has not been established although earlier studies found influences from Sweden and Switzerland (Seppinen 1996, 31; Purhonen 2006). But it could well be that these experts were given a grant to visit the United States or went there as part of their studies. In a different tradition of thinking about national infrastructures, however, Collier's and Lakoff's model might have to be reformulated somewhat. For example, in some cases, issues with health effects or environmental impacts might be seen as more significant infrastructure risks than threats to national security (Kaijser 1994, 21).

A summary of the history of infrastructure problematizations and crisis management in Finland is presented in Figure 3.3. It displays how concerns for basic provisions were first made official in the government initiatives for economic defence mobilization in 1929. During the Second World War, the concerns for infrastructural security were narrowed down and, after the war, preparedness of the civil sector was difficult on account of post-war political constraints. In 1955, infrastructure problems could be put back on the political agenda. Such problems included concerns with the total national defence, later exemplified by concrete efforts to secure storage and self-reliance should foreign exports be blocked. In the 1970s, critical arguments were raised, however, on the types of threats that had been and could be imagined in the context of total national defence.

Critical security experts wanted to address security of supply, which was not merely a matter of storage, but also of securing various "supplies" continuously (such as energy, transport, food, finance, and government). In 1992, this security of supply received its own legislation and organization, namely the National Emergency Supply Agency. This new legislation also incorporated the previous practices of storage security. The Finnish government produced its first list of society's basic technical structures in 1995, updating the aims of this policy periodically, and published three wider resolutions on the securing of the functions vital to society in 2003, 2006, and 2010. These new strategies show clear continuity with the older concerns for national emergencies, but especially the 2006 strategy started to develop the response to threats in a novel, non-calculative direction.

This chapter has also documented how Finnish concerns that might seem contemporary are still markedly similar to Finnish debates in the 1960s and 1970s on non-military threats, computerization, and dependence on electric energy. The effects of this continuity I would claim are visible throughout the new security strategies and discourse in general. Some of these effects have already been discussed in this chapter, but another more general comment is that the Finnish security discourse draws on old styles of reasoning in that they seldom seem to refer to new developments in the field of security. Consider *resilience*, a popular

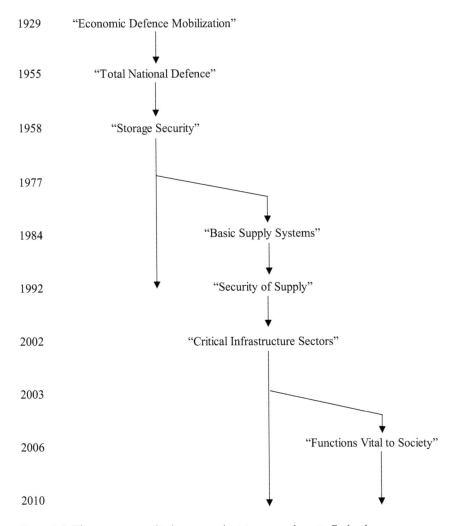

1929   "Economic Defence Mobilization"

1955   "Total National Defence"

1958   "Storage Security"

1977

1984   "Basic Supply Systems"

1992   "Security of Supply"

2002   "Critical Infrastructure Sectors"

2003

2006   "Functions Vital to Society"

2010

Figure 3.3 The emergence of infrastructural crisis preparedness in Finland
Source: Author

and influential concept in discussions in recent decades on national catastrophes and terrorism (Furedi 2007) and on earlier risk perception and risk assessment studies (Douglas & Wildavsky 1982; Hood et al 1992). Resilience is not mentioned at all in the 2003 and 2006 Finnish strategies on society's vital functions. This happens even if, as one might argue, they are precisely about improving resilience, not just about anticipating threats (as the strategies admit that is impossible to do in an exhaustive manner by a prior definition).

The concept of resilience is indeed used a number of times in the 2010 strategy. For example, psychological crisis tolerance has now become psychological resilience to crisis – maybe in an echo of one origin of the concept of individual resilience in psychological research (Krieger 2016). Nevertheless, there is still no glossary entry for the concept in the strategy. The central element of security thinking in Finland therefore seems to come from already existing practices, not just from more novel developments. Also, when infrastructure experts in Finland need to clarify their styles of reasoning to the general public, they still mention the tension between storage security and security of supply in works of history (Voimatalouspooli 50 vuotta 2006) as well as in popular articles (Sivonen 2007).

Non-calculable risk and reinvention of techniques

However, based on the historic approach in these chapters, the clearest difference between older security practices and current debates may be found on the level of concrete techniques that mitigate system vulnerabilities. In a way, all infrastructure protections have tried to find a balance between risk – probabilities and impacts of events that can be calculated – and uncertainty – aspects of events that cannot be calculated (O'Malley 2004). Storage security was most of all a calculative logic. The national security threat was already known, as it was always a military attack and the vulnerability of society's basic provisions could be mitigated by calculating how long raw resources would last in the eventuality of an attack and blockage of foreign trade. If there were uncertainties, they were perhaps only related to the reliability and validity of the data that was used in the calculations, and such uncertainties were not acknowledged in the official policies I explored.

Security of supply shifted towards greater uncertainty about the nature of potential crises, yet, it also emphasized that the level of security of supply and the duration of infrastructural crises in Finland should be calculated – although speculations on crisis duration, in practice always concerning a one-year-long supply crisis, were left out from the 2008 government decisions onward. The newest security practice – vital functions thinking – is in fact the direct opposite, at least when public strategies are considered. It draws on almost no calculations at all and tries instead to imagine worst-case scenarios and teach responsibilities to the actors that might face these scenarios. It would be easy to dismiss such perceptions of risk and vulnerability as culturally exaggerated (Furedi 2007) and, indeed, the contrast with the United Kingdom for example is marked.

In the UK National Risk Register (Figure 3.2), probabilities and harms are still mentioned, while the Finnish "risk and threat analysis" (Figure 3.1) contains no figures or statistics at all. Although even the UK figure is somewhat schematic, the degree of exactitude is greater than in the Finnish figure. Overall, the new strategies on Finnish security are simply short on numbers. They do not calculate how much electricity blackouts or other incidents cost, nor do they measure the number of their victims or provide exact probabilities of threat scenarios. The likely or less likely causes of blackouts are mentioned qualitatively in one

document (Puolustusministeriö 2009, 7–14), but there is no reference to risk levels, statistics, or simulations that produced this account. The key of the studied
infrastructural risk techniques, it seems, is not so much about quantifying probabilities and harms than about operationalizing what could happen when electric
power is down.

In many studies about power outage risk, in contrast, risk is derived by a quan-
tification or a semi-quantification of past incidents. One policy study (Doorman
et al 2004, 23–25) identifies over 20 unwanted events that can contribute to
power outages in Scandinavia and orders their interrelations into an "event tree".
It then calculates the probabilities of such chains of events by using various statistics and time series as well as expert judgements. Another reliability study plots
different already-experienced blackouts into a diagram by their magnitude and
probability and names this combination of the magnitudes and the probabilities
as "risk" (Kjølle, Utne & Gjerde 2012).

Even complex computational simulation models about blackouts – that do not
aim at measuring past catastrophes, rather than at "enacting" coming hazards
(Collier 2008) – seem to be motivated, to some extent, by a study of past records,
by the "logs of the frequency of blackouts versus their magnitude" (Fairly 2004).
In a different research context, an organizational study about cascading failures of
critical infrastructures notes that empirical reports do not "indicate a wide array
of unknown dependencies across infrastructures" and that "most cascades were
stopped quickly" (van Eeten et al 2011, 391). Again, it is systematically studied
reports of past incidents that measure risk – and from this premise, it is clear,
the more imaginative approach of the national threat scenarios could seem not
systematic enough.

Yet, at the same time, the vital functions strategies do also evaluate risk if
one understands risk not as a numerical method per se, but as a technique that
determines the impacts of future unwanted events. To begin with, the strategies
try to take infrastructure threats into account and sensitize actors such as ministries, authorities, and companies to them. The strategies rely on mechanisms
that assign responsibilities and resources to these same actors. And the strategies
propose concrete practices to monitor and test the success of the respective measures. But the methods to do all of these things are more imaginative than calculative: emphasis is placed on preparedness planning (enhancing anticipation) and
crisis exercises (enhancing resilience) rather than technical risk calculations.

This is, however, a credible way of dealing with unwanted events. As research
on the precautionary principle (Ewald 2002) and governing of future uncertainty
(O'Malley 2004) has pointed out, future harms cannot always be calculated.
They can also be imagined and governed through innovative techniques, such as
precaution, prudence, foresight, and rules of thumb (O'Malley 2004, 23). Such
approaches also go beyond the domain of risk researchers; in his discussion on
Iraq's weapons of mass destruction, whose known existence or non-existence
has received considerable scrutiny since, the US Secretary of Defense Donald
Rumsfeld famously popularized the terms *known knowns* ("things we know we
know"), *known unknowns* ("things we do not know"), and *unknown unknowns*

("the ones we don't know we don't know"). Rather than dismissing the Finnish security strategies and claiming that they are exaggerating threats and "inviting" catastrophes (Furedi 2007), it is plausible that these experts are charting such "unknowns" and developing new ways of dealing with them.

Yet, their novel security practices are not the only way of protecting the national territory from global uncertainties and managing these problems as risks when the electricity infrastructure is concerned. Between 1998 and 2007, the biannual national seminars of the policy association Finnish Energy Industries had nearly 90 presentations about energy market liberalization, the integrated Nordic and European electricity markets, and the public regulation of such forms of market competition. Over the same period, only six presentations dealt with security of electricity supply or interruptions. Official decisions on national security of supply concur with this market focus: a long way from the 1970s aspirations on national autarchy in energy resources, since 2008 the Finnish government has based security of supply on "international markets *and* national actions" (VN 2008, my emphasis).

This is not to understate the importance of more traditional infrastructural security thinking. On the contrary, if infrastructural security thinking deals with issues so seminal to the vitality of the society as a whole, why did it not appear on the industry's agenda more often? And how different is it from the thinking about free energy markets? I now turn to the popular, market-oriented style of reasoning about electricity to consider these issues.

References

Abele-Wigert, Isabelle & Dunn, Myriam (2006). *International CIIP Handbook 2006 Vol. I: An Inventory of 20 National and 6 International Critical Information Infrastructure Protection Policies.* Zürich: Center for Security Studies. Link accessed 25 November 2016: http://e-collection.library.ethz.ch/eserv/eth:31123/eth-31123-03.pdf

Auer, Jaakko (1973). Energiahuollon kriisivalmius ("Energy Supply Crisis Preparedness"). In Haukilahti, Väinö; Hyvärinen, Erkki; Korhonen, Keijo; Korte, Olavi; Löyttyniemi, Veikko; Savolainen, Aapo; Öhman, Gunnar; Valtanen, Jaakko & Makkonen, Lauri (eds) *Tietoja maanpuolustuksesta: Maanpuolustus turvallisuuspolitiikan osana* ("Information about National Defence: National Defence as Part of Security Policy"). Helsinki: Pääesikunnan koulutusosaston julkaisu (Finnish Defence Force's Defence Command Training Department), 138–144.

Brunner, Elgin & Suter, Manuel (2009). *International CIIP Handbook 2008/2009: An Inventory of 25 National and 7 International Critical Information Infrastructure Protection Policies.* Zürich: Center for Security Studies. Link accessed 25 November 2016: www.css.ethz.ch/publications/pdfs/CIIP-HB-08-09.pdf

Collier, Stephen (2008). Enacting Catastrophe: Preparedness, Insurance, Budgetary Rationalization. *Economy and Society* 37 (2): 224–250.

Collier, Stephen & Lakoff, Andrew (2006). Vital Systems Security: Anthropology of the Contemporary Research Collaboratory Working Paper no. 2. Link accessed 25 November 2016: http://anthropos-lab.net/ wp/publications/2007/08/workingpaperno2.pdf

Collier, Stephen & Lakoff, Andrew (2008). The Vulnerability of Vital Systems: How Critical Infrastructures Became a Security Problem. In Dunn Cavelty, Myriam & Kristensen,

Kristian Søby (eds) *Securing 'the Homeland': Critical Infrastructure, Risk and (In)security*. London: Routledge, 17–39.

Doorman, Gerard; Kjølle, Gerd; Uhlen, Kjetil; Huse, Einar Ståle & Flatabø, Nils (2004). *Vulnerability of the Nordic Power System: Report to the Nordic Council of Ministers*. Trondheim: SINTEF Energy Research.

Douglas, Mary & Wildavsky, Aaron (1982). *Risk and Culture: An Essay on the Selection of Technological and Environmental Dangers*. Berkeley: University of California Press.

Dunn Cavelty, Myriam (2008). Like a Phoenix from the Ashes: The Reinvention of Critical Infrastructure Protection as Distributed Security. In Dunn Cavelty, Myriam & Kristensen, Kristian Søby (eds) *Securing 'the Homeland': Critical Infrastructure, Risk and (In)security*. London: Routledge, 40–62.

Edwards, Paul (2010). *A Vast Machine: Computer Models, Climate Data, and the Politics of Global Warming*. Cambridge, MA: MIT Press.

European Council (2008). On the Identification and Designation of European Critical Infrastructures and the Assessment of the Need to Improve Their Protection. Directive 2008/114/EC. Link accessed 24 November 2016: http://eur-lex.europa.eu/LexUriServ/LexUriServ.do?uri=CELEX:32008L0114:EN:NOT

Ewald, François (2002). The Return of Descartes' Malicious Demon: An Outline of a Philosophy of Precaution. In Baker, Tom & Simon, Jonathan (eds) *Embracing Risk: The Changing Culture of Insurance and Responsibility*. Chicago: University of Chicago Press, 273–301.

Finnish Security and Defence Policy Report (2004). Prime Minister's Office: Publications 18/2004. Link accessed 25 November 2016: www.defmin.fi/files/311/2574_2160_English_White_paper_2004_1_.pdf

Furedi, Frank (2007). *Invitation to Terror: The Expanding Empire of the Unknown*. London – New York: Continuum.

Gaia Group & Net Effect (2005). Yhteiskunnan elintärkeiden toimintojen turvaamisen strategian arviointi ("Evaluation of the Strategy for Securing Functions Vital to Society"). Link accessed 25 November 2016: www.defmin.fi/files/249/2769_Yhteiskunnan_elintArkeiden_toimintojen_turvaamisen_strategian_arviointi.pdf

Häkkinen, Kaisa (2004). *Nykysuomen etymologinen sanakirja* ("An Etymological Dictionary of Contemporary Finnish"). Helsinki: WSOY.

Haukilahti, Väinö (1973). Taloudelliset voimavaramme ja niiden kehittäminen ("Our Economic Resources and Their Development"). In Haukilahti, Väinö, Hyvärinen, Erkki, Korhonen, Keijo, Korte, Olavi, Löyttyniemi, Veikko, Savolainen, Aapo, Öhman, Gunnar, Valtanen, Jaakko & Makkonen, Lauri (eds) *Tietoja maanpuolustuksesta: Maanpuolustus turvallisuuspolitiikan osana* ("Information about National Defence: National Defence as part of Security Policy"). Helsinki: Pääesikunnan koulutusosaston julkaisu (Finnish Defence Force's Defence Command Training Department), 113–120.

Hood, C. C.; Jones, D. K. C.; Pidgeon, N. F.; Turner, B. A. & Gibson, R. (1992). Risk Management. In Royal Society Study Group (eds) *Risk: Analysis, Perception and Management*. London: The Royal Society, 135–191.

Hustich, Ilmari (1982). Esipuhe ("Foreword"). In Massa, Ilmo (ed.) *Energia, kulttuuri ja tulevaisuus* ("Energy, Culture, and the Future"). Helsinki: Suomen Antropologinen Seura (The Finnish Anthropological Society) & Suomen Kirjallisuuden Seura (The Finnish Literature Society), 9–12.

Jahkola, Antero (1993). Energian tarpeen kehitys ja siitä laaditut ennusteet ("The Development of Energy Need and the Forecasts that Concern It"). In Keskinen, Risto (ed.) *Suomen energiatekniikan historia: teknis-historiallinen tutkimus energian tuottamisesta ja käytöstä*

Suomessa 1840–1980 ("The History of Finnish Energy Technology: A Technological-Historical Investigation of Energy Production and Use in Finland 1840–1980"). Tampere: Tampere University of Technology Publications, 115.

Kaijser, Arne (1994). *I fädrens spår: den svenska infrastrukturens historiska utveckling och framtida utmaning* ("In the Tracks of the Fathers: The Historical Development and the Future Challenges of the Swedish Infrastructure"). Stockholm: Carlsson.

Kananen, Ilkka (2011). Huoltovarmuuden toimintaympäristön muutoksia 1988–2011 ("Changes in the Operational Environment of Security of Supply 1988–2011"). In Valkonen, Niilo (ed.) *Sotataloustietoutta X: sotatalous murroksessa* ("War Economy Information X: War Economy at a Turning Point"). Helsinki: Sotatalousseura (War Economy Association), 3–20.

Kjølle, Gerd; Utne, Ingrid & Gjerde, Oddbjørn (2012). Risk Analysis of Critical Infrastructures Emphasizing Electricity Supply and Interdependencies. *Reliability Engineering and System Safety* 105: 80–89.

Krieger, Kristian (2016). Resilience and Risk Studies. In Burgess, Adam; Alemanno, Alberto & Zinn, Jens (eds) *Routledge Handbook of Risk Studies*. London: Routledge, 335–343.

Laki huoltovarmuuden turvaamisesta (Finnish Security of Supply Act) (2016). 18.12.1992/1390, amendments up to 8.6.2016 included. Link accessed 25 November 2016: www.finlex.fi/fi/laki/ajantasa/1992/19921390

Myllyntaus, Timo (1991). *Electrifying Finland: The Transfer of a New Technology into a Late Industrialising Economy*. Helsinki: ETLA.

O'Malley, Pat (2004). *Risk, Uncertainty and Government*. London – Sydney – Portland: Glasshouse Press.

Perrow, Charles (1999). *Normal Accidents: Living with High-Risk Technologies*. Princeton, NJ: Princeton University Press, updated edition (original 1984).

Perry, Ronald (2007). What Is a Disaster? In Rodrígues, Havidan; Quarantelli, Enrico & Dynes, Russell (eds) *Handbook of Disaster Research*. New York: Springer, 1–15.

Puolustusministeriö (Finnish Ministry of Defence) (2009). Pitkä sähkökatko ja yhteiskunnan elintärkeiden toimintojen turvaaminen ("Long Blackout and Securing the Functions Vital to Society"). Text written by Jaana Laitinen and Suvi Vainio. Link accessed 25 November 2016: www.defmin.fi/files/1436/pitka_sahkokatko_ja_yett.pdf

Purhonen, Mika (2006). Toimintaympäristön muutoksista huolimatta energia-alan huoltovarmuus on edelleen hyvä ("In Spite of the Shifting Working Environment, the Security of Supply of the Energy Sector is Still Good"). In *Voimatalouspooli 50 vuotta*. A history whose working group included Heikki Hartikainen, Eino Hälikkä, Leni Lustre-Pere, Timo Ristokankare, Maria Hallila, and Tuija Sorsa. Helsinki: Puolustustaloudellinen suunnittelukunta (Finnish Economic Defence Planning Authority) and Voimatalouspooli (Power Economy Pool), 6–7.

Ruostetsaari, Ilkka (1998). *Energiapolitiikka käännekohdassa: Järjestöt ja yritykset vaikuttajina vapautuvilla energiamarkkinoilla* ("Energy Politics at a Turning Point: Associations and Companies as Stakeholders in the Liberalizing Energy Markets"). Tampere: Tampereen yliopisto (University of Tampere).

Seppinen, Ilkka (1996). *Ahdinkoajan varalle: Taloudellinen puolustusneuvosto ja puolustustaloudellinen suunnittelukunta huoltovarmuuden kehittäjänä 1929–1955–1995* ("For Times of Distress: The Economic Defence Council and the Economic Defence Planning Authority as Developers of Security of Provision 1929–1955–1995"). Helsinki: Puolustustaloudellinen suunnittelukunta (Finnish Economic Defence Planning Authority).

Silvast, Antti (2014). The Protection of the Banking System as a Critical Societal Infrastructure. In Petropolous, Nicholas & Tsobanoglou, George (eds) *The Debt Crisis in the*

Eurozone (EZ): Social Impacts. Newcastle upon Tyne, UK: Cambridge Scholars Publishing, 459–480.

Sivonen, Hannu (2007). Mikä meitä oikein uhkaa – ja miten varautua erilaisiin uhkiin? ("What Actually Threatens Us – and How to Prepare Against Different Threats?") The publication of Official Statistics Finland. *Tieto & Trendit* 8: 26–29.

SSFVS (2006). The Strategy for Securing the Functions Vital to Society. A Finnish government resolution 23 November 2006. Authored by the Security and Defence Committee of the Finnish Ministry of Defence. Helsinki: Ministry of Defence. Link accessed 25 November 2016: www.defmin.fi/files/858/06_12_12_YETTS__in_english.pdf

SSS (2010). *Security Strategy for Society: A Finnish Government Resolution 16 December 2010.* Authored by the Security and Defence Committee of the Finnish Ministry of Defence. Helsinki: Ministry of Defence. Link accessed 24 November 2016: www.yhteiskunnanturvallisuus.fi/en/materials/doc_download/26-security-strategy-for-society

UK Cabinet Office (2015). *National Risk Register of Civil Emergencies, 2015 Edition.* London: Cabinet Office. Link accessed 25 November 2016: www.gov.uk/government/uploads/system/uploads/attachment_data/file/419549/20150331_2015-NRR-WA_Final.pdf

US Department of Homeland Security (2013). *National Infrastructure Protection Plan 2013: Partnering for Critical Infrastructure Security and Resilience.* Washington: Department of Homeland Security. Link accessed 10 October 2016: www.dhs.gov/sites/default/files/publications/National-Infrastructure-Protection-Plan-2013-508.pdf

van Eeten, Michel; Nieuwenhuijs, Albert; Luiifj, Eric; Klaver, Marieke & Cruz, Edite (2011). The State and the Threat of Cascading Failure across Critical Infrastructures: The Implications of Empirical Evidence from Media Incident Reports. *Public Administration* 89 (2): 381–400.

VN (Valtioneuvosto, Finnish Government) (539/2008). Valtioneuvoston päätös huoltovarmuuden tavoitteista ("Finnish Government Decision on Security of Supply Aims"). Link accessed 25 November 2016: www.finlex.fi/fi/laki/ajantasa/2008/20080539

Voimatalouspooli 50 vuotta (The Power Economy Pool 50 Years) (2006). *Voimahuollon varautumisen vaiheita 1956–2006* ("The Phases of Preparedness in Power Supply 1956–2006"). A history whose working group included Heikki Hartikainen, Eino Hälikkä, Leni Lustre-Pere, Timo Ristokankare, Maria Hallila, and Tuija Sorsa. Helsinki: Puolustustaloudellinen suunnittelukunta (Finnish Economic Defence Planning Authority) and Voimatalouspooli (Power Economy Pool).

YETTS (2003). Yhteiskunnan elintärkeiden toimintojen turvaamisen strategia ("The Strategy for Securing the Functions Vital to Society"). A Finnish government resolution 27 November 2003. Authored by the Security and Defence Committee of the Finnish Ministry of Defence. Helsinki: Ministry of Defence. Link accessed 25 November 2016: www.defmin.fi/files/248/2515_1687_Yhteiskunnan_elintArkeiden_toimintojen_turvaamisen_strategia_1_.pdf

Yle (7 January 2013). Fortumin sähköverkon myynti herättää pelkoa poliitikoissa ("Sale of Fortum's Electricity Network Generates Fear Among Politicians"). Written by Ari Hakahuhta. Link accessed 25 November 2016: http://yle.fi/uutiset/3–6485776

Part III

Competition and security in a liberalized electricity market

4 Materializing electricity markets

From power failures to deregulation

Does competition compromise resilience? This is what many critical social scientists have said when observing energy companies competing on the free power markets. Urbanist Stephen Graham (2009, 14) summarizes by noting that "the resilience of infrastructures may be severely compromised as they are actively reorganized to maximize profit" and the liberalization of infrastructures "is disruptive to reliable services". For one thing, market reforms fragment responsibilities among different organizations, rendering risk management difficult (de Bruijne & van Eeten 2007). Two urban scholars flag the impacts of deregulation and privatization in the electricity industry as increasing complexity, hampering communication, and intensifying competition (Byrd & Matthewman 2014). They conclude that in "a competitive environment, reliability and profits may be at cross-purposes" (Byrd & Matthewman 2014, 87). For example, by merely supporting competition, market reforms have neglected the maintenance of a public common good such as power lines, according to Charles Perrow (2008, 246). The earlier, more-or-less centrally planned and monopolistic electricity system in industrialized countries had provided a surplus of electricity and prioritized preemptive maintenance – in fact, this alleged "over-maintenance" became one of the many reasons for liberalization in the power industries (Berglund 2009; Thue 2013).

Yet, as others point out, in practice the relation between infrastructural reliability and competition is multidimensional and not always well understood. Empirical details of electricity network regulation (Hirsh 1999), infrastructure restructuring (Collier 2011), and high reliability management in electricity organizations (Roe & Schulman 2008) suggest considerably more nuance to the ways in which energy markets work in risk and security terms. A summary of these findings is that market liberalization certainly does not just neglect infrastructure security – but it does formalize and govern security in an original and specific manner, giving explicit attention to it in different ways than before (Collier 2011). To contribute more to this research problem, the following chapters of this book explore free market competition and the attaining of security in the liberalized energy market in Finland and the Scandinavian power market where

Finnish companies participate. The research question in this part of the book is: *how are electricity interruptions managed as risks in the liberalized electricity market in Finland and Scandinavia and what do these practices imply for the resilience of the electricity infrastructure?* The focus of this first, background chapter is about the opening of the electricity market to competition in Finland and other Nordic countries.

Curiously, the free energy market seems to be at once a highly standardized and a controversial objective. In the European Union, the deadline for completing the European Union's internal energy market was 2014. This has meant the removal of energy trade barriers, the separation of "competitive" and international energy generation from yet "monopolistic" and regionally based energy networks, harmonization of market rules and pricing policies, and, all over Europe, the right for energy consumers to choose their power supplier competitively (European Parliament & Council 2009). Such EU-wide laws can make the liberal energy market seem like a coherent objective shared among energy specialists, politicians, and citizens. But this has not always been the case – even if it is the case now. This chapter starts with an observation that is not entirely intuitive, but has been shown in many Nordic countries (Summerton 1995; Thue 1995; Ruostetsaari 1998; Högselius & Kaijser 2007) as well as in Western Europe in general (Lagendijk 2008, 204–210). This observation is that when discussions about liberalized electricity began in Europe in the 1980s and the 1990s, the energy industry generally opposed the free energy market reform, which was mainly driven forward by the public administration.

European governments were inspired by the early US energy deregulation debates, the European Economic Community's discussions about an internal energy market from the mid-to-late 1980s, and initial energy market restructurings in England, Wales, and Norway in 1990 and 1991 (Högselius & Kaijser 2007, 62; Lagendijk 2008, 204–210). The industry, on the other hand, had a specific sense that the existing electricity system already worked highly optimally (Högselius & Kaijser 2007, 74) and that electricity is already a competitive, an international, and a liberalized industry, although not necessarily in a way that would have been appreciated by policy makers (Lagendijk 2008, 204–210). Even in the United Kingdom, often the example of powerful privatization programmes, restructuring in the electricity supply industry was pursued by the Conservative government, but opposed by the industry's own Central Electricity Generating Board for causing alleged technical and economic risks (Winskel 2002). Similarly in the United States, electricity utility managers had created a regulated system precisely to protect it from competition, persisting until the 1970s (Hirsh 1999). Viewing the deregulation of Swedish electricity in the 1980s and the 1990s in their historical study, researchers Per Högselius and Arne Kaijser (2007, 75) were indeed compelled to ask: if the deregulation was opposed so intensively, how then did the reform rise on the political agenda and how was it accomplished in spite of opposition? This chapter is inspired by similar questioning, but I consider more closely how the question about infrastructural risks has been coded into the debates about a free energy market in Finland and the design and the regulation of this marketplace, also in Scandinavia.

The materials include a report by the lobby organization Finnish Energy Industries, then known as the Finnish Electricity Association SENER (2000), published five years after the official market opening and representing a useful view to contemporary problematizations of the free energy market. I also consider another more academic history by Finnish political scientist Ilkka Ruostetsaari (1998); academic studies about electricity deregulation particularly in the closely related energy regimes in Sweden (Kaijser 1994; Summerton 1995; Högselius & Kaijser 2007), Norway (Karlstrøm 2012; Thue 2013), and also in mainland Europe (Lagendijk 2008); a small number of Finnish and Nordic common market regulatory policy documents for comparison; and electricity expert interviews. My method of viewing the data stems from social studies of markets (Callon 1998a,b) and concerns uncovering who the economic agents of the energy markets are defined by experts, what kinds of transactions they are supposed to make, and how they handle externalities to the markets, especially power interruptions.

My key aim here is situating power failures in Finland and their governance as a risk in a historical background of deregulation. At the same time, the chapter introduces a number of key actors of Finnish electricity infrastructures and Nordic power markets that again appear in the subsequent empirical chapters. In its conclusion, this chapter also clarifies why, relatively soon, I left economic models about energy markets behind and went to study how the market is produced in practice: in control rooms.

Centralized and liberalized electricity

In Finnish energy policy, the oil crises of the 1970s had motivated two seemingly quite different responses. One was that "there should be as low as possible dependence on energy markets on a single provider. Governments were urged to guarantee that diverse energy markets are possible" (Ruostetsaari 1998, 29). On the other hand, the crises also emphasized the importance of cooperation among electricity producers and the significance of public interventions to secure national and regional energy supplies. Similarly ambivalent aims were also stressed in reports on the oil crises in Sweden: the issues included national energy security, but also the dynamic character of the energy sector and the need to put a price on market "externalities" such as blackouts (Kaijser 1994, 60–61; 233). Nonetheless, the Finnish Electricity Act of 1980, which replaced the former Act on Electricity Utilities from 1928, leaned more towards centralized planning than the free markets, just like the Swedish energy policy from 1975 (Kaijser 1994, 224).

The Finnish act enacted statutory, national and regional planning systems of electricity supplies. It divided Finland into twenty *cooperation districts for electricity supply*, larger than any single city and managed by a regional committee comprising electricity utilities, electricity wholesale companies (that sold generated electricity directly to utilities and industries), and electricity producers (Sähkölaki 1979, Section 4). The remit of these committees was producing a standardized plan for the purchases of electricity, for distributing it, and for its distribution regions, which was yearly approved by the Finnish Ministry of Trade and Industry. The nationally significant electricity production and transmission had its own respective planning arrangements, also yearly agreed this time by the Finnish government (Sähkölaki 1979, Section 3).

More than direct state control, this centralized regime operated through consensual decisions among political decision makers, authorities, and electricity producers (Ruostetsaari 1998, 34). Part of this faith in expert planning could have been motivated by energy consumption: at least in Sweden, it was expected that consumption would stagnate in the coming years, rendering future requirements and their risks more foreseeable (Kaijser 1994, 224). But if an electricity infrastructure being "stagnated" offered one argument for central planning, it soon also became an argument for intensifying market competition (Högselius & Kaijser 2007, 72).

The commissions from the sales of petrol and diesel were deregulated in Finland in 1984 and the public oversight of electricity prices ended in 1988 (Ruostetsaari 1998, 10). Many further deregulations in other sectors including trains and postal services were envisioned by the government of the liberal conservative Prime Minister Harri Holkeri (1987–1991) (Ruostetsaari 1998, 46). The electricity market liberalization was in its turn initiated in 1990 by the Finnish Ministry of Trade and Industry by founding an Electricity Utility Commission, followed by an Electricity Act Working Group in 1993. Hence, even if the European Union has become a major driver of liberalized electricity markets, these policy bodies predate Finland's EU membership in 1995 by several years.

Why were these bodies founded if another national energy "crisis" was not apparent and there was no obligation to deregulate electricity? One influence seems to have stemmed from a liberalistic rationale. According to official designations, the policy work was initiated so that the ownership structures, organization, and functions of electricity utilities would be reconsidered and more competition would be created in the electricity distribution (Ruostetsaari 1998, 41). Norway exemplifies a similar logic: there, the political pursuit of risk-free electricity had created a surplus of energy, which could not be traded in an efficient way and then called for establishing deregulated energy markets (Thue 2013, 227–230).

A number of more specific problems had also emerged and inspired energy market restructurings in Finland. In the late 1980s, investors had a rising interest in electricity utilities and several electricity utility sales and acquisitions had already been experienced (SENER 2000, 6). All Finnish electricity utilities were legal monopolies and sales became problematic: "the monopoly position gave possibility to make the customers pay for the costs of electricity utility sales" (SENER 2000, 6). The use of this as a policy argument for liberalization is also inverted as, at least in Sweden, many cities sold their electricity utilities precisely because they were uncertain about the effects and the risks of deregulation (Summerton 1995, 175). So, in a way, one reaction to deregulation motivated further deregulation.

A closely related issue to acquisitions was *vertical integration* – that is, the possibility that large electricity producers acquire local electricity distribution and start providing as well as generating electricity. In Sweden in 1992, the Minister of

Trade Per Westerberg, a strong proponent of market reform, even stated critically that "almost 100 percent of the Swedish energy markets is vertically integrated" (Kaijser 1994, 231). Such integration did not benefit users tied to monopolistic utilities and pricing; hence, the liberalization of electricity markets would be needed to engage consumers, again, by allowing competition (Ruostetsaari 1998, 42; Summerton 2004).

Starting from these different considerations, the Finnish policy bodies recommended that local electricity networks be opened to competitive entry by all energy generators; that retail sales of electricity be no longer a monopoly or subject to permit; and that the pricing and utility ownership be made more transparent. To minimize the likelihood of vertical integration, utilities would also be requested to unbundle, that is, split their generation, transmission, and distribution functions (Ruostetsaari 1998, 42).

A few additional suggestions were made by the Ministry of Trade and Industry subsequently. The first was public regulation of the free electricity markets through founding a specific Energy Market Authority (SENER 2000, 7). This approach, where market-based electricity companies and the social benefits that they produce are monitored by a public regulator, resembles the US energy markets and its private corporations and regulatory commissions monitoring these corporations (Hirsh 1999). It was also not the model established in Finland or Sweden before the 1990s, which had relied more on city utilities and centralized planning of the electricity infrastructure (Kaijser 1994, 60). Secondly, the two co-existing Finnish high-voltage electricity transmission companies – one a state-owned power company and another owned by large industries – would be given a legal system responsibility, which meant maintaining the stability of the national electricity transmission system. Here, hence, the market liberalization and the market act incorporated system security rather than hampering it, but formalized it in a new manner (see Collier 2011).

Public debates and statements followed this initial policy work, and there was an open hearing of the draft of the Electricity Market Act from almost 40 stakeholders in 1993. The market liberalization was supported by electricity buyers and business users in particular: for example, the Federation of Finnish Enterprises welcomed the reform to gain lower energy prices (SENER 2000, 7). On the other hand, many other statements worried about the status of small consumers, security of electricity provision, the fair treatment of customers, and the willingness of electricity companies to invest to their capacities and networks in a liberalized market (Ruostetsaari 1998, 46). According to SENER (2000, 7), however, electricity producers, sellers, and distributors opposed the reform most directly.

Four specific criticisms were raised by the Finnish electricity industry. Firstly, the schedule for the market opening was too hasty. Secondly, the level of consumers (at 500 kW of electric power, which is industrial customers) who can switch their energy provider should have been even higher. Thirdly, it was noted that Finnish electricity utilities had long-term contracts for wholesale energy that lasted until 1995 – indeed, in Sweden, many utilities had acquired such contracts especially to anticipate the deregulation (Summerton 1995, 176). However, if the market was to be opened in 1994 as planned and if electricity prices fell as a result of the liberalization, these companies bound by obligations faced financial losses. Fourthly, the founding of a public energy market authority was criticized by the energy industry, which preferred industrial interoperation rather than public regulation in general.

The Swedish energy market liberalization was prepared at the same time and was followed closely in Finland (Ruostetsaari 1998, 47). Overall, the Swedish energy industry was hopeful about new business opportunities and increasing competition. But it feared that the reform would tamper with the existing management of electricity that already provided low prices and high energy security (Högselius & Kaijser 2007, 76–138). An even critique was made in the continental Europe when the European Union's common electricity markets were initiated in the mid-to-late 1980s. Electricity companies said that the European electricity system was already "liberalized", had been "international" since the early-to-mid 20th century, and any alterations might compromise security and increase blackouts (Lagendijk 2008, 204–210).

In spite of the criticisms, the Finnish Electricity Market Act was presented to the Parliament in 1994 and enacted in 1995. The regulator, the Energy Market Authority, was founded in 1995 to oversee and support competition and grant permission to the electricity network operation and the building of high-voltage cables. In the following year, a single Finnish high-voltage electricity transmission company – the Finnish Transmission Network or later Fingrid – was founded and owned by the Finnish state, the state-owned power company Imatran Voima, the industrial power company Pohjolan Voima, a number of institutional actors, and insurance companies. Electricity distribution companies asked to be shareholders in Fingrid but were not included (SENER 2000, 10). The industry's criticisms concerning long wholesale contracts and regulation were not acknowledged in the new legislation, according to SENER (2000, 8).

Relatively few new issues or themes emerged in the years that followed the market liberalization. In 1997, the Confederation of Finnish Industries found that the costs of electricity were lower after the liberalization. The Finnish government's energy policy report to the Parliament in the same year noted that the electricity market was already relatively competitive and that small-scale electricity users could start switching their energy supplier, which they did in 1998 (SENER 2000, 13–14). The Finnish Energy Industries, in their turn, maintained their critiques about vertical integration and long-term contracts and managed to influence these issues somewhat in the late 1990s (SENER 2000, 19–20): limitations of utility market shares and loosening of long-term wholesale contracts were both taken into account legally.

Long power failures as a policy issue in Finland

A few years later, Finnish policy debates emerged about long electricity blackouts, although it was not new to consider such "public" issues in the context of Finnish liberalized energy. The first Finnish Electricity Market Act from 1995 already stipulated a number of "public" responsibilities to utilities such as fair and non-discriminatory pricing, universal electricity provision to all users, and prohibitions to interrupt electricity supplies in the winter months in houses with electrical heating. Hence, the market legislation incorporated security in a specific manner. When Finnish energy policies have talked about power outages, they have likewise not proposed regulations or arrangements that represent either public interventions or market competition to begin with. Rather, the balance has shifted both ways.

In a 1998 amendment to the Finnish Electricity Market Act (2004), the national electricity "systems responsibility" (Section 16) was added with the maintenance of a more financially framed "national balance responsibility" (Section 16b): hence, the responsibility about a national infrastructure was no longer merely about technical operability and reliability, but also about transparent and fair "terms of trade". On the other hand, in 1999, the act incorporated several new consumer protection considerations about electricity distribution errors, responsibilities, and compensations (Sections 26c, d, e), one year after allowing small-scale consumers to switch their supplier.

In 2001, two exceptionally strong storms Pyry and Janika struck Finland and doubled the yearly number of electricity supply interruptions compared to the whole previous decade (Kauppa- ja teollisuusministeriö 2006, 29). Swedish scholar Björn Wallsten has studied similar extreme weather events in Sweden and their relationship with electricity security of supply; he argues that these "events have had deep impact on the system culture through creating so-called 'formative events' in which a variety of technical and organizational measures has been implemented" (Berglund 2009, 1). Correspondingly in Finland, just like with national security of supply more generally (Chapter 3), exceptional storms became a strongly perceived risk to electricity supplies and helped challenge the earlier policies and legislation concerning the electricity market.

In 2002, an official evaluation about the major blackouts in 2001 (Forstén 2002) recommended that Finnish energy end users receive compensations from all blackouts that last longer than 12 hours, and this became operational in the electricity market act in 2003 (Section 27f). The aim was to "motivate electricity distribution owners to act in a manner that shortens the duration of interruptions" (Forstén 2002, 31–32), and to this end the report also suggested a maximum duration of six hours for an electricity interruption "even in exceptional conditions" (Forstén 2002, 2). A few years later, the Finnish Ministry of Trade and Industry suggested that customers or "entrepreneurs" critically dependent on electricity purchase their own private emergency power generators (Kauppa- ja teollisuusministeriö 2006, 56), though a similar idea had been afloat since 2002:

> Uninterruptible electricity distribution cannot be guaranteed. If the customer's production or other activities do not tolerate reasonable electricity distribution interruptions, then the customer should personally secure the electricity supply.
>
> (Forstén 2002, 35)

But as unattainable as risk-free electricity distribution may be, since 2008, Finnish electricity network companies have been "penalized" financially for each electricity blackout according to market regulation (Energiamarkkinavirasto 2007). In all of these examples, the public common effect of a blackout is transformed into a calculable risk in order to create a "fair", transparent, and market-based way of distributing harms across all energy consumers. Considering infrastructure risk in a broader sense, this I would argue is also what the energy market restructuring in Finland has been all about. Only recently has this logic been challenged by yet other "formative events" (Berglund 2009) through further difficult power failures in Finland, as I show.

A major Finnish storm on Boxing Day 2011 initiated a blackout that momentarily affected 570,000 customers and lasted for days for tens of thousands of customers (Energiateollisuus 2012). The power failure also led to an untypically wide public debate concerning the poor crisis communication and crisis preparedness among allegedly "private" energy companies, the impacts of the outsourcing of their maintenance, and the necessity of preventing similar storm damages in the future by burying electrical cables and considerably increasing monetary compensations for customer damages from blackouts. Participated in by large energy companies, Finnish ministries, emergency authorities, market regulators, workers' and employers' associations, and the media itself (Tennberg & Vola 2014), in the aftermath of these debates the Finnish Electricity Market Act was overturned in 2013.

Until around 2013, Finnish electricity law and regulation had mainly concerned ex-facto reactions (such as real-time energy pricing, fines and compensations, and trading on more-or-less real-time energy markets) to mitigate the effects of incidents such as peak energy demands, threats to functioning systems, and intermittent power generation after they have already occurred. In other words, the legislation had relied on *resilience* as a security strategy. However, the new Act from 2013 puts more consideration on *anticipation*, once again, just like the earlier strategies in centralized planning did. Electricity network operators must now make preparedness plans and provide instructions to their customers in the event of an interruption. Also end users can be variously engaged in this preparedness: for example, housing permits in Finland determine that detached houses have to have auxiliary heating systems (Jalas, Rinkinen & Silvast 2016).

In summary of the history here, Finnish electricity was based on a legal, centralized system of planning and permits starting from 1980. This arrangement was challenged in the late 1980s and early 1990s due to a number of critiques, which partly emerged from international discussions concerning liberalization and deregulation, but were also affected by practical issues and problematizations of Finnish electricity at the time. In my materials, hence, there was neither specific attachment to the Finnish system's optimality, like in Sweden, nor fears about impending blackouts if the system was altered, like in continental Europe.

The Finnish energy industry did initially oppose the market reforms, however. This was not because it was against deregulation and competition, but, one could argue, for the opposite reason: the industry worried, as it had since the 1980s,

that there would be increasing public regulation and interventions in the operation of electricity-providing companies should the government pursue a market
liberalization (Ruostetsaari 1998, 51). By 1990, Finland had the most competitive, private, and profit-oriented electricity sector in the Nordic countries (Thue
1995, 14). Part of its high-voltage transmission network was privately owned and
private manufacturing companies produced around 35–40% of Finnish electricity. Finnish public policies, it could be argued, have only been additions to this
logic, applying it rather than replacing it with strong public risk governance.
The recent years' events and overturning of the Electricity Market Act in 2013
suggest a new pathway and that the balance has tilted back to stronger public
risk governance through legislation, stipulating that energy companies must act
in the face of threats before they have occurred. I will now turn to the common
Nordic energy market to compare how these themes figure internationally.

Internationalizing business and its risks

The high-voltage electricity transmission system operators in Finland, Sweden,
Norway, Denmark, and Iceland have collaborated to forge a common international power system since 1963. They have interacted in a body called Nordel,
until 2009 when it merged with the European organization ENTSO-E. Nordel
was a forum for exchanging information, advice, and recommendations, but it
also facilitated early forms of international energy trading: as Norway, for example, has cheap hydropower while Sweden and Finland has thermal power capacity, the operators could have traded the power over the transmission grid (Kaijser
1995, 50–51). This practice is not exclusive to Northern Europe, for similar
aspirations and implementations concerning common European power networks
have figured in continental Europe since the early 20th century (Lagendijk 2008).

   Due to such forms of cooperation, the electricity transmission capacity between
Nordic countries had been relatively high for many decades in the late 1990s
(SENER 2000, 27). The basis existed then for a common, more systematic energy
stock exchange in the Nordic countries. In 2000, the following designation of
an energy stock exchange or a *pool* was produced: "A pool is a kind of a stock
exchange that gathers daily the sale offers from electricity providers for each half
an hour and determines the system's market price" (SENER 2000, 10). What is
important here in terms of risk is the time-scale: quite unlike long-term plans submitted to authorities, the stock exchange and its system price is reformulated on
a daily basis and measures events on the granularity of half an hour (in England
where the example is taken, but one hour in the Nordic markets).

   An analogical auction-based stock exchange has existed in Norway since 1971,
initially to manage problems created by intermittent hydropower (Karlstrøm
2012; Thue 2013). To import electricity if the waters did not flow, the utilities
set up a small-scale market for electricity trading between Norwegian regions and
parts of Sweden. Done in order to "organise a market for occasional power based
on decentralised decisions of supply and demand" (Thue 2013, 231), the market
actors would communicate their bids to a central computer in Oslo, which would

then calculate the energy market price by their combination. This initially small-scale stock exchange acquired great significance in economic theory: as means of providing efficient resource allocation and transparency in the situation where national self-sufficiency had left Norwegian producers with surplus electricity that it could not export at a reasonable price (Thue 2013, 229–230).

The Norwegian transmission company acquired the stock exchange and engaged in Norwegian-Swedish trading in 1996, coining it Nord Pool. Individual Finnish power companies have participated in Nord Pool since 1996. Nord Pool was introduced to Finland more systematically in 1998 after EL-EX, a stock exchange initiated by Finnish Option Brokers in the mid-1990s, was acquired by the transmission company Fingrid (SENER 2000, 11).

This is how the power market is supposed to work according to the stock exchange operator, Nord Pool Spot (2009, 3). There is a *wholesale market* which is Nord Pool and the *retail market* is where the end users buy energy; *producers* are electricity generators who place energy on sale on the Nord Pool wholesale market; the *retailers* buy this economic electricity from the Nord Pool wholesale market and sell it to the energy *end users*; and the *end users* buy and consume energy in a wide variety of ways and may, in some cases, participate in the market themselves by trading electricity.

These categorizations between producers, retailers, and other actors are clear and specific – contrary to all the issues associated with vertical integration in the Nordic countries (cf. Summerton 1995, 172). Hence, energy appears as any market commodity that rational economic agents trade: "When the electricity market is liberalized, electricity becomes a commodity like, for instance, grain or oil" (Nord Pool Spot 2009, 2). More specifically, energy-selling companies balance energy levels on two temporally related electricity markets.

Firstly, they use the Elspot market for monitoring and anticipating the supply and demand of the days ahead (Nord Pool Spot 2016a). The market is accessed through techniques called bidding and offering. An example bid and offer is produced by Nord Pool Spot (2009, 6–7). Here, the decisions that a company makes to trade energy are determined by the wholesale energy price; bids and offers are communications about how much energy in megawatt hours the company is willing to buy or sell for a certain wholesale price.

In this example, if the wholesale price is 40 euros per megawatt hour, the company bids to buy 10 megawatt hours from the stock. On the other hand, if the wholesale price is 60 euros per megawatt hour (or more), then the company offers to sell 30 megawatt hours to the stock. The rest of the energy required by consumers, and not acquired from the stock, can be generated locally by the trading company. Once every day, the energy market players make similar bids and offers for each hour of the coming day and further ahead. Nord Pool then combines all the bids to calculate the Nordic common system price of energy. This price, calculated for each hour of the day, determines how the local bids and offers play out.

A second energy market that gained importance a few years ago is called Elbas (Nord Pool Spot 2016b). Rather than concerning the day ahead like Elspot, Elbas is a real-time, hour-ahead marketplace that has operated in Finland and

Sweden since 1999, Germany since 2006, Denmark since 2007, and Norway since 2009. It works through bids and offers just like Elspot. Previously, Nord Pool Spot (2010) framed Elbas as an instrument of economic profit: in real time, economic agents can make just-in-time trading that increases their revenues. A few years later, Nord Pool related to the market more where unwanted events are concerned. Accordingly, the real-time market helps manage "incidents" such as shutdowns at nuclear power plants and wind power fluctuations (Nord Pool Spot 2013). The most recent explanation (Nord Pool Spot 2016b) removes the reference to nuclear shutdowns, but keeps acknowledging that "wind power is unpredictable by nature", the possibility of "exponential" growth in wind capac-ity all over the world, and that "this type of [real-time -AS] market can be a key enabler to increase the share of renewable energy in the energy mix." Hence, commercial players are supposed to reduce financial impacts in real time when an unanticipated incident such as intermittency occurs. In practice, the risk is mitigated by trading energy. The matter clearly is about financial risk more visibly than about security.

Nord Pool Spot states this separation by writing that the energy market's com-mercial actors deliver "only the prices (and the bills)" and "financial services":

> The commercial players are not and cannot be responsible for the security of supply. If a South Swedish retailer, for example, has bought electricity from a North Swedish producer, the North Swedish producer cannot guarantee that there will be electricity in the plug at the retailer's customers. What the com-mercial players deliver to each other and the end users are only the prices (and the bills). Hence, the commercial players deliver financial services only. The commercial players work in the domain which is changed when the electricity market is liberalized: the financial domain.
>
> (Nord Pool Spot 2009, 4)

However, at the same time, there is at least some "non-commercial" side of elec-tric energy as the exchange calls it (Nord Pool Spot 2009, 3). This "non-commercial" operator transmits and distributes the electricity from one region to another, but also appears especially when the energy is out of balance. Indeed, the operations on the two Nordic markets might not always be sufficient to reach an hourly balance between energy supply and demand. This may happen due to a number of reasons, as I discuss later in the control room chapters. In short, weather is a key factor, as it directly affects energy consumption and generation levels and is not wholly predictable on a minute-by-minute basis. When the local balancing on markets fails, the national high-voltage electricity transmission operator steps in and fills the gap with so-called balancing energy (Nord Pool Spot 2009, 5–7).

How does the national operator then acquire this balancing energy and what requirements stem from managing the reliability of a national electricity system? In 2008, I visited the Finnish electricity transmission company and interviewed its two managers responsible for system security. We sat next to a control room separated by a window – but not in the room, as this would not have been allowed before a thorough background security check. This is where the Finnish electricity transmission system is maintained through a number of computers and monitors. The transmission control room was continuously monitoring, predicting, and modelling the stability of the Finnish transmission system and its most critical interconnections to other countries. One key standard of this security practice is called the N-1 criterion. It states that no single component failure should compromise the system, or more formally coded "is an expression of a level of system security entailing that a power system is assumed to be intact apart from the loss of individual principal components (production units, lines, transformers, bus bars, consumption etc.)" (Nordel 2007, 67). Accordingly, the non-compliance with this criterion was a significant factor to the major blackout in Italy in 2003 (CRE & AEEG 2004, 7). Another practical matter, caused by local distributors, is about purchasing the gap-filling energy if it is needed. The transmission company does this from a separate balancing market, participated in by large industries which are compensated if they decide to lower their consumption due to national balancing needs. Hence, by means of such separate markets along with security principles, the risks of the Nordic common markets are constantly screened, anticipated, and distributed.

The public regulation of energy markets and networks

The public bodies that regulate energy markets and networks such as the Finnish Energy Authority are experts whose interest in risks, as could be expected, is more visible and stated. Market regulation can be generally understood as a "negative feedback system in which asymmetries, whether due to social, economic or technological factors are balanced by rules which may (or may not) be codified in legal statutes" (Boyd 2001, 4). Separate from ministries and legislators in many countries, market regulators have "quasi-legislative power by allowing them to make rules having the force of law" – although these rules can be and have been contested in courtrooms (Hirsh 1999, 31). The various theories, histories, and national specifics of electricity network and energy market regulation are, however, outside of my scope (see more details in Hirsh 1999; Boyd 2001). The Council of European Energy Regulators (CEER), a cooperation body of European national electricity and gas regulators, has published overviews of the European regulatory practices, including the Northern European countries, which I shall draw upon here.

According to the body, many European countries' electricity regulation shared a starting point until about 2000. This is because regulators operated through assigning price caps for the electricity network service that is billed from customers (CEER 2005, 31). Soon, however, the regulators noted that while managing one risk (overpricing), this mechanism created another. Even if prices are capped, electricity network companies might reduce their maintenance and investments to make a profit. And according to a popular line of thinking by economists (see Gramlich 1994), lack of investments in its turn directly influences the quality of infrastructure provision: "Price-cap regulation without any quality standards or incentive/penalty regimes for quality may provide unintended and misleading incentives to reduce quality levels" (CEER 2005, 31).

New electricity regulation models, increasingly popular in Europe from around 2005, strive to monitor this quality and motivate its improvements (CEER 2005, 31–32). In practice, statistics of quality are made public; "incentive" and "penalty" schemes are enforced to utilities to control their profits in terms of their quality of supply; and there is a growing number of arrangements that fix maximum durations for electricity blackouts and customer compensations for cases when the durations are not met. Along with compensations, however, the matter has also been about making customers aware of the costs of quality. Thus, specific emphasis has been laid on electricity customers' "expectations" and "their willingness to pay" for good-quality electricity (CEER 2011, 4). As CEER summarized it in 2010: "Results from cost-estimation studies on customer costs due to electricity interruptions are of key importance in order to be able to set proper incentives for continuity of supply" (CEER 2010, 9).

The following example about electricity quality regulation and blackouts concerns Finland, but corresponding instruments were in place in the mid-2000s in countries all over Europe including Sweden and Norway as well as the United Kingdom, Ireland, Italy, Portugal, Hungary, and Estonia (CEER 2005, 37). Between 2008 and 2011, the Finnish energy network quality regulation depended to a large part (although other measures were also deployed) on a method called Data Envelopment Analysis (DEA). Developed in the United States, like many other Finnish infrastructure risk models as I suggested earlier, and situated in a scientific tradition called operational research, the method calculates the technical "efficiency" of multi-output, multi-input production units or *decision-making units* (Charnes, Cooper & Rhodes 1978). In so doing it compares different decision-making units with one another, identifying the most efficient unit relatively and, in most contemporary applications, prescribing how the other units may improve their "efficiency" by altering their input, output, or both. While these aims may sound "neoliberal", the method's original intention was different: DEA was developed to study "public programs" and "decision making by not-for-profit entities rather than the more customary 'firms' and 'industries'", and it depended on data "not readily weighted by reference to (actual) market prices and/or other economic desiderata" (Charnes, Cooper & Rhodes 1978, 429). Doubtless such traits also made the method appealing to measure public electricity utilities and their efficiency.

The Finnish electricity regulation DEA model has the following formula for technical DEA "efficiency", that is, an utility's yearly outputs divided by inputs (Energiamarkkinavirasto 2007, 53).

$$DEA = \frac{u_1 * Energy + u_2 * Network + u_3 * Customers}{v_1\,(OPEX + TP + KAH)}$$

Most of the inputs at the bottom of equation and outputs at top of equation are relatively common sense. Factors such as an utility's operational expenses

(OPEX) and property value depreciation (TP) are obviously a "cost" from the quality point of view. An utility's "productions" include the financial value of distributed electricity during a year (Energy), as well as the length of the utility's electricity network (Network) and the number of customers served by the utility (Customers) to normalize the utility's size. The variables u_1, u_2, u_3, and v_1 are altered during a linear optimization to maximize "efficiency" relative to other utilities.

Along with these parameters, however, the customer's costs from blackouts (KAH) are an input. What does this mean in practice? Such costs have been first gathered by means of surveys (such as Silvast et al 2006). Based on these, the Finnish regulation model then concluded on the "pricing" for blackouts (Table 4.1). For example, an unexpected electricity blackout would cost 1.10 euros per one kilowatt of lost customer electric power and 11.00 euros per one kilowatt hour of lost customer electric energy (the difference between a kilowatt hour and a kilowatt, to put it briefly, is that a kilowatt hour measures the amount of energy you use, while a kilowatt measures the rate in which your appliances use it). Hence, if an average rowhouse in Finland used 2,850 kilowatt hours of energy in a year at the time of these perceived costs (Adato Energia 2008, 26), then a twelve hour's unexpected blackout in such a house would "cost" the customer (and the utility) about 43 euros, while a similar blackout for 100 rowhouses would "cost" 4,300 euros. The table also assigns other costs to planned interruptions and reclosing operations used by utilities to protect their systems that cause short-lived blackouts.

In the DEA input-output framework, such partly researched, partly constructed blackouts' "costs" are then combined with managing electricity risk: the more costly the blackouts the customers have had, the more electricity the utility now has to distribute, or the less expense and property it has to have in order to appear "efficient". What emerges is a loop between customers' risk perceptions and potential for profit. Between 2008 and 2011, the Finnish Energy Market Authority set each electric utility an efficiency target to a large part based on a DEA formula (Energiamarkkinavirasto 2007, 49).

The "harm" of a blackout and the techniques of its measurement have, I discovered, their own history. Often the "harm" it referred to as value of non-delivered electricity, not customer interruption harm like in Finland. According to an infrastructure and electricity expert who was familiar with the first Finnish studies that concerned these harms decades ago:

Table 4.1 The regulatory "pricing" of electric power failures in Finland between 2008–2011

Price/Euros	Per kilowatt (power)	Per kilowatt hour (energy)
Unexpected interruptions	1.10	11.00
Planned interruptions	0.50	6.80
Fast reclosing operations	0.55	-
Delayed reclosing operations	1.10	-

Source: Energiamarkkinavirasto 2007

The term interruption harm indicates that the customers experience black-outs as a harm and they should assess it. The perspective has not been similar elsewhere in the world, and one still hears talk about NDE (non-delivered electricity) or such. Previously, in Finland, such NDE values were calculated without asking customers.

But the assumption in the DEA model is the opposite to NDE: customers are asked to calculate the level of risk and these are factored in as an input variable. All answers, or their averages, play a part in minimizing electricity risk and distributing harms.

In cases like these, regulation works by supporting markets rather than by preventing their functioning and this seems to be more generally the case. NordREG (2009a, 18), the body of Nordic energy regulators, highlights this approach, for example, when noting that the body supports as little of the regulation of market-based energy end-user prices as possible. In practice, only Danish regulators controlled this pricing in 2006, although energy price changes are still more strictly controlled in all Nordic countries and especially in Finland (NordREG 2006, 57–61). According to another discussion by NordREG (2010, 10), the European Union's (European Parliament & Council 2009, 50) recent energy policy considerations for national public service requirements and vulnerable energy customers, while relevant – and already explicitly addressed in Finland, Denmark, and Norway (NordREG 2006, 56–57) – are more of an issue of national social welfare policy than international energy markets.

Likewise, considering national energy shortage mitigations during energy peak loads, the Nordic regulator body proposes that the arrangements "should be designed to minimize the adverse effects on price formation in the Nordic market" and in principle, the "market should be designed to solve peak load problems through proper incentives to market players" (NordREG 2009b, 5). Hence, yet again, the market mechanism should ideally deal with risk. Appropriately, the regulatory body's "vision" is as follows:

> All Nordic electricity customers will enjoy a free choice of supplier, efficient and competitive prices and reliable supply through the internal Nordic and European electricity market.
>
> (NordREG 2009a, 9)

What emerges here is not a regulator that governs risks and uncertainties through some kind of centralized command and control. Instead, regulation merely channels risks and uncertainties and creates possibilities for the markets to function. It internalizes externalities in a way envisioned already in the 1970s after the oil crisis and Nordic energy policy restructurings (Kaijser 1994, 60–61).

For most of the electricity utility and energy experts who I interviewed, public regulations were seen in a constructive manner. In particular, these regulations express what is important and then make it public: "the new standard compensation instruments [for customer blackouts] show that without electricity we do not have our society", one communication manager said in our interview. Another electricity use manager stressed that the new quality regulations are a positive development, because they make the expectations of authorities clear and explicit. In summary, then, the regulator intervenes in risks by creating a market for risks that functions alongside the markets for energy generation.

Markets, security, or both?

This chapter has been concerned with the relation between electricity risks, security, and market competition. Its key outcome concerns the way in which the categories of common risks and private profits were operationalized by contemporary energy market design and policies in Finland and the Nordic countries. In practice, it was often the market instruments that were keen to minimize both financial and technical risks. At the same time, public bodies also appeared to be in support of free enterprise. In some sense, market-based management of risk assimilated the prevention of technological risk in a manner that seemed almost automatic – at least to these actors. Only recent critical events in Finland seemed to have challenged this market-only logic by stressing anticipatory preparedness to power failures more than before, including in electricity legislation.

In previous studies, deregulated large-scale electricity infrastructures are seen as much more problematic and prone to failures for various reasons, as I discussed in the start of the chapter. This chapter, though, suggests that a large distributed energy marketplace can be something more unique than a hindrance to reliability or resilience. As critiques of free markets would note, energy market players do not need to consider electricity supply security in a substantive way and rarely have to think about the public or "common" status of regional electricity networks. Previously, electric energy suppliers were often bound together by physical proximity in a specific region; now, they are increasingly seen as economic agents who are bound together by contracts, risk calculations, and money and need not even be in the same country. Risk is hence distributed and managed on the systemic level of the international energy marketplace and other semi-markets for issues such as "national balancing energy" and "supply quality". European energy market policy documents support a similar line of reasoning: the internal European electricity market aims to provide choice, opportunities, trade, and efficiency as well as higher standards of service and contributions to security of supply (European Parliament & Council 2009, 1).

Yet, such an outcome of an analysis, while relevant, might be subject to a critique that has been levelled against the social studies of markets, particularly against sociologist Michel Callon (1998a,b). Anthropologist Daniel Miller (2002, 218) argues that by merely describing what economic agents are like, Callon's work ends up in "defence of the economists' model of a framed and abstracted market against empirical evidence that contemporary exchange rarely if ever works according to the laws of the markets". Likewise, an analysis of merely energy market policy documents – whose aim it is to convince their readers that the markets work like they are supposed to – could simply end up defending the models proposed in those papers by means of social science concepts. At the same time, much less consideration would be given to how the markets work in practice, all the time.

I found Miller's observation insightful after talking to the security managers in the transmission company. However, this was not because the electricity transmission would have functioned empirically in some other way than it was supposed to – rather, his argument drew my attention to an unintended effect of the free markets in the context of trust. One duty of transmission operation is about informing the market players about the grid capacity, that is, the technical basis of the markets. Among the numerous computers in the transmission control room was a screen with a normal web browser, viewing the public site that displays the said capacity. This is where transmission operators would also check if their web pages are displaying the correct information, because that is "what the market actors are viewing quite a lot", along with these same actors checking the Nord Pool regularly.

However, this public screen with real-time information then caused another effect: the local traders' anticipation of risks and their trust in the functioning electricity infrastructure began to affect prices. For example, if a transmission operator informs about a possible shortage of electric power, that according to the managers directly affects prices. SENER (2000, 28) claims likewise that a Nordic severe energy price spike in 2000 was not created by a concrete shortage of electricity generation rather than its anticipation; by "actors reacting to the announcements that Norwegian and Swedish transmission companies had made in the previous days about possible capacity problems".

Such issues highly relevant for risk are connected with concrete activities on the energy markets. Other examples were motivated from my interviews with the experts: for instance, we know how energy quality regulation and its optimization is supposed to work, but not so much how that regulation enforces "a specific number of maintenance workers and preparedness systems that have all been tailored to optimize the regulation model" as a CEO of a local electricity utility told me. Rich ethnographic studies have shown a corresponding result several times – namely that the practical management of electricity opens up new ways of understanding practices depicted by abstracted market models and regulations (de Bruijne & van Eeten 2007; Roe & Schulman 2008).

Not much more could be said about such pragmatic issues by exploring abstract energy economic models at least based on the examples in this chapter. A high-voltage transmission company, on the other hand, would not have been an easy site to access due to its sensitive practices and secret location. More fortunately, I was able to conduct interviews and a period of fieldwork in a local electricity distribution company in a Finnish city. I turn to this case and real-time resilience in organizations in the following chapters.

References

Adato Energia (2008). Kotitalouksien sähkönkäyttö 2006 ("The Electricity Use of Households 2006"). Research Report. Link accessed 25 November 2016: www.motiva.fi/files/1353/Kotitalouksien_sahkonkaytto_2006_-raportti.pdf

Berglund, Björn (2009). *Svarta svanar och högspänningsledningar – om försörjningstryggheten i det svenska elsystemet ur ett teknikhistoriskt perspektiv* ("Black Swans in the Power Grid – How Critical Events Has Affected the Security of Electricity Supply"). Dissertation,

Uppsala University, Disciplinary Domain of Science and Technology. Link accessed 10 October 2016: www.utn.uu.se/sts/cms/filarea/0901_Berglund.pdf

Boyd, Keith (2001). *Regulation and Innovation: The Case of Metering in Public Utilities.* Doctoral thesis, University of Edinburgh. Edinburgh: University of Edinburgh.

Byrd, Hugh & Matthewman, Steve (2014). Exergy and the City: The Technology and Sociology of Power (Failure). *Journal of Urban Technology* 21 (3): 85–102.

Callon, Michel (1998a). Introduction: The Embeddedness of Economic Markets in Economics. In Callon, Michel (ed.) *Laws of the Markets.* Oxford, UK: Blackwell Publishers, 1–57.

Callon, Michel (1998b). An Essay on Framing and Overflowing: Economic Externalities Revisited by Sociology. In Callon, Michel (ed.) *Laws of the Markets.* Oxford, UK: Blackwell Publishers, 244–269.

CEER (Council of European Energy Regulators) (2005). *3rd CEER Benchmarking Report on Quality of Electricity Supply.* Brussels: Council of European Energy Regulators ASBL. Link accessed 25 November 2016: www.autorita.energia.it/allegati/pubblicazioni/vol ume_ceer3.pdf

CEER (Council of European Energy Regulators) (2010). *Guidelines of Good Practice on Estimation of Costs due to Electricity Interruptions and Voltage Disturbances.* Brussels: Council of European Energy Regulators ASBL. Link accessed 25 November 2016: www.energy-regulators.eu/portal/page/portal/EER_HOME/EER_PUBLICATIONS/ CEER_PAPERS/Electricity/2010/C10-EQS-41–03_GGP%20interruptions%20and%20 voltage_7-Dec-2010.pdf

CEER (Council of European Energy Regulators) (2011). *5th CEER Benchmarking Report on Quality of Electricity Supply.* Brussels: Council of European Energy Regulators ASBL. Link accessed 25 November 2016: www.ceer.eu/portal/page/portal/EER_HOME/EER_ PUBLICATIONS/CEER_PAPERS/Electricity/Tab/CEER_Benchmarking_Report.pdf

Charnes, A.; Cooper, W. & Rhodes, E. (1978). Measuring the Efficiency of Decision Making Units. *European Journal of Operational Research* 2 (6): 429–444.

Collier, Stephen (2011). *Post-Soviet Social: Neoliberalism, Social Modernity, Biopolitics.* Princeton, NJ: Princeton University Press.

CRE (Commission de Regulation de l'Energie) & AEEG (Autorita per l'Energia Elettrica e il Gas) (2004). Report on the Events of September 28th, 2003 Culminating in the Separation of the Italian Power System from the other UCTE Networks. Allegato A – delibera n. 61/04. Link accessed 25 November 2016: www.autorita.energia.it/allegati/ docs/04/061-04all.pdf

de Bruijne, Mark & van eeten, Michel (2007). Systems that Should Have Failed: Critical Infrastructure Protection in an Institutionally Fragmented Environment. *Journal of Contingencies and Crisis Management* 15 (1): 18–29.

Energiamarkkinavirasto (Finnish Energy Market Authority) (2007). Sähkön jakeluverkonhaltijoiden hinnoittelun kohtuullisuuden arvioinnin suuntaviivat vuosille 2008–2011 ("Guidelines for Evaluating the Reasonableness of Pricing of Electricity Distribution Network Owners for 2008–2011"). Dnro 154/422/2007. Helsinki: Energiamarkkinavirasto.

Energiateollisuus (Finnish Energy Industries) (2012). Loppuvuoden sähkökatkoista kärsi 570 000 asiakasta ("570,000 Customers Suffered from the Year's End's Blackouts"). Press release 19 January 2012. Link accessed 25 November 2016: www.energiaviesti.fi/uutiset/ loppuvuoden-sahkokatkoista-karsi-570–000-asiakasta.html?p739=14

European Parliament & Council (2009). Concerning Common Rules for the Internal Market in Electricity and Repealing Directive 2003/54/EC. Directive 2009/72/EC. Link

accessed 25 November 2016: http://eur-lex.europa.eu/LexUriServ/LexUriServ.do?uri=
CELEX:32009L0072:en:NOT

Finnish Electricity Market Act (2004). 386/1995, amendments up to 1772/2004 included. Unofficial translation by the Finnish Ministry of Trade and Industry. Link accessed 25 November 2016: www.finlex.fi/en/laki/kaannokset/1995/en19950386.pdf

Forstén, Jarl (2002). Sähkön toimitusvarmuuden parantaminen ("Improving the Reliability of Electricity Distribution"). Report for the Finnish Ministry of Trade and Industry. Link accessed 25 November 2016: www2.energia.fi/myrsky/pdf/toimitusvarmuus.pdf

Graham, Stephen (2009). When Infrastructures Fail. In Graham, Stephen (ed.) *Disrupted Cities: When Infrastructure Fails*. London: Routledge, 1–26.

Gramlich, Edward (1994). Infrastructure Investment: A Review Essay. *Journal of Economic Literature* 32 (3): 1176–1196.

Hirsh, Richard (1999). *Power Loss: The Origins of Deregulation and Restructuring in the American Electric Utility System*. Cambridge, MA: MIT Press.

Högselius, Per & Kaijser, Arne (2007). *När folkhemselen blev internationell: elavregleringen i historiskt perspektiv* ("When the Swedish Welfare State's Electricity Became International: The Deregulation of Electricity in a Historical Perspective"). Stockholm: SNS Förlag.

Jalas, Mikko; Rinkinen, Jenny & Silvast, Antti (2016). The Rhythms of Infrastructure. *Anthropology Today* 32(4): 17–20.

Kaijser, Arne (1994). *I fädrens spår: den svenska infrastrukturens historiska utveckling och framtida utmaning* ("In the Tracks of the Fathers: The Historical Development and the Future Challenges of the Swedish Infrastructure"). Stockholm: Carlsson.

Kaijser, Arne (1995). Controlling the Grid: The Development of High-tension Power Lines in the Nordic Countries. In Kaijser, Arne & Hedin, Marika (eds) *Nordic Energy Systems: Historical Perspectives and Current Issues*. Canton: Science History Publications, 31–54.

Karlstrøm, Henrik (2012). *Empowering Markets? The Construction and Maintenance of a Deregulated Market for Electricity in Norway*. Doctoral thesis, Faculty of Humanities, Norwegian University of Science and Technology (NTNU). Trondheim: NTNU.

Kauppa- ja teollisuusministeriö (Finnish Ministry of Trade and Industry) (2006). *Sähkönjakelun toimitusvarmuuden kehittäminen: Sähkön jakeluhäiriöiden ehkäisemistä ja jakelun toiminnallisia tavoitteita selvittäneen työryhmän raportti* ("Developing the Supply Security of Electricity Distribution: The Report by the Working Group that Explored the Prevention of Electricity Supply Failures and the Practical Targets for the Supply"). Helsinki: Kauppa- ja teollisuusministeriö.

Lagendijk, Vincent (2008). *Electrifying Europe: The Power of Europe in the Construction of Electricity Networks*. Doctoral thesis, Eindhoven University of Technology. Amsterdam: Aksant Academic Publishers. Link accessed 25 November 2016: http://alexandria.tue.nl/extra2/200811526.pdf

Miller, Daniel (2002). Turning Callon the Right Way Up. *Economy and Society* 31 (2): 218–233.

Nord Pool Spot (2009). *The Nordic Electricity Exchange and the Nordic Model for a Liberalised Electricity Market*. Lysaker: Nord Pool Spot. Link accessed 25 November 2016: http://nordpoolspot.com/globalassets/download-center/rules-and-regulations/the-nordic-electricity-exchange-and-the-nordic-model-for-a-liberalized-electricity-market.pdf

Nord Pool Spot (2010). The Elbas Market. Website. Link accessed 10 November 2010: www. nordpoolspot.com/trading/The-Elbas-market/

Nord Pool Spot (2013). Intraday Market. Website. Link accessed 3 June 2013: www.nord pool spot.com/How-does-it-work/Intraday-market-Elbas/

Nord Pool Spot (2016a). Day-Ahead Market. Website. Link accessed 26 October 2016: www.nordpoolspot.com/How-does-it-work/Day-ahead-market-Elspot-/

Nord Pool Spot (2016b). Intraday Market. Website. Link accesssed 26 October 2016: www.nordpoolspot.com/How-does-it-work/Intraday-market/

Nordel (2007). The Nordic Grid Code 2007: Nordic Collection of Rules. A collection of common rules for the interconnected Nordic electricity transmission grids. Outdated after Nordel was incorporated by the European association ENTSO-E in 2009.

NordREG (Nordic Energy Regulators) (2006). The Integrated Nordic End-User Electricity Market: Feasibility and Identified Obstacles. Report 2/2006. Eskilstuna: NordREG. Link accessed 25 November 2016: www.nordicenergyregulators.org/wp-content/uploads/2013/02/NordREG_Integrated_End_user_Market_2_2006.pdf

NordREG (2009a). Peak Load Arrangements: Assessment of Nordel Guidelines. Report 2/2009. Oslo: NordREG. Link accessed 25 November 2016: www.nordicenergyregula tors.org/wp-content/uploads/2013/02/Peak-Load-final-21.pdf

NordREG (2009b). Market Design: Common Nordic End-User Market. Report 3/2009. Oslo: NordREG. Link accessed 4 June 2013: www.nordicenergyregulators.org/uplo ad/Reports/Market_Design_Common_Nordic_end-user_market_20090507.pdf

NordREG (2010). NordREG Approach to the 3rd Legislative Package on Retail and Consumer Issues. Report 1/2010. Eskilstuna: NordREG. Link accessed 25 November 2016: www.nordicenergyregulators.org/wp-content/uploads/2013/02/NordREG-approach-to-the-3rd-package_retail-and-consumer-issues.pdf

Perrow, Charles (2008). *The Next Catastrophe: Reducing Our Vulnerabilities to Natural, Industrial and Terrorist Disasters.* Princeton, NJ: Princeton University Press.

Roe, Emery & Schulman, Paul (2008). *High Reliability Management: Operating on the Edge.* Stanford, CA: Stanford Business Books.

Ruostetsaari, Ilkka (1998). *Energiapolitiikka käännekohdassa: Järjestöt ja yritykset vaikuttajina vapautuvilla energiamarkkinoilla* ("Energy Politics at a Turning Point: Associations and Companies as Stakeholders in the Liberalizing Energy Markets"). Tampere: Tampereen yliopisto (University of Tampere).

Sähkölaki (Finnish Electricity Law) (1979). 319/1979. Link accessed 26 October 2016: www.finlex.fi/fi/laki/alkup/1979/19790319

Sähkömarkkinalaki (Finnish Electricity Market Act) (1995). 386/1995. Link accessed 26 October 2016: www.finlex.fi/fi/laki/alkup/1995/19950386

Sähkömarkkinalaki (Finnish Electricity Market Act) (2013). 588/2013. Link accessed 26 October 2016: www.finlex.fi/fi/laki/alkup/2013/20130588

SENER (Finnish Electricity Association) (2000). Vapaan sähkön lyhyt historia: Suomen sähkömarkkinoiden avaus ja kipupisteet ("The Brief History of Free Electricity: The Opening and the Pain Spots of Finnish Electricity Markets"). A discussion paper by the Finnish Energy Industries, then Finnish Electricity Association. Helsinki: SENER.

Silvast, Antti; Lehtonen, Matti; Heine, Pirjo; Kivikko, Kimmo; Mäkinen, Antti & Järventausta, Pertti (2006). *Keskeytyksestä aiheutuva haitta* ("The Harm Caused by an Interruption") Espoo: Teknillinen korkeakoulu (Helsinki University of Technology) and Tampereen teknillinen yliopisto (Tampere University of Technology).

Summerton, Jane (1995). Coalitions and Conflicts: Swedish Municipal Energy Companies on the Eve of Deregulation. In Kaijser, Arne & Hedin, Marika (eds) *Nordic Energy Systems: Historical Perspectives and Current Issues.* Canton: Science History Publications, 169–186.

Summerton, Jane (2004). Do Electrons Have Politics? Constructing User Identities in Swedish Electricity. *Science, Technology, & Human Values* 29 (4): 486–511.

Tennberg, Monica & Vola, Joonas (2014). Myrskyjä ei voi hallita: Haavoittuvuuden poliittinen talous ("Storms Cannot Be Controlled: The Political Economy of Vulnerability"). *Alue ja Ympäristö* 43 (1): 73–84.

Thue, Lars (1995). Electricity Rules: The Formation and Development of the Nordic Electricity Regimes. In Kaijser, Arne & Hedin, Marika (eds) *Nordic Energy Systems: Historical Perspectives and Current Issues.* Canton: Science History Publications, 11–30.

Thue, Lars (2013). Connections, Criticality, and Complexity: Norwegian Electricity in Its European Context. In Högselius Per; Hommels Anique; Kaijser, Arne & van der Vleuten, Erik (eds) *The Making of Europe's Critical Infrastructure: Common Connections and Shared Vulnerabilities.* London: Palgrave Macmillan, 213–238.

Winskel, Mark (2002). Autonomy's End: Nuclear Power and the Privatization of the British Electricity Supply Industry. *Social Studies of Science* 32 (3): 439–467.

5 Monitor screens of market risks on an electricity trading floor

Electricity risk, control rooms, and everyday work

The previous chapter described the emergence of the free energy market in Finland and Scandinavia, the traits of its key players, and how Nordic energy market trading is designed. I also addressed some of the techniques that are applied to minimize price risks, balance national energy levels, and regulate the electricity networks in situations in which the market mechanism is not viewed as adequate for providing reliable electricity to all customers. The theory of liberalized electricity and its risk management hence goes roughly as above. Yet, at the same time, relatively little is known about the ways in which the energy market is produced in the immediate contexts of everyday work (Heath & Luff 2000, 10–12; see Özden-Schilling 2016 and Roe & Schulman 2008 for exceptions). This chapter addresses the gap in knowledge by studying the management of electricity and energy markets in a Finnish electricity company.

Many sources suggest that the control room is the appropriate field site for such an inquiry. The control room is a centre where infrastructure systems are overseen and managed, computer monitors abound, and communication devices are deployed to interact with different organizational units (de Bruijne 2006). An established field site of workplace studies (Heath & Luff 2000) and emerging in urban studies (Luque-Ayala & Marvin 2016), infrastructure control rooms are also the subject of many organizational studies (e.g. de Bruijne 2006; de Bruijne & van Eeten 2007; Roe & Schulman 2008; Steenhuisen 2009). These studies have brought together the topics of technological risks and reliability with ethnographic methodologies and broader public policy and management themes. In doing so, they have found that a crucial but rarely acknowledged element of infrastructural reliability is human control room operators. Infrastructure risks, as these researchers see it, are not so much anticipated and prevented as continuously produced in the control room work and its more-or-less real-time adjustments (Roe & Schulman 2008, 114–115).

The fieldwork for many of these earlier organizational studies was conducted in California, where the situation lent particular relevance to their findings. In 1998, energy generation in California was transferred from large integrated electricity utilities to independent private companies. These companies sold their energy on competitive wholesale markets, where local electricity distributors traded it in turn to energy end consumers. Pushed to purchase electricity increasingly in real time and faced with the ability of large energy suppliers even to fix prices, major Californian electricity utilities could no longer meet the electricity demand of their customers. The State of California had to intervene by buying electric power and supporting the utilities.

In organizational theory, the case of this Californian "electricity crisis" immediately suggests a risk: that of almost unavoidable cascading power failures due to the complexity and interconnectedness of the energy system. This perspective stems from sociologist Charles Perrow's (1999) classic *Normal Accidents: Living with High Risk Technologies*, which compared various human-built systems (e.g. nuclear power plants, air traffic, DNA recombination, space missions) and characterizes their two related traits: interactive complexity and tight coupling. The first trait refers to the degree of unexpected interactions among system components; the second to the pace in which effects propagate from one component to the other. When interactive complexity and tight coupling are both high in a system, accidents – damaging, unintended, and disrupting events – become difficult to anticipate and, over time, almost inevitable, hence the term *normal accidents*.

According to Perrow (1999, 97), the earlier, monopolistic, and regional power supply was tightly coupled, but was a relatively linear rather than a complex system, with the vertical integration of the energy supply chain and a limited number of organizations supplying electricity. Yet, the liberalization of these systems now suggests a growing number of organizations, more competition, new more-or-less real-time market relationships, and hence unexpected complex interactions and normal accidents, as Perrow (2008) himself and several others have predicted with regards to power supplies on the markets (van der Vleuten & Lagendijk 2010; Byrd & Matthewman 2014).

However, the above organizational field studies have not found what Perrow anticipates about normal accidents. Instead, they observed that energy system operators coped with these major restructurings and challenging working conditions by applying their working habits or *skills*. These are, more formally, their different "performance modes" that were tailored to the situational options of the workers and the volatility of the energy systems (Roe & Schulman 2008, 42–48): *just-in-case* (when the system's volatility is low, but there is a high number of options, which also means a high degree of redundancy); *just-in-time* (high system volatility and high number of options, requiring real-time flexibility); *just-for-now* (high system volatility, but low options, requiring "quick fixes"); and *just-this-way* (low system volatility and low options, which is a purposeful short-term emergency solution). The human controllers' ability to switch among such performance modes kept the infrastructures running even if normal accidents should have been almost inevitable, according to Perrow. Hence, the systems can continue to work with better forms of management and a culture of safety. In organizational literature, this argument is named as *high reliability theory* (Rochlin, La Porte & Karlene 1987; La Porte & Consolini 1991; Rochlin 2003).

My concern here is not whether Perrow was "right" about system accidents – if that can even be shown or disproved by evidence, given that Perrow is interested in looming rather than just-experienced catastrophes (Silvast & Kelman 2013). To me what is more interesting is how the focal point seems to tilt away from disastrous power failures and back towards techniques and practices – to the anticipation of unwanted events through present means such as preparedness, learning, or threat analysis, and bouncing back from disruptions after they have occurred.

Inspired by this interest in how infrastructures, their risk management, and markets work in practice, three themes of inquiry are developed in this chapter. The first theme situates a general curiosity about a Finnish electricity market control room and its technological artefacts. This interest follows from workplace studies and science and technology studies (STS) in particular: they argue that technological artefacts are salient for the continuous production and coordination of workplace activities. While there are various artefacts in an electricity control room, these workplaces' staff operates largely on computer monitors. This situation was different before the energy market liberalization in Finland. Before this period, electric energy was commonly traded over the phone. Hence the first theme of inquiry explores some of the specificities about how trading energy gets done on the computer monitor rather than, for example, over the phone with known business partners (for a parallel discussion on currency traders, see Knorr Cetina & Bruegger 2002, 166). Several STS works support this focus: from currency trading through to monitoring infrastructures (Latour & Hermant 2006), civil engineering (Suchman 2000), and protein modelling (Myers 2008), material computer screens bring specific interactions and information together in particular ways that affect practices on an ongoing basis (Silvast 2011).

The second theme zooms closer to the production of market-based bids and offers on these computer screens. In liberalized electricity, bids and offers have become a primary tool for attaining market exchanges from Scandinavia to the US Independent System Operators who have similar duties to the Nordic power stock exchange (Özden-Schilling 2016). In the control room of my fieldwork, to form an energy market bid and offer, megawatt hours and prices have to be entered into a monitor. Electricity hence acquires economic value and such values are always the result of work and efforts, according to literature on the social studies of markets (see Çalışkan & Callon 2010, 5–14). More specifically, this theme concerns how electricity's values are monitored in the control room and what screens are used to calculate these values.

The third theme of inquiry develops the previous themes further by discussing the extent to which monitor screens affect electricity market values and risks in the daily practices of control room work. My claim is that the bids on control room monitors have a degree of agency in that they participate in disciplining and routinizing, and thus ordering the control room work (MacKenzie 2009, 9). I wish to explore this ordering further by focusing on the "breakdown" between what might be called bidding logic and the more intuitive actions of workers themselves. Another way to phrase this is what happens when the bid does not add up and how might "screens" work to restore order and hence affect the management of market risks.

At the same time, as I showed in this book's Part II, the electricity control room workers also manage an infrastructure whose functioning is critical to a number of other provisions. Failure to provide electricity is thus a risk in that it is an unwanted event whose impacts need to be minimized (O'Malley 2004). When I speak of control room monitors and their screening effects, this chapter is hence particularly interested in the way in which control room workers anticipate and mitigate – or "screen" – unwanted events through computer monitors.

Two electricity control rooms

I went to do interviews and observations at an electricity distribution company in a Finnish city first in 2007 and then in 2008. Due to policies for creating energy markets by separating or *unbundling* regional monopolies from competitive units (Graham & Marvin 2001), the company had two control rooms. These rooms, here called the *energy market control room* and the *electricity distribution control room*, were responsible for electric energy trading and real-time management of the electricity grid. The energy market control room belonged to a company which also produces energy: this organization thus included both *retailers* and *producers*, to use the terminology of the previous chapter. The electricity distribution control room was owned by a separate network company. The control room was responsible for the management of the distribution grid, while yet another private company handled maintenance work in the field. In this chapter, I analyse the market control room and, in the next chapter, explain the history of policies for separating energy markets from networks and how that had affected the working practices and operator roles of both the distribution control room and the market room.

Figures 5.1, 5.2, and 5.3 display the arrangement of the two control rooms. Both rooms have one or two operators. The operators were titled as technicians and most of them were trained in energy generation technology, which is a vocational degree; however, about half of them, in correspondence with their new duties, received a brief course as brokers after the energy market was liberalized. I interviewed all twelve employees who worked in the two rooms and carried out around 20 hours of participant observation of their work.

As can be seen, these people sit in front of several computer monitors, observe these monitors, and use the computer in response to the day-to-day routines, real-time situations, and signals that the monitors display. Various communication devices are also present and provide opportunities to interact with actors situated elsewhere, such as maintenance teams and power producers. The rooms share the same premises, but are separated by a window and a door. Both rooms also share the same kitchen.

Figure 5.1 above shows various different computer monitors in the market room. Most of them display a different image while one is blank. The photographs and the map in Figure 5.3 show that there are altogether eight monitors in front of the worker. The monitors that appear in the background of the

Figure 5.1 Inside the energy market control room

Source: Antti Silvast 2007

Figure 5.2 Inside the electricity distribution control room
Source: Antti Silvast 2008

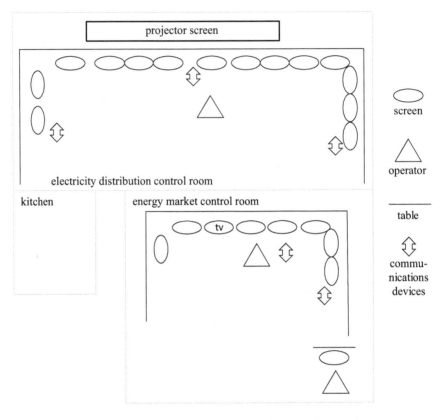

Figure 5.3 The map of neighbouring electricity control rooms of a Finnish city

photograph through the door are from the other control room. Based on my field notes, these monitors display from left to right:

1   Information on the production of electricity (possibly non-interactive).
2   Information on the electricity network (possibly non-interactive). An extended work desk from monitor 1.
3   A television (not on in Figure 5.1).
4   Email software and information on temperatures. Information on the production of district heating (possibly non-interactive).
5   An extended work desk from monitor 4.
6   Spreadsheet software. Interface to the day-ahead Elspot energy marketplace.
7   A graph on the balance between electricity production and electricity consumption.
8   Interface to the real-time Elbas energy marketplace.

According to my notes, the workers interacted mostly with their email and spreadsheets (4–6) and market-related monitors (6–8). These brief field notes outline the diversity that computer monitors can figure in control room work practice. The next section explores this diversity further in relation to how computer monitors screen economic actions in the control room, the first main theme of my inquiry.

Trading on monitor

As the previous chapter explained, the energy producers in Finland trade energy in a large-scale transnational Nordic power exchange, called Nord Pool. Based on talking to the control room workers and observing their work, it appears that the first salient characteristic of Nord Pool trading on the screen is its disciplined nature. For example, bidding and offering on the Nord Pool obliges workers to complete electronic forms on monitors and submit them by a certain time, as well as intensely follow the Nordic market situation on an hour-by-hour, if not minute-by-minute basis. When asked about changes in the trading of energy, one of the operators recollected how energy trading used to be "much more casual" over the phone. The same worker concludes that the "work has become much more exact" after the introduction of Nord Pool. Several other workers confirmed that they were not as financially accountable prior to today's market. For example, if prior to the market restructuring the company was imbalanced regarding electricity production and consumption, the electricity transmission company managed the gap for a price that was affordable according to several workers.

Another important feature of Nord Pool trading is its volume. It is not obligatory for electricity companies to take part in the Nord Pool collaboration. Instead, companies might rely on their own local power plants or trade energy outside the Nord Pool market. In practice, however, most of the electricity supplied in the company seemed to be traded through Nord Pool. It would seem that this trading provides the companies with certain benefits. This brings me to my third point.

As mentioned in the previous chapter, the situation created by Nord Pool is markedly different from previous practices of trading energy in that the whole market operates in real time. Nord Pool is also used for trading electric energy for the next and the following days, but the energy trading on Nord Pool continues up to one hour before the delivery of the energy. According to Nord Pool Spot's (2010) homepage from some years ago, there were two underlying reasons for initiating this practice: real-time trading of energy "reduces the risk of imbalance (between energy consumption and production)" but it also provides "the opportunity for better prices than in the day-ahead market" and "opportunities for economical profit for all participants". More recently, the stock exchange has considered Elbas when real-time risks and their mitigation are concerned. Specifically, it has noted that buyers and sellers can "trade volumes close to real time to bring the market back in balance", such as if a nuclear power plant fails or more and more "unpredictable" wind power is deployed by the participating countries (Nord Pool spot 2013, 2016a).

In our interviews the operators were clear that these economic profits are shared also by consumers: one of them told me that the goal was to acquire cheaper electric energy to lower the prices for the city dwellers. With all these different aims in view, these are rather binding considerations by the Nord Pool. It is apparent that energy trading that strives to minimize electric power imbalance and acquire financial profit in real time compels the workers to observe and study the market continually, day and night.

The "screened" relationship between control room practice and the Nordic energy market is hence specific for many reasons. International economic exchanges are not new in Scandinavian electricity supply – a cable between Skåne in Sweden and Zealand in Denmark went online in 1915, while Finland and Sweden were interconnected by 1959 and Norway and Sweden first in 1960. Early in the history of modern electricity networks, "companies and official bodies in the Nordic countries . . . realised that there were significant benefits to be gained from collaborating and utilising whichever energy source was the most advantageous at the time in the various countries" (Nordel 2007, 6).

At the same time, the market shown on the monitors seems to enhance and augment economic activities and relationships in specific and original manners. The workers are submitted to discipline and visible trading, which works through software and routine inputting of bidding numbers on computer terminals. These software and routines tell the workers what they should do: for this hour of the day, the company will buy or sell a certain amount of energy, for a certain price per unit.

Electricity companies are hence assumed by the market software to calculate their maximum profit and financial risks in a variety of ways offered by the devices. When the Nordic "system price" of energy is calculated in the Nord Pool collaboration, it is similarly assumed that the calculation corresponds with the economic model of supply and demand. The Nordic price of the energy is determined by economic equilibrium – that is, the point where the price of producing energy by all the participating companies is equal to the desire of buying energy by the companies (Nord Pool Spot 2016a). It is obvious even from this brief introduction that the current anonymous online trading on monitors is different from the previous practice of trading with business partners and other companies over the phone (see also Knorr Cetina & Bruegger 2002, 167).

It is also apparent that computer monitors, computer software, and market bids and offers can extend or "distribute" (MacKenzie 2009, 16–19) the capabilities of the control room workers. Two numbers (quantity and price) for each hour of the day is, at least in some respects, effective for making sense of a large distributed electricity network and a market that is comprised hundreds of companies from tens of different countries. But as the social studies of markets argues, final market prices are one thing but their production is a different matter (see Çalışkan & Callon 2010, 5–14). How does electricity gain its quality as a value to be inputted into the Nord Pool bid and offer? This question denotes a second theme of my inquiry and is assessed in the following section.

Screening electricity values

One of the workers, whom I interviewed in the night shift after the order for that day had already been sent, described the day-ahead Elspot bid and offer in this way:

> In the morning shift we make the next day's prognosis, where the power plant's generation power is defined based on the weather situation and from there the electricity. From there on we also send to Norway [to the energy stock exchange] the order, which has for each hour the information on which price we are willing to sell and buy [energy].

At 13:00 each day, the company communicates to the Nord Pool stock exchange about the prices for which it is willing to sell and buy energy during the following day. However, the worker points out that there is something behind the number: the prognosis of buying and selling energy is based on the ongoing weather situation. From a strict economic perspective this is not obvious. The weather affects people's demand for heat, but in Finnish cities it is not normal to have buildings with electrical heating. The energy market room is hence not selling heat as a commodity as such.

One reason for the weather predictions can be found in the structure of the energy production that the workers are managing. This and many other Finnish towns rely on district heating – a system where heat is generated in centralized power plants from wood, oil, and other fuels and distributed to people in the form of hot water in pipes. Furthermore, district heating and electric energy are generated inside the same power plant. Heat generation is the primary product of the plant but it also generates electricity as a kind of side product. Therefore, when people need more heat it requires the generation of more district heating, which then also generates surplus electricity. That is why the workers need to acknowledge the following day's weather when making the bids for Elspot.

Based on direct observations and interviews with the workers, predicting the weather situation is a complex and varied practice. In everyday life we may assess the weather by simply going outside or looking at the sky. However, in the control room this does not suffice. Instead the weather has to be transformed into a number for each hour of the following day. What is needed, thus, is some kind of weather "screen". Like weather predictions of meteorological institutes, data on the weather situation has to be "[g]athered together, added up, standardized, and averaged out" (Latour & Hermant 2006, 10). Upon asking about the matter, it turns out that the workers are doing more to this end than following weather predictions on television or the Internet. When I asked about the use of weather predictions, a worker explained:

> Yes, we have separate services, so that these temperatures are as accurate as possible. So here it is [shows me a spreadsheet on a computer monitor - AS], this day's weather. In fact this has been done this morning, there's the thing

that we have to make this spot offer by one o'clock, telling what we want to buy. Here are the predicted temperatures. And here is a sort of comparison day, where the temperature for instance has been as close as possible and usually also the day of the week has to be the same, because there are differences between a Saturday and a weekday.

The respondent notes the weather prediction service provided to the company. However, determining the status of the weather situation merely starts here. The prediction is entered into a spreadsheet on the monitor where each hour of the day is juxtaposed with various data, not only on the temperature, but also on the predicted electricity consumption, as several workers confirmed. The computer monitor is hence an essential interface to the weather as the monitor mediates or "screens" between weather data and the number that the workers want to produce.

As the worker remarks in the quote above, it is particularly important to find a comparison day; a day that has had similar temperature and consumption patterns as the predicted day. The same days of the week are preferred as working days tend to have different energy consumption patterns to the weekend. Contingencies in the following day's local electricity production also have to be taken into account, such as stopping a power plant for maintenance or starting one for the winter months. As I observed from a worker who had to handle such a situation, staying up-to-date with these kinds of events requires making constant phone calls with the local power plants. In other words, technical reliability was anticipated and trust in functioning systems was generated by interacting with the producers.

One can see therefore that the Elspot order is not just drawing on individual economic thinking. Instead, the order has to be "screened" in diverse and, from a strictly economic perspective, unpredictable ways. Different computer monitors are studied, archival data are gathered, and phone calls to the local power plants are made before the control room workers can make "our estimate of electricity production and distribution" or the Elspot bid to the Nord Pool. The bid is merely an end result of a long chain of elements that works together to produce an estimate of the next day's electricity.

On another side of the energy market chain, other experts are analyzing how the energy markets work. Working in the US context, anthropologist Canay Özden-Schilling (2016) describes an even process among these analysts to my control rooms. Striving to foresee how the US regional system and market operators, Independent System Operators, will act, the market analysts need to mimic closely the kind of bidding and offering I described above:

To predict how the Independent System Operators (ISO) will compute prices and bid or offer accordingly, traders must study a variety of factors that go into price making – demand, supply, and congestion. To get a hold on demand, they must study weather, because consumers' electricity usage depends largely on weather conditions. To get a hold on supply, they must study the age, capacity, and fuel type of various generators and predict how much and at what price they will be willing to offer 1 MW/hr of electricity. To get a hold on congestion, they must study the properties of the electric infrastructure, for instance, how much power specific transmission lines are able to hold.

(Özden-Schilling 2016, 71)

At the same time, my interviews and observations indicate that the important practice of prediction is still missing from these accounts. One aspect was continually repeated when I discussed the Elspot prediction. When I asked about it without observing the actual making of the prediction, the answers were brief and general. When I asked the worker to show the making of the prediction on the spreadsheet on the monitor, the answers were much more detailed. I do not consider here that some workers were less precise than others. Rather, the making of the Elspot bids on the computer screen had become a *habit* (Kilpinen 2000), which can be difficult to describe and was easier to explain in practice next to the monitor. One of the experienced workers even reported that he used his "gut feeling" to predict energy demand on any one day of the week:

> Tuesday, Wednesday, Thursday, they could be similar to each other in the middle of the week, then you have Friday, Saturday, Sunday, even Monday, they are little bit different. But that starts from your guts in a sense, that you somehow suspect that they have some small difference.

A habit, pragmatist theory argues (Kilpinen 2000, 57), is a generalization from particular experiences. One can also assume here that the worker has predicted the following day's energy on several occasions. Therefore he has a "hunch" that he can rely on for every occasion he makes a prediction.

To sum up, producing an electricity market bid is neither an automatic routine nor is it simply based on economic or other theories. It is not the kind of work that can easily be done with computer software alone. As a worker explains, "they have not succeeded in developing reliable prediction software for this [work]. Something was developed recently, but it did not turn out to be better than we are." But nor is a prediction made by a skilful and trained worker on his own necessarily more effective. Producing a value for electricity, in brief, is a matter of skilfully using technologies and consulting other people: one might say that the habits of workers are co-configured with technological artefacts and social interactions and one requires the other (Suchman 2000; Myers 2008). Control room practices rely on monitors but it is also the case that the monitors themselves enliven the local control room practices, habits, and interactions.

Bids, offers, and order

The previous section documented the role of monitors and diverse forms of "screening" in producing Elspot bids that predict the energy flows for the following day. However, the work of the control room does not stop at predicting.

The electricity supply has to be managed in real time, hour by hour, even during the night shift. On one of the computer monitors that face the operator there are two graphs. These show the predicted difference and the actual difference between energy consumption and energy generation. The latter is measured every three minutes and requires action if it deviates markedly from the prediction. The predicted and actual balance between consumption and generation should be as close to each other as possible in order that the company does not generate too much or too little energy. The requirement is not only technical: the company's participation in the electricity market also sets it a legal obligation for "balance responsibility" in the distribution area (Finnish Electricity Market Act 2004, Section 16b).

By and large it seems that the predictions made on the previous day are seldom markedly inaccurate. After the next day's prediction has been made, it even appears that there is not a great deal of continuous activity. For example, the workers could carry out an interview with me while working and they were allowed to watch programmes on television. The latter is possible as the management has put a television set in the control room to serve as "a breathing space for the operators". However, when I discussed this further, it turned out that the notion of having time for less intense "breathing spaces" is itself somewhat problematic in the context of this kind of work.

All the operators in my study emphasized the ever-changing contexts of day-to-day practice and the monitors certainly heightened this intensity. Even while the work might seem quite similar from day to day, the following conversation illustrates how hard it is to pinpoint the work either as completely routine-like or constantly changing:

Interviewer: Is this work routine-like or does it change daily?
Operator: Well, it changes in principle. Or it is kind of similar, but every moment is a matter of guesswork. There is no particular moment where you could put your feet up on the table, moments when the shift would go through without disturbance. No situation is hundred percent sure. For example, you cannot predict what the temperature is going to be and the work depends on the temperature so much.

Hence, not much happens but the worker's main task is to stay alert. One of the workers summarized energy trading as watching a campfire: "You have to be constantly keeping up a small flame. That is, you mustn't fall behind the energy stock exchanges." Another worker emphasized how the district heating makes the infrastructure "alive" all the time:

The process is alive all the time. And we try to keep up with the district heating network and as a counterweight to it. It's alive all the time. When we make some guess about the temperature and what could be the consumption, it's a living process even though there have been similar temperatures in the past. It's alive and production is alive too.

For yet another operator, "this work is always about making adjustments, there is no crystal ball. You cannot do the electricity stock exchanges beforehand so that it goes dead-on. This work changes from moment to moment." For example, the weather might change and alter the levels of energy production and consumption; or it might become dark enough for the city's street lights to come on, which creates a marked shift in the required level of electricity production, yet tends to occur at slightly different hours of the day.

But even though the rapid changes in daily conditions cannot always be predicted, there are several ways of improving the balance between energy use and production. The local power generation plants, which are owned by the same parent company, can be requested to produce more energy. To this end the control room workers have a phone that connects them with the plant's workers. A second option is to use the real-time online electricity stock market Elbas to purchase more energy or sell extra energy. This option operates on the monitor and on the market and I will assess it further in the light of the chapter's theme.

Elbas is in operation 24 hours a day and 7 days a week, with exchanges being made up to 1 hour before the delivery of energy (see Nord Pool Spot 2016b). Like with Elspot participation, the market is done online. A computer monitor introduces the participant with other market actors' bids and offers to buy or sell energy for selected hours for a defined price. The operator can also make his or her own anonymous bid and offer on every even hour. The company's own energy purchasing and selling in the stock market appear in green on the monitor and whenever I observed there were several such trades in action.

The principal tool for doing the Elbas trading is another monitor, already mentioned with the prediction practices, which shows a computer spreadsheet that provides temperatures, consumption patterns, and electricity generation information. The spreadsheet is studied by the worker to produce a new estimate of the consumption and generation balance and exactly on the hour, to make a bid and an offer on the Elbas market, thus correcting the energy balance. The numbers are hence estimates and are updated hour by hour; it is apparent here that the market numbers on control room computer monitors do not need to be treated as stable facts. Instead, the numbers gain their quality as facts by once in while performing as fleeting snapshots that can often be interchanged with new ones when the situation demands it.

It is not always the case that balancing work is so flexible. Instead, it is possible that both practices of correcting the energy balance fail. The parent company might not have enough local generation and the worker might not be in time to purchase it from the market either. Technically, this would result in an electricity supply failure. In practice, however, the national high-voltage electricity transmission operator steps in to fill the gap between production and consumption. This gap-filling electric energy is called "balancing energy" (Fingrid 2016) and the electricity distribution company is charged for it afterwards.

The charge for this balancing energy is not a fine. But the charge is not always affordable either, which, according to the workers, was the case before the energy market liberalization. Instead, the gap-filling electricity is "bought" (by coercion) from a separate balancing marketplace. The prices of this electricity are highly unpredictable. According to one of the operators, the balancing prices cannot really be known beforehand. Another is explicit that he does not want the company to "take a lot of energy" from the national transmission operator. One of the operators even thinks that the balancing energy can cause "serious economic risk situations". The balancing energy is hence screened to the control room in terms of financial accountability rather than, for example, a sort of public intervention, as was the case before the shifts of recent decades. However, the control room workers do not seem to want to be accountable for using this energy and hence avoid it.

This balancing energy and its costs, it might be claimed, is another disciplinary technique that gives the control room workers an incentive to be responsible economic actors. A different interpretation is also possible and goes closer to the previous studies of electricity control rooms and operator responses to volatile situations. Perhaps the workers want to feel that they are decisive with the monitors and their screening effects and not let the national operator fix the energy imbalance. We would then be observing an active effort to control the risk of imbalance in the local practice by keeping a high number of options open. Or to take the conclusion one step further, perhaps the control room operators take some degree of pride in sorting out problems locally even if this means that they have to make "just-in-time" real-time decisions and work under pressure (Roe & Schulman 2008, 88).

Markets, monitors, numbers, and habits

This chapter has explored the interrelationship between the role of monitors in an electricity control room and the management of electricity supply. Specific attention was paid to computer monitors that depict the Nordic energy market for electricity control room workers. Three themes guided the inquiry of these monitors and their effects: the specificity of "screened" market relations; the production of monitored market values; and the effects and adjustments of these values in the context of everyday work. It was shown how the depictions of the markets enable the control room workers to predict the levels of electricity production. It was also documented how these workers are engaged in balancing energy production and consumption as they created local adjustments to the balancing based on working habits, interactions, and knowledge of real-time risks such as weather fluctuations. Situation-specific layers were hence constantly added onto the control room monitors.

The findings in this chapter indicate that risk-based habits and technological artefacts such as monitors are not separate items in the control room setting. As was shown, computer monitors, like operational decisions and procedures in the previous studies on electricity control rooms (e.g. Roe & Schulman 2008), need to be understood and used in specific situated ways by the workers to play a legitimate role in everyday practices. Engineering skills can hence mediate technological artefacts. Indeed, it does not seem that the monitor-mediated global energy markets are "everything" for control room practice. This contrasts with a finding about currency traders, who appear to be engaged with monitored markets all the time (Knorr Cetina & Bruegger 2002, 168), but certainly artefacts such as computer monitors can mediate local practices on an intense, ongoing basis. It was shown, for example, how computer monitors may discipline control room work, extend the calculative capabilities of the control room workers, make weather status more tangible, and become part of a habit when an action that has worked repeatedly on a monitor is a resource to be drawn upon when giving risks conscious reflection. Overall, the chapter stressed a process of mutual shaping which was going on: the monitors continuously shape local work practices while local work practices continuously shape how the monitors are used.

I wish to conclude by relating the last point to broader debates on markets and risks. In many social science discussions, it is established that risk is the property of an individual and his or her risk culture. This approach is called the theory of *risk perception* (Douglas & Wildavsky 1982; Lupton 1999). Yet, the findings here suggest a somewhat different conclusion on risks and the management of uncertainties. Ethnographic knowledge from the energy market control room adds to the understanding of risk, as control room risks are not so much managed or "perceived" by controllers alone. Rather, we can observe a distributed assemblage of people, habits, monitors, numbers, and market mechanisms that continuously work together to produce a reliable infrastructure service in ever-shifting conditions (MacKenzie 2009). These socio-technical assemblages reveal how market-based electricity supply is supposed to work, help manage risks, and stay resilient, and hence demand more attention from researchers, especially if the economization of energy continues to gain support.

References

Byrd, Hugh & Matthewman, Steve (2014). Exergy and the City: The Technology and Sociology of Power (Failure). *Journal of Urban Technology* 21 (3): 85–102.

Çalışkan, Koray & Callon, Michel (2010). Economization, Part 2: A Research Programme for the Study of Markets. *Economy and Society* 39 (1): 1–32.

de Bruijne, Mark (2006). *Networked Reliability: Institutional Fragmentation and the Reliability of Service Provision in Critical Infrastructures*. Doctoral thesis, Technical University of Delft, Faculty of Technology, Policy and Management. Delft: TUD Technische Universiteit Delft.

de Bruijne, Mark & van Eeten, Michel (2007). Systems that Should Have Failed: Critical Infrastructure Protection in an Institutionally Fragmented Environment. *Journal of Contingencies and Crisis Management* 15 (1): 18–29.

Douglas, Mary & Wildavsky, Aaron (1982). *Risk and Culture: An Essay on the Selection of Technological and Environmental Dangers*. Berkeley, CA: University of California Press.

Fingrid (2016). Balancing Power Market. Website. Link accessed 26 October 2016: www.fingrid.fi/en/customers/Balance%20services/management/powermarket/Pages/default.aspx

Finnish Electricity Market Act (2004). 386/1995, amendments up to 1772/2004 included. Unofficial translation by the Finnish Ministry of Trade and Industry. Link accessed 25 November 2016: www.finlex.fi/en/laki/kaannokset/1995/en19950386.pdf

Graham, Stephen & Marvin, Simon (2001). *Splintering Urbanism: Networked Infrastructures, Technological Mobilities and the Urban Condition*. London: Routledge.

Heath, Christian & Luff, Paul (2000). *Technology in Action*. Cambridge, UK: Cambridge University Press.

Kilpinen, Erkki (2000). *The Enormous Fly-Wheel of Society: Pragmatism's Habitual Conception of Action and Social Theory*. Doctoral thesis, University of Helsinki, Department of Sociology. Helsinki: Department of Sociology Research Reports, No. 235.

Knorr Cetina, Karin & Bruegger, Urs (2002). Traders' Engagement with Markets: A Postsocial Relationship. *Theory, Culture & Society* 19 (5/6): 161–185.

La Porte, Tod & Consolini, Paula (1991). Working in Practice But Not in Theory: Theoretical Challenges of "High Reliability Organizations". *Journal of Public Administration Research and Theory* 1 (1): 19–48.

Latour, Bruno & Hermant, Emilie (2006). *Paris: Invisible City*. The original printed version in French is Latour, Bruno & Hermant, Emilie (1998). Paris ville invisible. Paris: La Découverte-Les Empêcheurs de penser en rond. Link accessed 25 November 2016: www.bruno-latour.fr/sites/default/files/downloads/viii_paris-city-gb.pdf

Lupton, Deborah (1999). *Risk*. London: Routledge.

Luque-Ayala, Andrés & Marvin, Simon (2016). The Maintenance of Urban Circulation: An Operational Logic of Infrastructural Control. *Environment and Planning D: Society and Space* 34 (2): 191–208.

MacKenzie, Donald (2009). Ten Precepts for the Social Studies of Finance. In MacKenzie, Donald (ed.) *Material Markets: How Economic Agents are Constructed*. Oxford, UK: Oxford University Press, 8–36.

Myers, Natasha (2008). Molecular Embodiments and the Bodywork of Modeling in Protein Crystallography. *Social Studies of Science* 38 (2): 163–199.

Nord Pool Spot (2010). The Elbas Market. Website. Link accessed 10 November 2010: www. nordpoolspot.com/trading/The-Elbas-market/

Nord Pool Spot (2013). Intraday Market. Website. Link accessed 3 June 2013: www.nord pool spot.com/How-does-it-work/Intraday-market-Elbas/

Nord Pool Spot (2016a). Day-Ahead Market. Website. Link accessed 26 October 2016: www.nordpoolspot.com/How-does-it-work/Day-ahead-market-Elspot-/

Nord Pool Spot (2016b). Intraday Market. Website. Link accesssed 26 October 2016: www.nordpoolspot.com/How-does-it-work/Intraday-market/

Nordel (2007). The Nordic Grid Code 2007: Nordic Collection of Rules. A collection of common rules for the interconnected Nordic electricity transmission grids. Outdated after Nordel was incorporated by the European association ENTSO-E in 2009.

O'Malley, Pat (2004). *Risk, Uncertainty and Government*. London – Sydney – Portland: Glasshouse Press.

Özden-Schilling, Canay (2016). The Infrastructure of Markets: From Electric Power to Electronic Data. *Economic Anthropology* 3 (1): 68–80.

Perrow, Charles (1999). *Normal Accidents: Living with High-Risk Technologies*. Princeton, NJ: Princeton University Press, updated edition (original 1984).

Perrow, Charles (2008). *The Next Catastrophe: Reducing Our Vulnerabilities to Natural, Industrial and Terrorist Disasters*. Princeton, NJ: Princeton University Press.

Rochlin, Gene (2003). Safety as a Social Construct: The Problem(atique) of Agency. In Summerton, Jane & Berner, Boel (eds) *Constructing Risk and Safety in Technological Practice*. London: Routledge, 123–139.

Rochlin, Gene; La Porte, Tod & Roberts, Karlene (1987). The Self-Designing High Reliability Organization: Aircraft Carrier Flight Operations at Sea. *Naval War College Review* 40 (4): 76–90.

Roe, Emery & Schulman, Paul (2008). *High Reliability Management: Operating on the Edge.* Stanford, CA: Stanford Business Books.

Silvast, Antti (2011). Monitor Screens of Market Risks: Managing Electricity in a Finnish Control Room. *STS Encounters* 4 (2): 145–174.

Silvast, Antti & Kelman, Ilan (2013). Is the Normal Accidents Perspective Falsifiable? *Disaster Prevention and Management* 22 (1): 7–16.

Steenhuisen, Bauke (2009). *Competing Public Values: Coping Strategies in Heavily Regulated Utility Industries.* Doctoral thesis, Technical University of Delft, Faculty of Technology, Policy and Management. Delft: TUD Technische Universiteit Delft.

Suchman, Lucy (2000). Embodied Practices of Engineering Work. *Mind, Culture & Activity* 7 (1/2): 4–18.

van Der Vleuten, Erik & Lagendijk, Vincent (2010). Interpreting Transnational Infrastructure Vulnerability: European Blackout and the Historical Dynamics of Transnational Electricity Governance. *Energy Policy* 38 (4): 2053–2062.

6   Enacting markets and security in neighbouring electricity control rooms

International electricity and the grid in a city

I have now discussed the monitors and their screening effects in one control room of an electricity distribution company in Finland. As I also briefly mentioned, the electricity distribution company I studied had two control rooms. This is an effect of infrastructural "unbundling" (e.g. European Parliament & Council 2003, 2009): when electricity networks and generation are separated, there is an opportunity also to separate workers in line with their new specialized tasks. In practice, the separation could have been done in a number of different ways. As one of the workers told me, there had been discussions about moving the market control room from the company's offices to the electric power plant owned by the same company. On the other hand, the other electricity transmission company which I briefly went to in Finland had just one control centre where all operators sat. Hence, in that case, there were just separate desks for different duties (markets and technical) rather than several rooms.

Nevertheless, in the distribution company at the time of the study, the two control rooms neighboured each other separated by a wall. In principle, the operators worked for a different organization and were not supposed to "know" about each other's activities. In practice, they could have easily talked with each other because there was an open door and they shared the same kitchen. This spatial arrangement raised my curiosity about how markets and security are enacted in these two neighbouring but different specialized compartments of the organization.

The duties of the two rooms also suggest wider considerations about spatiality. The market control room operated in the international Nordic energy market, Nord Pool. Following urban scholars such as Stephen Graham and Simon Marvin (2001), one could say that such international infrastructural markets represent "transnational connectivity" (Stephen & Simon 2001, 100) and a "globalized economy driven by liberalized flows of capital, technology, and information" (Stephen & Simon 2001, 103). A globalized market assumes the perfect mobility of money and information, which it facilitates through tools such as computer screens, discussed in the previous chapter. Two sociologists (Centeno & Cohen 2010, 3–4) explain the global economy as a system of high complexity:

comprising multiple parts that act individually, whose interactions aggregate to emergent outcomes, that then feedback to individual actors. Ideally, these types of interactions come together in the market:

> Ranging from face-to-face negotiations between a single buyer and a seller to the electronic auction of derivatives among millions, markets essentially match the supplies of goods and services with the demands for the same. Markets allocate the flow of goods and payments according to the intrinsic logic of a balance between needs and offers.
>
> (Centeno & Cohen 2010, 12–13)

International electric power markets expect this allocation of energy services with energy demands, too. However, I should clarify that the Nord Pool market allows only day-ahead and hour-ahead trading and hence is more restrictive on how buyers and sellers can meet than any generic economic marketplace. The aim of perfect mobility, facilitated by the market, is further hampered in practice when more tangible networks such as electricity are considered.

Infrastructures such as electricity grids are also "inevitably fixed and embedded in produced space" (Graham & Marvin 2001, 192). Global markets are hence "founded" in a territory when seen through the tangible infrastructures that they operate through. In my case, the company traded power to gain lower energy prices in Nord Pool, but also maintained the city's electricity grid in the other control room. The faults and blackouts handled in the latter site are local and territorial phenomenon – at least they have local effects, such as specific city blocks darkening. As for their causes, between 2007 and 2011 near to my fieldwork, only 4 to 7% of interruptions in customers' electricity distribution in Finland were initiated by causes outside of the local electricity network. Over the same period, faults caused by local acts of nature were considerably more common (40 to 65% of all faults) and even technical, structural, and operational errors (7 to 15%) exceeded outside culprits (Energiateollisuus 2016). Based on these statistics, a crucial element of the risk of blackouts is in everyday work practices and its situated conditions, such as local weather. The relation between the global energy markets and the city that they "pass through" (Graham & Marvin 2001, 184) can then be uncovered more by comparing my study's two control rooms, their expertise, and kinds of risk management.

This chapter discusses the different kinds of expertise and risk techniques in two neighbouring electricity control rooms and asks how markets and security are enacted in each respective site by control room technicians. The scope of this comparison is also informed by themes studied in Parisian control rooms by philosophers Latour and Hermant (2006, 27): I want to compare, on the one hand, how material flows of electricity are monitored and made tangible in the two control rooms and, on the other hand, how the electricity flows themselves are controlled and steered to minimize risks. In their study, Latour and Hermant (2006) lay particular emphasis on the diversity of urban control rooms: each infrastructural control room, accordingly, "captures a different matter, different aggregates, different behaviours, a different physics" (Latour & Hermant 2006, 79), a useful premise here, too, to consider two different control rooms and their risk management.

However, while the chapter discusses the way in which financial risks and technical security risks diverge in the two rooms, I also consider whether these risks can interweave and incorporate each other in control room decision-making. This research object corresponds to what sociologist Michel Callon (1998) calls overflowing of economic frames: issues that are external to the typically restricted frames of economic decisions. The models that regulate electricity quality, summarized in Chapter 4, suggest that externalities such as power failures should be internalized on a routine basis by economic agents. The key finding of this chapter, however, is that mixings of financial risk and technical security risk issues and techniques, while they do exist, often remain invisible to the workers who deal with them. In everyday practice, infrastructure provision is split into different social worlds just as recent energy market policies have predicted. The implications of the critical notion – that the crisis resilience of infrastructures may be compromised when profits are maximized on the free energy market (Graham 2009, 14) – will hence also be explored in more depth. How problematic is it that both security and markets are at stake when the Nordic electricity supply is considered? The two separate control rooms, their placement side by side, and distinct risk expertise offers one documentation of how these two aims are combined as a practical matter. Before moving to my ethnographic results, the following starts with the history of how this separation in the electricity organization came to be.

Unbundling comes to town

As energy histories have shown (Hughes 1983; van der Vleuten 2004; Lagendijk 2008), vertically integrated infrastructures, managed more-or-less centrally by natural monopolies, were once seen as almost unavoidable to pursue control, efficiency, and expansion of complex technological systems such as electrical supply. These public systems operated on many scales: initially serving cities, then subnational regions, entire nation states (Hughes 1983), and expanding more over national borders (Lagendijk 2008). From the 1960s onwards, however, economists and policy makers begun to problematize this public influence in infrastructure industries. In practice, modern infrastructures were starting to break down, cities suffered from urban sprawl rather than being integrated through networked infrastructures, and social and cultural critiques attacked the notion of rational centralized technological and urban planning in general (Graham & Marvin 2001).

Emerging economic theories addressed these issues by creating more room for commercial interests in infrastructure provision (Gramlich 1994). These restructurings sought to split (i.e. *unbundle*) infrastructures into segments, or "service packages", that operate independently and competitively and can be selected by consumers on infrastructure markets – such as the generation of electric energy or train provider – and into more physical infrastructures that remain monopolistic and are not duplicated – for example, the electricity network or physical rails of train transportation (Graham & Marvin 2001, 138–175). The markets that these moves have aimed at are international and the objectives that they pursue have been constructed as universal: such as increasing efficiency, competitiveness, customer choice, and market-based calculation, hence supporting the "global logic of supply and effective demand" (Collier & Ong 2005, 13). The underlying purpose has also been relatively straightforward: by supporting economies of scale, the liberalization and transnational integration of national infrastructures aims at increasing the efficiency and the output of the world economy (Cohen & Centeno 2010). The full integration of energy markets in the European Union, for example, illustrates this goal at the European scale (European Parliament & Council 2009).

The Finnish power sector prior to its liberalization conforms to this theory of vertical integration, later shifted by unbundling. In contemporary law in the centralized electricity supply, only a single organizational actor provided electricity: the electricity utility, "a company or an establishment that produces or distributes electricity or provides it for other than its own use" (Sähkölaki 1979, Section 1). Requiring a ministerial permit from 15 to 40 years, the permission for operating an electricity utility could only be given to a Finnish citizen, a domestic community, or a domestic establishment (Sähkölaki 1979, Section 2).

Following liberalization, in the new Electricity Market Act from 1995 (Sähkömarkkinalaki 1995), the actors had changed and clearly splintered in so doing. A *distribution system operator* was tasked with operating local electricity networks, meaning placing the system at the disposal of anyone against payment, hence transporting electricity from one "trade participant to another" (Sähkömarkkinalaki 1995, Section 1). Amid the commercial terminology, this remained permit-based and a regional monopoly, but allowed by the energy market authority rather than a ministry, for an open term, and with no requirement of being Finnish (Sähkömarkkinalaki 1995, Section 2). An *electricity seller*, in its turn, a person, community, or establishment, could either do *bulk-sale of electricity* to retailers and large consumers or *retail sale of electricity* directly to electricity consumers (Sähkömarkkinalaki 1995, Section 1). As the law required, these new actors also were to *unbundle* the electricity systems from trade by separation of "any electricity system operations from other electricity trade operations and the electricity trade operations from its other trade operations" (Sähkömarkkinalaki 1995, Section 28). In practice, at this point, unbundling simply meant separate income statements and balance sheets – in cities, for example, a municipality's engagement in electricity trade should have accounting unconnected to any other municipal activities (Sähkömarkkinalaki 1995, Sections 29–30).

This relatively soft unbundling became problematic initially at a more European scale. The European Union's first 1996 electricity market directive, enacting common rules to complete a single electricity market in Europe, had provisions on unbundling: all EU member states were to have separate accounting for electricity generation, transmission, and distribution in electricity companies (European Parliament & Council 1996, Chapter IV). However, this legal attempt coincided with a number of horizontal mergers between European electricity companies, often across national borders (Karlström 2012, 128–129). By simply unbundling profit statements and hence focusing on flows of market information, vertical integration in the electricity system had apparently not been prevented. Hence, in the European Union's second electricity market directive in 2003, the unbundling requirement became markedly stricter: legal forms, organization, and decision-making would also be unbundled in electricity provisions (European Parliament & Council 2003, Article 15).

The Finnish Electricity Market Act (2004) was amended in 2004 with unbundling in view. For network operators that transmitted more than 200 gigawatt hours of electricity during three years, *legal unbundling* separated the legal forms, organization, and decision-making of their electricity systems, generation, and sales. For operators that served more than 50,000 customers, *operative unbundling* meant that the same person could not act as the managing director or as a member of board in generation, sales, and network activities.

Already in 2002, however, the company of this study had been split, if not yet "unbundled", into seven parts that were termed as "business operation units" and aimed toward "customer orientation" and founding a "process organization" of new "expert organizations" (Electricity company 2002, 14). One was an energy centre (that I call the *energy market control room*) operating on the Nordic electricity and derivatives and European emissions markets; another was for sales of electricity and district heating. There were also units for energy production in power plants; district heating, including gas provision; business support; business development; and finally electricity distribution, the single remit of an integrated utility more historically. In 2005, following the Finnish unbundling act, the city divided this electricity distribution into two further corporations – a single network company, regulated by the energy market authority, and another company for building and maintenance – which were opened up to competitive entry by other providers. It is these new task divisions – mainly between the network company, the maintenance companies, and the energy market centre – which I observed play out in my fieldwork.

In terms of their tasks the network company would continue to "use the electricity network, maintain, plan, and build the same as before the incorporation" (Electricity company 2005, 16). The professional backgrounds in this organization would be mostly technical, accordingly. The energy centre of the free energy markets, on the other hand, was meant to operate on "constantly changing energy, derivatives and emission trades markets and supports the attainment of the city's energy business targets" (Electricity company 2005, 15). Its tasks included financial balance reports, certain research and service development activities, and, significantly to the company, managing "market risks".

During daily work, the energy market control room would do the following according to its manager in the company's annual report:

> In practice, the work is about continuously analyzing a whole formed by many variables, about making prognoses, and about optimization. The most significant variables on the whole are the weather situation, the prices of

fuels, the electricity and heating need of the end customers, as well as the market prices of electricity and emission permits.

(Electricity company 2005, 15)

While most of the centre's workers had a technical background, financial expertise would be stressed during future recruitments. Market risks had also became important a few years earlier when the company lost money on the energy markets and then pursued "risk management models". These models, accordingly, managed to "create a procedure that protects us from the variance of profitability, caused by surprising shifts in electricity and fuel prices" (Electricity company 2004, 10). As a result, the company had decided to become a seller rather than a buyer on the Nordic markets where prices continued to rise throughout the early 2000s.

In spite of this sharp market focus, the energy centre remained part of the city's electricity company: a municipal energy establishment founded in the late 19th century and among the first urban electricity utilities in Finland. In 2009, the city incorporated their electricity supply and ended something that had "started in 1888, the utility's life as a municipal establishment" (Electricity company 2008, 13), as a CEO put it in the annual report that followed. My fieldwork in this company happened in 2007 and 2008 during a phase between the two transitions described here. The unbundling and the restructuring that preceded it had already been carried out a few years earlier. The incorporation of the utility itself was a few months ahead. The following examines ethnographically how the staff managed to reinforce and reproduce their changing organizations as local order during day-to-day working practices.

Energy market control room and monetary issues

The key responsibilities of the market control room have been outlined in the previous chapter. Summing up, the workers almost continuously bought and sold on the Nordic common energy markets and also coordinated local electricity production. The previous chapter also noted that rather than just make predictions for the day ahead – and draw upon archives, weather predictions, and experiential "hunches" – it was increasingly the control room worker's task to stay alert to the markets and their fluctuations, as well as to unanticipated situations such as weather changes that impacted on energy generation or consumption levels.

As diverse as these duties are, all of them are still reducible to economic actions according to the unbundling of electricity. As Nord Pool Spot (2009, 4) stressed, energy market players "deliver to each other and the end users only the prices (and the bills)". They do not deliver electricity locally all the way to the customer. Instead, it is another "non-commercial" operator who takes care of the technical electricity supply. The management of risk of this supply is hence, in principle, diffused into locations other than the market room.

Such strict division of labour seemed to reflect the way that operators talked about their work in terms of risks and security. One worker did not wish to talk about "things that do not belong to the work here". This reaction was especially noticeable when I mentioned the concept of security. An experienced operator showed a similar attitude during a conversation. I asked what happens should a power plant fail, something which I proposed to be "an exceptional situation". The operator first argued that he did not think this situation was exceptional and then responded after a lengthy pause:

Operator: There's nothing else to it. District heating has so many additional heat plants. The only thing is that money gets burned.
Interviewer: So it's just costs then?
Operator: Yes, there's not . . . there's no security risk. Except if a boiler explodes, then the risk is for the boiler men. But there's nothing else. If a plant is dropped out of production, you scrape together the energy and heat from elsewhere.

In this case, the risk – a notion that the worker did not agree with – was only measured in money terms. More specifically, even if the situation increased uncertainty, it would have been distributed among market players and visible only as a small price fluctuation on the Nordic markets.

A similar response emerged from other workers concerning the effects of a blackout. As a strictly economic problem, a blackout is not a similar "risk" to these workers as it is technically for end users. The matter is primarily financial: when a blackout occurs, the company ends up with undelivered energy which should be deflected away from the network by trading it on the energy markets. Having said that, the market control room workers clearly were concerned about the consequences of electricity blackouts to customers, but as far as their work was concerned, it did not involve fixing blackouts as a technical breakdown, but finding the correct levels of generation.

In summary, then, the workers operated in an economic frame and did not seem to acknowledge security risks as part of their work even if they found such risks important in other respects. On the other hand, this issue could have also been terminological. Perhaps there were anticipations of security threats, just not organized under the concept of risk. Exceptional energy-related crises and disasters are relatively rare in the Nordic countries and I was unable to observe any. But the operators had experienced catastrophic failures – such as major blackouts after severe storms – so like in the above interview, I asked them about what possible exceptional situations that energy trading could face.

In general, the workers could only remember one or two occasions when something serious had happened during their long careers. One of the workers thought about a dangerously leaky pipe in the district heating networks, which then resulted in one of the company's own power and heat generation plants shutting down. As the energy market exchanges have already been planned ahead, this would cause serious problems with energy market brokering (differently from the above worker, according to who you just "scrape together" the missing energy from elsewhere).

When imagining the aftermath of this leaking water pipe, the operator explained:

> It could be that a power plant goes offline. Then we start to repair it and then we start the power plants in a way and then trading is all mixed up, but it gets put back in order step by step. If you start to build from scratch and you don't know exactly what the activation time of a power plant is, then you simply have to guess what it is.

When I asked for more details, it turned out that this step-by-step recovery was carried out in close practical coordination with other organizations:

Interviewer: What kinds of means do you have to repair things? Do you communicate with others?

Operator: We communicate with the district heat control room regarding what is the situation, so we get information ourselves. The power plant communicates between these control rooms about what to expect.

Interviewer: Is it very different then from normal working when there is an exceptional situation?

Operator: You have to be more in contact to get information and they don't always have the information either and then we try to guess and you have to be play with that and against the markets. You have to guess how much you have to buy and how much the power plants will possibly generate.

Interviewer: Lots of guessing?

Operator: It is guessing. Part of it comes of course from experience, but everyone experiences it differently, each individual's experience is always different.

The solving of exceptional crises, thus, requires tinkering, improvizations, situational awareness, and ongoing interactions between different organizations. But it is not outside of the scope of the control room working habit: rather, habit or "experience" was one resource through which such issues can be resolved.

In another type of event, energy brokering on the markets could cause problems with prices. From the early 2000s, an operator recalled what he called a "senseless event": the so-called "Black Monday" of the Nordic energy stock exchanges. Finnish energy end customers were protected from rapid price alterations (NordREG 2006, 59), but this was clearly still a severe issue for the control room.

> It was a situation that suddenly on Monday, when our spot market order came, the prices of that Monday were terrible. They were senseless, they were like the maximum prices that the energy stock exchange could have. We did not have enough electricity and then we had to buy it from the markets and it was terribly expensive. My colleague who operated that day of course had to face the worst of it.

I then prompted him about what the operators did when the price spike arrived. He replied that the management of the price spike is "just very much dependent on luck, on the kind of prognosis and order that I have made for the following day". Normal habits such as prognosis and ordering thus determined the response. I tried to ask whether new "Black Mondays" are possible and the worker said, "I guess they are possible the same way as any situation in the world. I bet no-one could have anticipated this two or three months before, you can never know about market forces."

Finally, I asked about the way in which the organization prepares for price spikes. The response was that "they come as surprises. Of course our prices are protected, but that is the protection side and we don't know anything about it." Undoubtedly, the anticipation of the price spike as a security threat was not part of the normal working habits of this room.

In many ways, the recourse to habits is an understandable response when considering the energy market. The common Nordic markets do not shut down even in an unusual crisis and economic transactions have to be produced even in exceptional situations. This according to the operators is also a limitation of simulated crisis exercises that they sometimes attended. When I asked about crisis training, one operator responded that market prices vary from one situation to the other and thus cannot be simulated:

> In practice we don't have anything like that, that we would for example simulate something. Because they are so hard to carry out, when you never know about those market prices, when even if you have some major situation, nobody knows the market prices. And they cannot be simulated either.

While a preparedness plan that deals with exceptional crisis situations has in fact been part of the training of the operators, in practice it depends on whether it is read carefully or not:

> In principle everyone has had to receive it and in principle everyone gets it. Then it is everyone's own responsibility how much you read it. But of course it can be found in a file.

To sum up, it seems that the operators in the market room work in a state of a real-time flexibility (Roe & Schulman 2008, 42–48), although this seems hardly problematic in the context of work. The risks were distributed in the markets, local energy consumers were protected from rapid price fluctuations, and it would seem that even exceptional crises could be solved by problem-solving and everyday habits. Issues about security of electricity supply, on the other hand, were delegated to the second control room.

Electricity distribution control room, technical monitoring, and maintenance

The electricity distribution control room maintains that the generated energy is distributed to energy consumers in the geographical distribution region. To this end, the workers of the control room monitor and adjust a number of "inputs" and "outputs". These included the electric voltages along the distribution network, the standard frequency of the electric voltage, and the stability and temperature of electric network components (see Roe & Schulman 2008, 27–28) – but not the price of the generated energy, which is managed by the energy market control room.

Like the market room, the network room has an operator who sits in front of a semicircle of several computer screens. The operators also face a large wall-sized video screen, used for doubling the smaller screens. This setup ensured that the screens are constantly watched as intensively as or even more intensively than in the market room.

My field notes indicate that the control room monitors most commonly display a map. Some of these are normal landscape maps, while others are more schematic, industrial control system depictions of the electricity distribution network. Yet other screens show databases where information about faults can be entered and reviewed later on by other workers. Furthermore, two monitors in the room display a video camera showing a site of the electrical grid. Finally, television is also available and clearly visible in the video wall in Figure 5.2.

While the offices of the two electricity control rooms resemble each other, their working tasks were highly specialized. Most workers in my study had the same training, were of similar age, and they had worked in the same control room prior to the energy market restructuring in the mid-1990s. During my study, however, only one worker still operated both the control rooms. He made the following characterization of the work tasks:

> The energy market control room is like keeping watch of a camp fire. You have to constantly keep a small flame burning, that is, you shouldn't fall behind the energy stock exchanges. Working in the distribution control room, on the other hand, is like being a tin soldier. Things don't happen all the time, but when someone calls you have to be ready on the spot.

What he saw hence was a marketplace that has to be constantly "made" by economic actors. The electricity grid, in its turn, was managed primarily through reactive monitoring and maintenance tasks.

In particular, three responsibilities were required in the distribution control room: firstly, maintaining a functioning electricity distribution system; and in so doing, secondly, maintaining the reliable provision and (as the worker said) "physical well-being of the energy customers"; and thirdly, managing the electricity distribution grid in such a manner which avoids large-scale material losses. This is what happens during daily work:

> We monitor the electricity grid and also use remote operated stations and switches and other accessories. And the normal use is that when a load change causes a situation or because of building operations, the switching of the energy grid has to be occasionally changed.

This operator continued that the most typical routine in a working day is the remote testing of newly installed components (e.g. lines, transformers, power stations) of the electricity grid in cooperation with teams of mechanics who are outside "in the field". The continuous monitoring task also covers the oversight of so-called "waste power" that electricity cables contain.

More acutely, the components of the grid trigger alarms when their voltage, current, or temperature exceeds a certain level. One operator had not counted how many alarms there had been in a single day, but an event list on a computer screens showed 36 pages of events for that particular day. Not all of these events set off an alarm, however, as some are solved by automatic fail-safe devices. When an alarm occurs, the task is to first report the details of the fault to a computer system, then determine whether a maintenance team is needed and, if it is, to send the team into the field and coordinate the fieldwork in relation to the information on the control room computer screens.

Thus far, what is at stake is relatively straightforward. In some sense, risks were not just mitigated, but seemed instead to be removed to increase security. This was also suggested by the methods of solving a fault, which were highly standardized by the workers. The steps taken are discussed in the following:

Interviewer: Are there many rules that are followed even though situations change?

Operator: Well, of course there are security and other sets of rules about what should be done. You have to go according to them. And every operator has to have the same point of view about those things. That doesn't change according to who sits here.

Thus, on the one hand, the working practice of the room follows strict rules and standards when "security" is considered. On the other hand, the way "security" is guaranteed is still to some extent dependent on circumstances: as the technician continued, "each fault is a little different and you have to consider separately each time how to act." Another operator reflected on a similar tension between security and on-the-spot actions:

> In principle electricity work is usually highly standardized. If everyone follows the standard, then it is highly structured. There is a problem, however, that when you go to a work site, the situation might vary greatly. And then comes your own adaptation about how you want to do things.

Here, one part of unpredictability stems from the actual worksite. Another stems from the need to maintain the welfare of customers. As a rule, maintenance work requires that the electricity grid is shut off to avoid dangerous electric shocks. Yet this practice while secure also makes a trade-off: some customers will inevitably lose their electricity supply during the maintenance. One operator highlighted this when he pointed out that each maintenance needs to be done in a manner that does not pose "unreasonable harm to other customers".

I was able to observe one occasion when an operator fixed a customer fault. This maintenance started from a phone call from a household customer, who could, it should be stressed, call these operators directly. This is not an obvious convention: it might have been considered distracting that operators were inter-rupted by customers during a fault. Nonetheless, the technician first talked with the customer who reported lights blinking at his or her home. The technician then determined if this fault was the responsibility of the electricity company. Eventually he decided to send a maintenance team into the field. The problem was at the customer's home and not on the company's electricity grid. However, blinking lights might indicate a "ground fault" which entails a potential risk of electric shock to the customer. He found the location of the house on a computer map, phoned an outsourced maintenance team, and told them about the techni-cal details of the fault. He determined how many other houses would have to, "in the worst case" as he added, be cut off from electricity distribution during the fixing of the fault and he waited for the maintenance team to get to the house of the customer. He then interacted with a computer screen and started writing a fault report. He talked with the maintenance team on the phone again once they arrived. Finally after several attempts at finding the cause of the fault at the customer's house, he determined together with the maintenance team that this was not a "ground fault" after all, but a loose electricity line, typical of "these old battlefront soldier houses" as he noted to me. He then concluded the fixing by sending the maintenance team off and checked the details about their working hours for their billing.

The point that emerges from this detailed description is that there were diver-gent aspects in the maintenance work. Only some of them involved a stand-ardized control of risks and uncertainty. The above example also illustrates improvizations, independent decisions, teamwork, skills, help from computer systems, practical rules of thumb, and knowledge of the local region.

Considering risk management, it is visible that the threat that is anticipated shifts gradually as the situation unfolds. Firstly, what occurs is blinking lights, suggesting perhaps a coming blackout for the customer. The operator, however, foresees a dangerous ground fault due to the blinking. Maintenance is sent and it is considered how many others customers will have a blackout due to the fixing. Therefore, the prevention of one risk causes another, in this case a risk of a power failure for other customers unrelated to the initial fault. After a long period of work, the operator realizes that the fault was not a ground fault. Instead, it was sagging lines, which could have been expected in this kind of housing area. In summary, the nature of these blackout threats can change almost minute by min-ute. Different habits and experience are drawn upon when observations become anomalous and information is added. Making urban life and its risks visible in a specific manner, the result of these rich working practices is an "establishment of new ways of seeing the city and its infrastructures", as urban scholars Andrés Luque-Ayala and Simon Marvin (2016, 2) suggest.

This style of reasoning, furthermore, is it seems not something that is only carried out on the backstage of using formalized risk management techniques. On the contrary, a print out of a fault report I received from another Finn-ish electricity distribution company in 2005 shows how the conception of an electricity fault developed: in correspondence with shifting cues in subsequent working situations.

Short circuit current X Ampere [all details omitted and replaced with large alphabets -AS]. We went through the wire, the cause of the fault was a long birch branch that had gone through the wire at the address Y. The position of the fault was not found. Wind 2.4 meters per second southeast. Checked according to notice (a loud bang was heard) a construction site near the place Z. The location of the fault was between the roads U and V. A dry twig flown on the line.

Here, while the report is not as detailed as the ethnographic example above, it is still clear that the operators determined the location and the cause of the fault – a dry twig on the electric wire – only gradually. Also, this happened only after inaccurate cues (i.e. a report of a loud bang near a construction site) had been verified.

Such a logic that deals with incidents little by little by adjusting habits seemed to be prevalent even in exceptional situations. The last serious incident an operator recalled was two major Finnish storms in 2001, called Janika and Pyry. More than 800,000 Finnish customers suffered from a temporary blackout and over 1,600 households were without electricity for more than five days (Kauppa- ja teollisuusministeriö 2006). What might seem like a catastrophe, however, was more mundane in the control room context. The first effect the operator recalled was that one extra operator was brought in to help with fixing the network. Few other remarks suggested that this blackout had been an unmanageable crisis. Rather, there was a hint of muted optimism about learning from these events. Some methods first applied during these storms – such as writing working steps on post-it notes and then discarding the notes after the steps were completed – were still in use as an operator remarked. In a way, hence, the crisis had been absorbed by control room working practice.

Risk-based habits and spatial issues

This chapter has studied the different scales of electricity risk by considering risk techniques and their use in two electricity control rooms, managing separated or "unbundled" electricity infrastructures. Material was gathered by interviewing the control room workers and observing their working routine ethnographically. From this vantage point, the market control room demonstrated how risks are distributed and hedged in the markets, so that even exceptional crises it would seem could be resolved by the skilful actions of the workers. The distribution room involved more formalized prevention of hazards with significant assistance from working experience and localized experience. Even in this room, some degree of market competition and optimizations had been introduced: the workers calculated the working costs of fixing the electricity grid, determined whose financial and legal responsibility the fault is, and contracted for outsourced maintenance teams.

In spite of such "overflows" between market-based risks and technical risks, the management of security risks and financial risks was clearly separate. Considerations about infrastructures and spatiality started this chapter and provide another perspective when dealing with this result. When "situating" global competitive infrastructures in a local territory, my study found that the co-existence in this case study of global markets with a local city's electricity infrastructure was not seen as very problematic by the two control rooms' operators. Instead, it seems that the two functions of the company (markets and technical distribution) had been separated and "unbundled" effectively. The study's method involved ethnographic presence in the control rooms and even though this stay was relatively short, it did not seem to me that the workers were not telling "what is really going on". What emerges rather is what seems like an effective way of dealing with local technical risks, while also meeting contemporary demands for cost-effectiveness in electricity. This also marks a contrast to rebundling of these splintered networks which is partially taking place in other locations such as operation centres in cities that aim to combine emergency, weather, police, traffic, and other information rather than fragmenting it (Luque-Ayala & Marvin 2016).

Furthermore, in everyday work, I would suggest that this separation of expertise was achieved not only by rules, norms, organizations, or even walling off different parts of the organizations. Rather, what kept the different worlds of risk so much apart were the different working habits of the two control rooms' workers. The energy market requires certain habits such as making bids every hour and ordering energy for the day ahead. The management of the electricity grid in its turn demands other habitualized actions such as reacting to faults on the spot when they occur. Clearly, the market-based habits carried out on computer screens were relatively detached from the situations in the local grid. The grid-based habits, on the other hand, generated knowledge applicable to specific local issues such as kinds of housing in the city. Such habits have their own specific effects, as shown by the working situations and their risk management. Indeed, it seems that even an exceptional crisis cannot easily hamper the logic, the effectiveness, and the durability of a habit. As the examples demonstrated above, a crisis was often absorbed rather than becoming a catastrophe. Lay people who use electricity, as I will show in the next chapter, display very similar habitualized responses to power failures – although as I will also discuss, these habits are not always acknowledged by expert discourses about electricity use and its risks.

References

Callon, Michel (1998). An Essay on Framing and Overflowing: Economic Externalities Revisited by Sociology. In Callon, Michel (ed.) *Laws of the Markets*. Oxford, UK: Blackwell Publishers, 244–269.

Centeno, Miguel & Cohen, Joseph (2010). *Global Capitalism: A Sociological Perspective*. Cambridge, MA: Polity Press.

Collier, Stephen & Ong, Aihwa (2005). Global Assemblages: Anthropological Problems. In Ong, Aihwa & Collier, Stephen (eds) *Global Assemblages: Technology, Politics, and Ethics as Anthropological Problems*. Malden: Blackwell, 3–21.

Electricity company (2002). Annual Report. Anonymized source, in possession of the author.

Electricity company (2004). Annual Report. Anonymized source, in possession of the author.

Electricity company (2005). The City's Energy Business Operations. Anonymized source, in possession of the author.

Electricity company (2008). The City's Energy Business Operations. Anonymized source, in possession of the author.

Energiateollisuus (Finnish Energy Industries) (2016). Sähkön keskeytystilastot ("Electricity Interruption Statistics"). Link accessed 27 October 2016: http://energia.fi/tilastot-ja-julkaisut/sahkotilastot/sahkon-keskeytystilastot

European Parliament & Council (1996). Concerning Common Rules for the Internal Market in Electricity. Directive 96/92/EC. Link accessed 27 October 2016: http://eur-lex.europa.eu/legal-content/EN/TXT/?uri=CELEX%3A31996L0092

European Parliament & Council (2003). Concerning Common Rules for the Internal Market in Electricity and Repealing Directive 96/92/EC. Directive 2003/54/EC. Link accessed 27 October 2016: http://eur-lex.europa.eu/legal-content/EN/TXT/?uri=CELEX%3A32003L0054

European Parliament & Council (2009). Concerning Common Rules for the Internal Market in Electricity and Repealing Directive 2003/54/EC. Directive 2009/72/EC. Link accessed 25 November 2016: http://eur-lex.europa.eu/LexUriServ/LexUriServ.do?uri=CELEX:32009L0072:en:NOT

Graham, Stephen (2009). When Infrastructures Fail. In Graham, Stephen (ed) *Disrupted Cities: When Infrastructure Fails*. London: Routledge, 1–26.

Graham, Stephen & Marvin, Simon (2001). *Splintering Urbanism: Networked Infrastructures, Technological Mobilities and the Urban Condition*. London: Routledge.

Gramlich, Edward (1994). Infrastructure Investment: A Review Essay. *Journal of Economic Literature* 32 (3): 1176–1196.

Hughes, Thomas (1983). *Networks of Power: Electrification in Western Society, 1880–1930*. Baltimore, MD: Johns Hopkins University Press.

Karlstrøm, Henrik (2012). *Empowering Markets? The Construction and Maintenance of a Deregulated Market for Electricity in Norway*. Doctoral thesis, Faculty of Humanities, Norwegian University of Science and Technology. Trondheim: NTNU.

Kauppa- ja teollisuusministeriö (Finnish Ministry of Trade and Industry) (2006). *Sähkönjakelun toimitusvarmuuden kehittäminen: Sähkön jakeluhäiriöiden ehkäisemistä ja jakelun toiminnallisia tavoitteita selvittäneen työryhmän raportti* ("Developing the Supply Security of Electricity Distribution: The Report by the Working Group that Explored the Prevention of Electricity Supply Failures and the Practical Targets for the Supply"). Helsinki: Kauppa- ja teollisuusministeriö.

Lagendijk, Vincent (2008). *Electrifying Europe: The Power of Europe in the Construction of Electricity Networks*. Doctoral thesis, Eindhoven University of Technology. Amsterdam: Aksant Academic Publishers. Link accessed 25 November 2016: http://alexandria.tue.nl/extra2/200811526.pdf

Latour, Bruno & Hermant, Emilie (2006). *Paris: Invisible City*. The original printed version in French is Latour, Bruno & Hermant, Emilie (1998). Paris ville invisible. Paris: La Découverte-Les Empêcheurs de penser en rond. Link accessed 25 November 2016: www.bruno-latour.fr/sites/default/files/downloads/viii_paris-city-gb.pdf

Luque-Ayala, Andrés & Marvin, Simon (2016). The Maintenance of Urban Circulation: An Operational Logic of Infrastructural Control. *Environment and Planning D* 34 (2): 191–208.

Nord Pool Spot (2009). *The Nordic Electricity Exchange and the Nordic Model for a Liberalised Electricity Market*. Lysaker: Nord Pool Spot. Link accessed 25 November 2016: http://nordpoolspot.com/globalassets/download-center/rules-and-regulations/

the-nordic-electricity-exchange-and-the-nordic-model-for-a-liberalized-electricity-market.pdf

NordREG (Nordic Energy Regulators) (2006). The Integrated Nordic End-User Electricity Market: Feasibility and Identified Obstacles. Report 2/2006. Eskilstuna: NordREG. Link accessed 25 November 2016: www.nordicenergyregulators.org/wp-content/uploads/2013/02/NordREG_Integrated_End_user_Market_2_2006.pdf

Roe, Emery & Schulman, Paul (2008). *High Reliability Management: Operating on the Edge.* Stanford, CA: Stanford Business Books.

Sähkölaki (Finnish Electricity Law) (1979). 319/1979. Link accessed 26 October 2016: www.finlex.fi/fi/laki/alkup/1979/19790319

Sähkömarkkinalaki (Finnish Electricity Market Act) (1995). 386/1995. Link accessed 26 October 2016: www.finlex.fi/fi/laki/alkup/1995/19950386

van der Vleuten, Erik (2004). Infrastructures and Societal Change: A View from the Large Technical Systems Field. *Technology Analysis & Strategic Management* 16 (3): 395–414.

Part IV

Lay people, experts, and electric power failures

7 Everyday habits as a risk response

Prepared households?

In everyday life, practices of energy use are often inconspicuous and not always apparent to their carriers (Shove 2003). The electricity network itself is typically underground or hidden inside walls, electrical transformers sit in basements, and power plants tend to be on the outskirts of towns (Lehtonen 2009). This infrastructure as such is certainly not always invisible – consider, for example, the key role of electricity as a symbol of state modernity in many places (Graham & Marvin 2001; Larkin 2013), including the electrification of Finland in the 20th century (Myllyntaus 1991). However, on the more mundane scale, our actions are dependent on the functioning of these infrastructures through a great number of other practices and everyday technologies, ranging from electrified heating and air conditioning to lighting, cleaning, the storing and preparing of food, media technologies, alarm systems, and computing (Star 1999; Southerton, van Vliet & Chappells 2004).

As I have now shown in this book, the indispensability of electricity has not been lost on experts. In Chapter 3, I presented expert discussions that draw on a heightened concern over vulnerabilities and infrastructures. Infrastructures are now increasingly framed as society's *vital systems* (Collier & Lakoff 2008). Infrastructural breakdowns, such as blackouts, water supply contaminations, cyber threats, fiscal crises, and major industrial accidents, have become perceived as a significant source of vulnerability for the whole Finnish society (SSFVS 2006; SSS 2010), other nation states (Brunner & Suter 2009), and international institutions such as the European Council (2008). Similarly, the energy industries in Finland have established many years ago that the desired level of security is 99.9 percent reliability for all energy customers (Energiateollisuus 2010).

These societal threat scenarios and worries over reliability are not just situated on some macro level of the economy and the government. Rather, the day-to-day effects of power cuts have become an important topic for emerging national security initiatives and energy policy programmes (Forstén 2002; Kauppa- ja teollisuusministeriö 2006; see Heidenstrøm & Kvarnlöf 2017). Some while ago, the Finnish Ministry of Defence (Puolustusministeriö 2008) issued an information campaign on electricity blackouts, written by two professional journalists. An image from this campaign (not reprinted here) shows how energy users cope with the loss of sewage and heating: water is poured into the toilet and a fireplace and sleeping bags help one keep warm (Puolustusministeriö 2008, 6; 12). The information guide also includes several written instructions, like this:

- "If the tap works, only use it for the most indispensable needs."
- "If a blackout lasts more than an hour, store water in a clean container."
- "In a prolonged power outage, the authorities will provide water."
- "Always keep bottled water or juice in your home."

(Puolustusministeriö 2008, 5)

Both with regard to blackouts that are imminent and those that occur, households are hence expected to be *prepared*. In a slightly different but related context, they are also expected to calculate the levels of risk. As seen in Chapter 4, energy market regulation now increasingly stresses the "quality" of electricity distribution. In Finland, the monitoring of this quality in its turn critically depends on information from the energy users to measure the economic worth of reliable energy supply. Such worths are assessed in surveys such as the one in Figure 7.1. Filled with questions about multiple power failures and their economic effects, the survey assumes that all energy users are rational economic actors who should calculate more frequently the value of energy use and the financial risk of electricity blackouts (Silvast & Virtanen 2014).

The Finnish electricity experts who I interviewed also showed corresponding worries about consumers' "unawareness" concerning risks. According to a user expert in one company, everything today is dependent on electricity and demands for reliable electricity supply are therefore high. As the same company's

---

Question 16. Evaluate the economic value of the damages or harms that expected and unexpected power cuts. The electricity cuts are 1 second, 12 hours or 36 hours long and they occur in winter during the week at

power cut duration	unexpected power cut	pre-announced	the most harmful time (e.g. 18:00–20:00)
1 second	_____ euros		_____
2 minutes	_____ euros		_____
1 hour	_____ euros	_____ euros	_____
12 hours	_____ euros	_____ euros	_____
36 hours	_____ euros		

Figure 7.1 A customer survey, 2004, asks what power cuts cost, among more than a dozen similar questions

Source: Translated from Silvast et al 2006, 104

use engineer remarked, electricity consumption is "easy and convenient, fast and efficient" and these "same elements belong to the market economy". Everyone "wants to use electricity", but not many "want to think" what is behind functioning systems. When electricity became widely diffused throughout society, "safeguards were forgotten to save money". Electricity has become a basic necessity or is taken for granted and when "this basic necessity, this taken-for-granted thing is missing, then we don't know what to do". This is why the effects of blackouts are so severe according to experts, for the skills needed for preparedness have been forgotten.

This relatively general discussion about energy-dependent users was, however, based on concrete communication. A particularly crucial communication channel was the utility fault phone line. The utility user expert remarked that there does not have to be a large electricity supply failure before people phone the customer line expecting help or compensation. This helpline was an essential part of the studied utilities and none of the companies had outsourced it. Still, the experts seemed to think that the customers who phone in do not always acknowledge the nature of the electricity supply system and its management and the inevitability of occasional supply failures.

These are not exceptional considerations within industries such as electricity supply. The capabilities of technology users and the involvement of users in production processes have become a "fact of life" in industrial strategizing, technology scholars Sampsa Hyysalo, Elgaard and Oudshoorn (2016, 3) write. At the same time, the connection of technology designers with users is a long-standing aspiration in business and academic circles starting from the early 20th century consumer research (Hyysalo, Elgaard & Oudshoorn 2016, 5–20).

With infrastructures, the problematic of user risk has found different expressions in electricity histories. One early example was the mitigation of electric fires and electric shocks in appliances and electricity networks. From early to the mid-20th century electric shock and fire risks were understood markedly individually: hazards were minimized not only by building standardized safe equipment, but also by establishing security norms to human actors and training them for safer conduct (Aarrevaara, Nurmi & Stenvall 2004). Initial electrical appliances were connected with another individualistic risk rationale when they were sold to homes: machines such as refrigerators and washing machines would save time and rationalize household work, women's in particular (Pantzar 1999). In Finland, the Finnish Electricity Association, today's Finnish Energy Industries, produced specific "electricity propaganda" in the 1930s to further this increasing and rational use of electricity that would also be about mitigating household risks, such as careless use of technology, at the same time (Kemppainen 2004).

Perhaps the worries above, about everyday risks due to infrastructural breakdowns, are merely a new expression of representation of users in the earlier and still existing risk discourses on electrical hazards and rational household electricity use. The attempts to survey the costs of blackouts can clearly also be relevant in several contexts from market regulation to consumer protection and insurance. Nonetheless, often these worries take a disciplinary bias, contrasting to the range of disciplines that liaison with industrial strategies to understand users – from collaborative design to cultural studies and human-computer interaction (Hyysalo, Elgaard & Oudshoorn 2016). Lay people's experiences of electricity supply breakdowns tend to be understood through rather hypothetical uses constructed by energy experts and, increasingly, economic assumptions about rational behaviour. This final empirical chapter of the book addresses this issue through a social science orientation that studies electricity supply interruptions closer to real "people out there" (see Hyysalo & Johnson 2016). The research question is: *how do lay people reconstruct blackouts and their effects as risks in households and bounce back from these disruptions?*

My main conceptual inspiration in addressing this question comes from American pragmatist philosophy. Many members of this school, such as Charles S. Peirce and John Dewey, explored a notion significant to the theme of this chapter and the book in general, namely *habits* (see also Trentmann 2009). Habits, by simple definition, are actions that have been repeated and that have become a resource for decision-making (Kilpinen 2000, 57). Pragmatists have been particularly interested in the interruptions of such habits, in surprises and doubts that disrupt action and generate the need to resume habits. Accordingly, a habit is effective only as long as it is not interrupted by a surprise, which can lead to the formation of new habits. This idea is called the circularity of action (Kilpinen 2000, 58–60; 217–228).

In the previous chapters, such interrelations between habitual actions or thoughts and doubts were identified in the problematizations of national security thinking and everyday work in two electricity control rooms. Yet, furthermore, the notion of circularity of action also addresses household blackouts rather directly. It focuses on the pressure that blackouts generate to deliberate on our actions while lacking an infrastructure that supports routines and actions that are not always conspicuous and immediately apparent (Star 1999; Shove 2003). Without electricity and lighting, for example, appliances can no longer be used, staircases are dark, computers cease to work, credit cards cannot be used, and lifts stop working.

According to pragmatists, the objective in such situations is to think about those options that are proposed by the disruptive situation (Kilpinen 2000, 217–228). As I did not observe any experienced blackouts directly, however, the vantage point became more specific, namely to view how people reconstruct blackouts in habit-based terms (Ullberg 2005; Revet 2013). If habits and their doubts are not separate from each other, then both offer a useful view to study the circularity of action (Kilpinen 1998). As people explained how they have recoursed to their habits and this helped them cope with complex blackouts, I also uncovered specific valuations about actions and actors that are reliable, fair, voluntary, trustworthy, or not. Furthermore, conceptualizations, values, and meanings about blackouts – or the "culture of blackouts" – are also of relevance in this context and are discussed more in the chapter's conclusion (see Nye 2010).

Another influence in my study is disaster research (see Dynes & Drabek 1994), which has developed many lines of inquiry into how "natural" and other disasters affect individuals and communities. Drawing on disaster anthropology in particular (Ullberg 2005; Revet 2013), I treat people not as victims of a blackout, but as active agents that reconstruct blackout events in specific and original ways – for example, by repeatedly interacting with experts or by relating the blackouts to memories about past risks. I was also inspired by a phase approach to disaster and crisis (Perry 2007, 7), which closely resembles the above-mentioned pragmatist circular notion of action. According to this approach, a crisis first escalates, which here means that something happens prior to a blackout to make households vulnerable to electricity interruptions, then comes the disaster event, the actual blackout, and the final phase is the recovery, which entails the post-disaster resuming of day-to-day conduct. We shall see how such circularity is manifested when my informants talk about blackouts in their homes. The material of these final chapters comprise interviews with Finnish households and a consumer survey.

Low-risk breaks

All interviewees in my end-user study had experienced power failures – events that the industry, market regulators and security experts now increasingly deem as catastrophic. Investigating these experiences, I discovered some surprising aspects of blackouts. One initial finding was that blackouts were not always particularly catastrophic events in the context of everyday life. Instead, most respondents tended to emphasize that a blackout does not cause marked damage or harm. Many stressed skills: a capable person manages to be without electricity, as long as this person acts responsibly and has prepared for a blackout. Other people, on the other hand, were not always that prepared, according to my interviewees. Thus a woman in her 30s, a kindergarten teacher, noted that she coped with blackouts well while children might not cope. Another interviewee, a retired woman, told about the wood stove that heats her old house and emphasized that she would have "no worries" during a blackout, but that her neighbours would:

> Personally I have no worries, there is a wood stove here as this is such an old house. But then the neighbour's house doesn't have wood heating, so they started to complain (during a long blackout) that it is starting to be a little bit chilly.

Her actions hence did not end in a crisis during a power failure. Rather, the interviewee managed to continue key everyday habits – at least those that require heating – even though the electricity supply was interrupted. Her neighbour, as can be seen, suffered from a different situation. The house became chilly and made everyday life increasingly difficult, especially during a long blackout.

Everyday preparedness and skills can hence mitigate the risks caused by blackouts. But even this assumes that people wish to anticipate blackouts in everyday life. However, nearly all of my informants – whether they appeared to be prepared or not – seemed relatively relaxed about blackouts. They were also explicit that not all blackouts are especially harmful. A female student said that "blackouts have not caused her any harm personally", while an academic man in his 30s mentioned that "he might even accept one more blackout in a year". On some level, it seems that everyday practices were simply allowed to stop due to the failing electricity. A sense of fatalism – the passive acceptance of future dangers that have been already determined – emerged in these blackout reconstructions I studied.

For example, for a young female student, an electricity failure meant a kind of halt and was a good excuse to stop doing things that require electricity such as cooking and studying. When asked what kind of halts she would accept in particular, she pointed to "natural" causes and commented "you should not try to mess with natural problems". A 35-year-old man, an IT expert, concurred that major storms inevitably led to blackouts: "When natural phenomena are concerned, one cannot of course do anything about electricity supply interruption." An academically trained woman, around 45, made the effects of such inevitable breaks very clear when she said that it is "actually rather positive every once in while to enjoy the forces of nature" – referring to a blackout that had been caused by acts of nature.

Some might view such fatalism and even excitement about blackouts as a non-rational risk response. For example, the responses described above were not based on calculations or even semi-calculations about levels of risk. The responses would perhaps not have led to further preparedness measures: if blackouts simply happen and one then copes with their effects and waits for the power to come back on, why try to anticipate such breakdowns? However, as the analysis progressed, it became more apparent that this fatalism was still based on rationalizations. In particular, people accepted some blackouts, but only in selected special cases which signified a relaxing break. For instance, I asked a 35-year-old woman if she saw a positive side to blackouts. It turns out she did, but she also thought about why she would want her everyday life to be interrupted:

> Of course the blackout offers a possibility to light the candles and spend a kind of primitive moment without computers and televisions. You're forced to sit on the couch with people and talk. It shouldn't really be the electricity company who decides when we do this, but it is a positive side to a blackout.

A blackout therefore offers a "primitive" non-electrified moment, but such a moment is acceptable only when it is voluntary, or at least feels like it (the blackouts I was studying were, according to the definitions given to the interviewees, not a planned interruption by the utility). If the blackout felt somehow "enforced" by the electricity company, however, the interviewee was not particularly happy. A distinction seems to figure between interruption situations that feel familiar and voluntary and those system failures which are simply imposed on people. The latter situations initiated thoughts of actual harm and provoked criticism against electricity companies.

Difficult concrete harms

The people I studied did not understate all effects of electricity blackouts. But in order to raise concern the electricity failure had to have a significant effect, such as frozen foods melting, water freezing, or the contents of a hard disk drive disappearing. In a 45-year-old woman's summer cottage, the freezer caused distress:

> In our summer cottage the freezer starts almost jumping around the house after the electricity is on again, it goes somehow out of sync. Luckily my husband knows how to deal with these kinds of issues. I couldn't do anything but just stand there horrified and watch.

This blackout was hence "horrific" although it was also framed as a matter that could be dealt with through knowledge and skill. One appliance stopped working and the respondent needed skills to fix it; in this case, the skills were supplied by her husband.

Being without electricity or at least using less energy may be expected when spending time at a summer cottage. One interviewee, on the other hand, had much more persistent problems with electricity blackouts. Practically all the appliances of this woman in her 40s and her family were electric, from regular appliances to air conditioning, water fountains, and an electric car. Altogether she had almost 150 separate appliances that required electricity, which she counted for me when I was interviewing her over the phone.

I found this subject through an electricity company, who knew I was studying consumers; the woman had made several complaints to this company. The problem was that the customer lived in an area which was classified as a rural area. In comparison to cities, such areas have longer electricity lines and a relatively large number of open-air electric cables and transformers. These open-air components are particularly subject to weather, trees, and animals, which damage overhead cables and transformers and can cause short, but frequent, blackouts. This was precisely the problem in the woman's house.

The interviewee stressed that blackouts cause multiple actual harms and not only infrequently but on a day-to-day basis. Such constant harms often cannot be understood by people who, as she remarked, do not "live surrounded by the latest contemporary technology". She told me that such people may talk about the way in which blackouts symbolize a halt and a relaxing break. Experienced infrequently, blackouts may be acceptable, but as frequent occurrences, they become unbearable:

> For us a blackout is not just an interruption. It's that we can't cope with a situation where every morning the phones may start to beep at five in the morning, so that the whole family wakes up. Because this is a new house, everything is automated. And if there's a blackout and for some reason a program is erased, then certainly it's a nuisance that you have to spend an hour to enter the data again. For a person who doesn't have this equipment it's just a matter of resetting the digital clock. But we live in a house where everything works with electricity and modern technology is complex.

Hence, as can be seen, it was taxing to constantly reflect on blackouts and she wanted her technology simply to work without having to reset it every morning. The finding comes close to pragmatist ideas: habits are reassuring and people feel secure when repeating them. Reflection, on the other hand, is merely one form of action and is a manageable reaction when interruptions are relatively infrequent; more frequent disturbances and the constant need of reflection, however, can become intolerable.

Other interviewees did not have such catastrophic experiences as the number of their appliances was much smaller. However, some household practices even in these homes indicated a particular vulnerability to blackouts. Consider the deep freezer, where one of the interviewees stored a large amount of food. A blackout may destroy the contents of the freezer and hence, very suddenly, undo the investment of gathering the contents in the first place. The same happens if a blackout destroys the contents of the hard disk drive: as a man in his 30s remarked, a blackout might erase "an irreplaceable piece of work". Other practices need to occur at a certain time and place and can be vastly affected by blackouts: for example, as remarked by a woman in her 30s, she would not want to have a blackout when she needs to hand in her thesis, or more mundanely, to go to a party or watch a television series.

In all of these cases, the severity of a blackout seems to be an issue which pertains to time: the regularity of blackouts, the time of their occurrence, and the amount of effort required afterwards. A related aspect of time concerns efforts that have already been made: for example, the contents of a hard drive are so valuable because much effort was invested in producing them and the same is true for the contents of the deep freezer. In the automated home above, the respondent had invested in the modern technology of her house. Equipment was purchased, installed, and maintained most likely at a high cost – but this equipment was not prepared to handle the damage done by constant electricity blackouts. Affluent homes were in general the most vulnerable to the failures of their infrastructures.

Awareness and blame

Among industries, the uncertainty around blackouts is often framed around effective communication from energy companies to customers (Tennberg & Vola 2014). The same topic also found its way into a customer survey on the impacts of blackouts, commissioned by the lobby organization Finnish Energy Industries. This survey concluded:

> Inadequate awareness is the most severe harm from blackouts and as the cut prolongs the melting of freezers and the lack of a water supply also raise alarm. 60 percent of those who had experienced blackouts felt that the lack of knowledge about the duration of the blackout is one of the biggest experienced harms.
>
> (Energiateollisuus 2012)

Lack of information was thus seen as the key issue. And to mitigate this harm, electricity companies should obviously raise people's awareness about blackouts.

Raising awareness is, in its turn, an aim relative to the kind of knowledge that is seen as important. What the lobby considered as awareness, based on the above, was measured magnitudes and durations; concerning, for example, which regions are affected by blackouts and when the power comes back on. Such information was indeed of value and even seemed reassuring during a blackout to the people I interviewed. Today, some electricity companies in Finland also offer their customers automated text messages to communicate these matters during a power failure.

Yet, at the same time, my informants were clearly not unaware of other catastrophic potentials of power failing. When asked to consider a serious blackout, the respondents reported multifarious "what-if" scenarios and discussed their own dependence on electricity. One interviewee thought about what would happen if the temperature was minus 25 degrees Celsius in the winter, whereas another thought that a blackout "makes you aware of the whole system's vulnerability and you start to feel sort of stupid, as you are so dependent on electricity". These common-sense comments, it might be noted, are not markedly different from qualitative national threat scenarios, discussed earlier in this book.

However, the catastrophic effects of a blackout were also never mentioned in connection with any blackout that the interviewees had experienced. Catastrophic considerations of infrastructures, it seems, are simply not very tangible when making sense of actual harms. This also made preparing for blackouts difficult for a woman in her 40s:

> Somewhere in the back of your head you have these fallbacks, like what if. And you think about purchasing an emergency heating system, about whether you should get one. But then when the electricity starts up again and is not interrupted, it's easy to forget about it.

Thus, as the interviewee suggests, the trust that the power comes back may be making preparedness less common. However, it is unlikely that if people had mistrusted their utilities they would have then been more prepared. Preparedness, in many ways, was delegated to be the responsibility of the infrastructure provider whether it could be trusted or not. From this premise, people also criticized electric provision not as a complex large-scale infrastructure that sometimes fails, but as an organization that acts according to a specific profit-seeking business logic.

When asked about what causes a blackout, nearly all interviewees concurred: in addition to natural acts, the most common perceived reasons were the liberalization of the energy markets, trees growing next to electricity lines, and the downsizing of energy network maintenance. The respondents also acknowledged "force majeure" accidents – fatalism about "natural" disasters, described above, indicated the same thing – but also talked critically about the profit-seeking of energy organizations. A woman in her 60s thus said that electricity blackouts reduce her trust in the whole electricity supply system, particularly if it "turns out that work has not been done adequately". Another – a woman in her 30s – would never accept breakdowns if they are due to the energy company acting irresponsibly. A heightened worry concerned whether energy companies are doing their part and taking care of risk mitigation.

It would perhaps be tempting to interpret this finding simply as a reduction of complexity. That is to say, perhaps the blackout – originally, a complex system-level failure of interconnected components and networks – needed to be reduced to more mundane and comprehensible explanations in everyday life. Such explanations would have kept the electricity infrastructure hidden rather than open its functioning to debate. Maybe the subjects just wanted to keep using the system, without having to think about it too much. The profit-seeking of utilities would have been a scapegoat that achieved this end.

However, a different interpretation is also possible and offers another conclusion. The subjects in my study clearly worried about Finnish electricity infrastructures. They talked about catastrophic failures and were concerned about the privatization of infrastructure utilities. This is understandable. Lay people must continue to use energy and they expect the energy supply to be reliable. Liberalization of utilities caused uncertainty because people were not quite aware of what it does to the regular availability of electricity and the continuation of everyday habits. A disastrous breakdown could be looming and this accounted for an increased sense of awareness.

Surveying power failures

To explore the commonality of my findings from households, I carried out a questionnaire study. 556 forms were posted and 115 households replied, making the response rate 21%. This relatively low rate in itself suggests that many lay people in Finland are not particularly worried about blackouts, a finding also made in the interviews. Nonetheless, due to this limited sample, the results from the survey are somewhat tentative and cannot be generalized to the Finnish population nor the regions that were studied.

Both a rural area and a city received the questionnaires and responded in nearly corresponding rates, though relatively more replies came from the rural area. The majority of the respondents lived in a detached house heated by electricity – the most common heating source in Finland – and the average number of people in a household was two. Every second respondent worked in a technical profession, although many other occupations were also represented (including for example teachers and health professionals). Overall, 70% of the respondents were male, and more than half of the subjects were in their 60s or older. Finally, the clear majority of these respondents had experienced a blackout in the past year. It is tempting to claim that those subjects who had suffered from difficult actual harms from blackouts also tended to respond to the questionnaire. However, even if this was the case, concern about blackouts was not always visible in the survey results.

Instead, the sense of fatalism that was visible in the interviews also figured in the survey responses. When asked about coping without electricity, the respondents thought they could live three days without tap water, four days without cooking, six days without lights – longer than without media appliances – nine days without cleaning, and even longer without computers and a number of other technologies (Table 7.1). As in the interviews, the refrigerator and freezer appeared as the most critical technologies to blackouts.

When checked against the number of blackout experiences, area (rural or city), gender, and age, the order of appliances in Table 7.1 changed hardly at all. What changed more, however, were the reported durations. Those who had experienced a blackout in the past year tolerated blackouts for a much shorter time than others and were especially concerned about loss of lights. People who lived in rural areas were less stressed about the interruptions of water supply and information and communication technologies than those who lived in cities. Women, on the other hand, were more worried about blackouts than men all in all, particularly about lights, cleaning, and warm water as well as mobile phone batteries, Internet use, and computers. The significance of age varied more across technologies: people over 60 were less worried about lights and toilets than younger people, but were more worried about the functioning of dishwashers, mobile phone batteries, and media appliances.

Another already-mentioned recent survey about blackouts' effects in Finnish homes (Energiateollisuus 2012) found the same result as I did: the melting of the fridge or the freezer was still the most critical harm with regard to home appliances, although darkness and the lack of an Internet connection were seen as more serious in 2012 than in my study in 2005. The newer survey also controlled for gender, age, and the experience of blackout in the interpretation of its results. Accordingly, women were visibly more worried about the uncertainty of the duration of a blackout, while men were more concerned about the lack of an Internet connection and television. People under 35 worried relatively more

Table 7.1 How many days households thought they could cope without different electric appliances and functions

Days	Appliance or function
1	Refrigerator, freezer
2	Toilet, heating in the winter
3	All water (warm and cold)
4	Cooking
5	Media appliances
6	Lights
7	Batteries (e.g. mobile phone), credit cards
8–9	Washing machine, cleaning
10	Computer, dishwasher
11	Internet
12	Heating in the summer
13–18	Housekeeping and gardening

about the Internet and less about heating. Overall, as in my survey, women were again more worried than men about the impact of blackouts.

This observation that gender affects the understanding of power failure risk may reveal wider gender roles concerning household technologies. The mechanization of household work began in the 20th century in the United States as part of a model of a future home, which designers and engineers in Finland appropriated rather directly (Pantzar 1999). This allegedly more rational home was reliant on electrical appliances and carried with it assumptions about gender: the emerging electrified household involved women doing the household work, men providing for the family (Kemppainen 2004). Electric power interruptions might reveal this assumption of the household as women's workplaces: the interruption of electricity is associated with the work that is undone. Similar preconfigurations of technology persist in energy: for example, the marketing of energy and heat technologies is strongly shaped by the alleged gender of their user (Jalas & Rinkinen 2016).

Even sharper differences were uncovered when the experience of blackouts was considered in 2012. Those subjects who had experienced a blackout of more than five hours stressed the importance of freezers, fridges, cooking, and water. On the other hand, the television and the Internet became decreasingly less significant as the experienced power cut prolonged. Being in a blackout hence seems to make an impact on the way in which people anticipate electricity interruptions in households; this suggests, in its turn, that people can remember risks and learn from them. As only 12 of my survey respondents had experienced a blackout of more than three hours, I cannot unfortunately compare the effect of the duration of a long blackout in my data.

In sum, fridges and freezers are clearly vulnerable to a blackout and important to many people in Finland, particularly when the power cut is prolonged. But the above cross tabulations also show that social background affects how reflective people were about blackout damages. City dwellers, women, and those who have experienced blackouts seemed to worry more than others, while the significance of age is more varied with different technologies. Nonetheless, we can see that fatalism about blackouts was at least a gendered and regional phenomena as well as being experiential: people might have learned to be less fatalistic after having experienced what blackouts can do.

My interviewees and survey respondents concurred on a number of other issues, too. Those who had experienced blackouts reported especially that blackouts draw their attention to the societal impacts of power cuts, to the opening of energy markets, to their own energy consumption, to electricity price, and to their own preparedness, in that order. The subjects hence clearly worried about the social and societal side of electricity supply risks, much more than about legal issues or technical structures, which I also asked about.

Both surveys mentioned here also show that respondents are generally prepared. In 2005 as well as 2012, the majority of those studied had candles, matches, flashlights, and batteries in case of a power cut and many also had a fireplace. In my survey, almost half of the subjects were considering purchasing an uninterruptable power supply for their computers or even their own emergency power generator. So, although the interviewees suggested that people do not always prepare even if they plan to, the survey respondents still at least wanted to anticipate blackouts in their homes. Perhaps this is due to the issue at hand: social and societal issues can pertain to blackouts and become alarming due to the multiple impacts of not having an infrastructure. One might even say that power failures motivate imaginative precautionary thinking about what may happen to everyday infrastructures that support diverse societal activities.

Power failures and the multiplicity of household risk

This chapter discussed everyday habits and their interruptions and analysed the ways in which Finnish individuals and households reconstruct the effects of electricity supply interruptions, or blackouts. While directly affected by blackouts, ordinary people have typically played quite a limited role in these matters. In the classics of science and technology studies (e.g. Hughes 1983; see van der Vleuten 2004), consumers most often appear as an abstract energy "demand" that rarely comes directly into contact with their electricity utilities, which have become large-scale technological systems. Many – though not all – national blackout threat scenarios (see Chapter 3) concern different official societal institutions and organizations rather than lay people. Energy market regulation (see Chapter 4) in its turn pinpoints questions about quality, responsibility, and compensations. In these legal and financial considerations, lay people may figure, but often merely as rational consumers who expect a certain quality of service and are compensated if this standard is not met.

At first, the study in this chapter seemed to support the view that people are generally passive about their energy supplies and risks. Many people simply accepted that electricity blackouts can happen, especially when they were caused by perceived "acts of nature". They downplayed the effects of these "inevitable" power failures and did not see it necessary to respond to the events or anticipate their onset. Many blackouts, in fact, have been somewhat different events than collective catastrophes to those who have experienced them. The analysis of blackouts and culture by Nye (2010, 173–204) found sociability and friendliness, solidarity and breakdown of hierarchies, and many forms of unforeseen collective behaviour in the New York blackout in 2003. He names blackouts such as these "liminal moments" (Nye 2010, 83) that unite people for a limited while.

The further the analysis went, however, the more apparent it becomes that what is at stake is not just a simple fatalistic culture of risk (Langumier & Revet 2010; cf. Douglas & Wildavsky 1982) or a "liminal moment" shared by everyone (Nye 2010, 208). Rather, there were various kinds of blackouts and different people had a variety of responses to them. The acceptance of a power failure varied according to gender, to age, to region, and especially to memory about past blackouts. To be acceptable, a blackout also had to feel "voluntary" rather than imposed from above. Such an acceptable electricity supply interruption, it was anticipated, should not halt those household practices that were perceived as important – and it also did not prevent less significant practices regularly or all the time.

In fact, temporality explained the seriousness of the blackout in at least three senses. Firstly, a blackout should not interrupt everyday habits on a regular basis. Secondly, a blackout should not occur at a time when people have planned to do something else that requires functioning electricity. And thirdly, a blackout should not impact on tangible objects which are the result of time and investment – such as the equipment of a technologized home, the contents of the freezer, or a computer's hard disk drive.

Some blackouts were hence reconstructed as more serious than others. Confronted with difficult actual harms, another, almost opposite, risk response to fatalism emerged: many people wanted to prepare for blackouts using, for example, wood stoves and fireplaces. In this fashion, household skills and resources were emphasized by the possibility of power failing (Trentmann 2009; Rinkinen 2013; Heidenstrøm & Kvarnlöf 2017). It was viewed by some that reasonable people should know how to cope with blackout situations. People also wanted to ensure that a blackout would not disturb everyday routine that much and criticized utilities for downsizing their maintenance and their other risk management. A study of a long and difficult ground water contamination in a Finnish village shows corresponding results: the water supply interruption, which went on for many months and while disrupting everyday life, was not generally considered a serious problem and most people coped with it individually and with the help of others (Lahti 1998). Lahti (1998) also talks about these people as fatalists, but clearly his subjects were not just passively accepting the effects of the water cut.

According to my study, however, reflective anticipations, cooperation, and even criticisms are rarely sustained in everyday life when energy supplies function. This is perhaps not that surprising in the context of habits. Simon Marvin and Beth Perry (2005) have shown a similar result in the context of a fuel crisis in the United Kingdom, when the crisis created a number of innovative strategies for motoring when fuel was scarce. However, when the fuel crisis was over, few of these new behaviours were instituted in everyday life. Marvin and Perry (2005, 99) point to the duration of the crisis as a relevant factor: as the crisis was over in a relatively short time, there were insufficient repetitions to forge new general habits. Instead, old habits were swiftly reestablished when fuel again became available.

One general issue that pertains to the understanding of such infrastructure breakdowns, as well as their status as risks, is knowledge practices. At the moment, much of the risk management in electricity is based on the status of already occurred events. We know that over the last decades, cities and rural networks have had different frequencies of blackouts in Finland (Energiateollisuus 2016). It has also been measured what past blackouts have been financially worth to people (e.g. Silvast et al 2006; Energiamarkkinavirasto 2007) and scholars have striven to uncover probabilities and harms to calculate risk levels of blackouts (Kjølle, Utne & Gjerde 2012). Such measured knowledge is, of course, relevant and important for many ends – ranging from consumer protection to potential applications in the insuring of energy networks. Yet, it would seem that a statistical style of reasoning tells relatively little about what happens when electricity is interrupted. Specifically, statistics give almost no explanation about the fears that people have when expressing concern about uncertain failures of everyday infrastructures.

Social scientists, too, are beginning to pursue understandings of technology users, infrastructure breakdowns, and the resulting uncertainties. Some highlight through blackouts the fragility of everyday life and the flexibility of people's habits (Trentmann 2009; Rinkinen 2013; Heidenstrøm & Kvarnlöf 2017), yet other research (Ullberg 2005; Höst et al 2010; Alapuro 2011; Collier, Cox & Grove 2016) on failing infrastructures has highlighted a particular aspect of the phenomenon. This is that failures of infrastructures – which are public common goods from the perspective of their consumers (Gramlich 1994) – may motivate collective action. It could be said that actions such as public protests mediate between the dissatisfaction of end users and the technological-economic rationality of expert decision makers (Alapuro 2011). And in other contexts, failures of large supplies have even become perceived as a political statement of their own. For instance, Nye (2010, 205–232) stresses three significant new collective phenomena that represent our "energy culture" and address the shifting status of blackouts: the social movement of people choosing to live "off the grid" of infrastructures; the growing societal importance of local self-reliant and more resilient energy generation; and voluntary "greenouts" or Earth Hours in which the lights are dimmed for a specific time to highlight how climate change can be mitigated.

Such actions and their study will be highly relevant, especially in the coming years as energy systems are shifting to greater sustainability (Southerton, van Vliet & Chappells 2004; Verbong & Geels 2007). The most common and important starting point here has been to view the political collective actor – or active consumer – as a rational and reflective actor. In the majority of these cases, it is easy to agree: public protests but also disaster information centres, public emergency power generators, local self-generation, or voluntary greenouts might not have been initiated had it not been the rational intentions of reflective actors. If the presumption is that users will learn by doing when managing electricity risk themselves, considerable, long-term work is required to sustain these new practices (Nielsen 2016).

At the same time, especially in the longer term, everyday habits also continue to have their own consequences and inertia as concerns electricity and its use (Shove 2003). And according to the study in this chapter, the effects are particularly visible when power fails. The results outlined in this chapter might hence provide a new angle to the contemporary discussions about energy systems and risks. Rather than assuming that all people are rational consumers or political decision makers – or victims of a disaster, as sometimes portrayed by catastrophe mitigation (Revet 2013) – the results demonstrate how people reconstruct blackouts, anticipate their effects, and adopt adaptive habits as fast as possible even after the lights go out.

References

Aarrevaara, Timo; Nurmi, Veli-Pekka & Stenvall, Jari (2004). Luottamuksesta normi-ohjaukseen: Sähköturvallisuuden hallintotavan muutos siirryttäessä teollisuusvaltiosta hyvinvointivaltioon ("From Trust to Norm Control: The Change of Governance in Electricity Safety from the Industrial State to the Welfare State"). *Tekniikan Waiheita* 22 (1): 41–58.

Alapuro, Risto (2011). Goods, Res Publica, Actors Networks and Collective Action. In Kharkhordin, Oleg & Alapuro, Risto (eds) *Political Theory and Community Building in Post-Soviet Russia*. London: Routledge, 31–56.

Brunner, Elgin & Suter, Manuel (2009). *International CIIP Handbook 2008/2009: An Inventory of 25 National and 7 International Critical Information Infrastructure Protection Policies*. Zürich: Center for Security Studies. Link accessed 24 November 2016: http://www.css.ethz.ch/publications/pdfs/CIIP-HB-08-09.pdf

Collier, Stephen; Cox, Savannah & Grove, Kevin (2016). Rebuilding by Design in Post-Sandy New York. *Limn* 5 (7). Link accessed 14 November 2016: http://limn.it/rebuilding-by-design-in-post-sandy-new-york/

Collier, Stephen & Lakoff, Andrew (2008). The Vulnerability of Vital Systems: How Critical Infrastructures Became a Security Problem. In Dunn Cavelty, Myriam & Kristensen, Kristian Søby (eds) *Securing 'the Homeland': Critical Infrastructure, Risk and (In)security*. London: Routledge, 17–39.

Douglas, Mary & Wildavsky, Aaron (1982). *Risk and Culture: An Essay on the Selection of Technological and Environmental Dangers*. Berkeley: University of California Press.

Dynes, Russell & Drabek, Thomas (1994). The Structure of Disaster Research: Its Policy and Disciplinary Implications. *International Journal of Mass Emergencies and Disasters* 12 (1): 5–23.

Energiamarkkinavirasto (Finnish Energy Market Authority) (2007). Sähkön jakelu-verkonhaltijoiden hinnoittelun kohtuullisuuden arvioinnin suuntaviivat vuosille 2008–2011 ("Guidelines for Evaluating the Reasonableness of Pricing of Electricity Distribution Network Owners for 2008–2011"). Dnro 154/422/2007. Helsinki: Energiamarkkinavirasto.

Energiateollisuus (Finnish Energy Industries) (2010). Verkkoyhtiöt haluavat eroon pit-kistä sähkökatkoista ("Network Companies Want to Get Rid of Long Blackouts"). Press release 14 September 2010. Link accessed 3 June 2013: www.energia.fi/ajankohtaista/lehdistotiedotteet/verkkoyhtiot-haluavat-eroon-pitkista-sahkokatkoista

Energiateollisuus (Finnish Energy Industries) (2012). Kuluttajatutkimus sähkökeskey-tyksistä ("A Consumer Survey about Electricity Interruptions"). A survey carried out by YouGov Finland. Link accessed 3 June 2013: www.energia.fi/kalvosarjat/kuluttajatutkimus-sahkokeskeytyksistaenergiateollisuus-ry

Energiateollisuus (Finnish Energy Industries) (2016). Sähkön keskeytystilastot ("Electricity Interruption Statistics"). Link accessed 27 October 2016: http://energia.fi/tilastot-ja-julkaisut/sahkotilastot/sahkon-keskeytystilastot

European Council (2008). On the Identification and Designation of European Critical Infrastructures and the Assessment of the Need to Improve Their Protection. Directive 2008/114/EC. Link accessed 24 November 2016: http://eur-lex.europa.eu/LexUriServ/LexUriServ.do?uri=CELEX:32008L0114:EN:NOT

Forstén, Jarl (2002). Sähkön toimitusvarmuuden parantaminen ("Improving the Reliability of Electricity Distribution"). Report for the Finnish Ministry of Trade and Industry. Link accessed 3 June 2013: www2.energia.fi/myrsky/pdf/toimitusvarmuus.pdf

Graham, Stephen & Marvin, Simon (2001). *Splintering Urbanism: Networked Infrastructures, Technological Mobilities and the Urban Condition.* London: Routledge.

Gramlich, Edward (1994). Infrastructure Investment: A Review Essay. *Journal of Economic Literature* 32 (3): 1176–1196.

Heidenstrøm, Nina & Kvarnlöf, Linda (2017). Coping with blackouts: A practice theory approach to household preparedness Manuscript in review.

Höst, Martin, Kristofersson Nieminen, Tuija, Petersen, Kurt & Tehler, Henrik (2010, eds). *FRIVA – risk, sårbarhet och förmåga samverkan inom krishantering* ("FRIVA – Risk, Vulnerability, and Capability to Co-operate in Crisis Management"). Lund: Media Tryck.

Hughes, Thomas (1983). *Networks of Power: Electrification in Western Society, 1880–1930.* Baltimore, MD: Johns Hopkins University Press.

Hyysalo, Sampsa, Jensen, Torben Elgaard & Oudshoorn, Nelly (2016). Introduction to the New Production of Users. In Hyysalo, Sampsa; Jensen, Torben Elgaard & Oudshoorn, Nelly (eds) *The New Production of Users: Changing Innovation Collectives and Involvement Strategies.* London: Routledge, 1–42.

Hyysalo, Sampsa & Johnson, Mikael (2016). User Representation: A Journey towards Conceptual Maturation. In Hyysalo, Sampsa; Jensen, Torben Elgaard & Oudshoorn, Nelly (eds) *The New Production of Users: Changing Innovation Collectives and Involvement Strategies.* London: Routledge, 75–100.

Jalas, Mikko & Rinkinen, Jenny (2016). Stacking Wood and Staying Warm: Time, Temporality and Housework around Domestic Heating Systems. *Journal of Consumer Culture* 16 (1): 43–60.

Kauppa- ja teollisuusministeriö (Finnish Ministry of Trade and Industry) (2006). *Sähkönjakelun toimitusvarmuuden kehittäminen: Sähkön jakeluhäiriöiden ehkäisemistä ja jakelun toiminnallisia tavoitteita selvittäneen työryhmän raportti* ("Developing the Supply Security of Electricity Distribution: The Report by the Working Group that Explored the Prevention of Electricity Supply Failures and the Practical Targets for the Supply"). Helsinki: Kauppa- ja teollisuusministeriö.

Kemppainen, Riia Maria (2004). Kodin hyödyksi – jokaisen iloksi. Suomen sähkölaitosyhdistyksen sähköpropaganda 1930-luvulla. ("For the Benefit of Home – for the Pleasure of Everyone: Finnish Electricity Association's Electricity Propaganda in the 1930s.") *Tekniikan waiheita* 22 (1): 24–40.

Kilpinen, Erkki (1998). Creativity Is Coming. *Acta Sociologica* 41 (2): 173–179.

Kilpinen, Erkki (2000). *The Enormous Fly-Wheel of Society: Pragmatism's Habitual Conception of Action and Social Theory.* Doctoral thesis, University of Helsinki, Department of Sociology. Helsinki: Department of Sociology Research Reports, No. 235.

Kjølle, Gerd; Utne, Ingrid & Gjerde, Oddbjørn (2012). Risk Analysis of Critical Infrastructures Emphasizing Electricity Supply and Interdependencies. *Reliability Engineering and System Safety* 105: 80–89.

Lahti, Vesa-Matti (1998). *Riskiyhteiskunta vesilasissa* ("Risk Society in a Water Glass"). Helsinki: Yliopistopaino.

Langumier, Julien & Revet, Sandrine (2010). Disasters and Risks: From Empiricism to Criticism, Paris, France. *E-Newsletter of the Disaster and Social Crisis Research Network* 11 (41): 5–7.

Larkin, Brian (2013). The Politics and Poetics of Infrastructure. *Annual Review of Anthropology* 42: 327–343.

Lehtonen, Turo-Kimmo (2009). How Does Materiality Matter for the Social Sciences? In Colas, Dominique & Khakhorin, Oleg (eds) *The Materiality of Res Publica: How to Do Things with Publics.* Newcastle upon Tyne: Cambridge Scholars Publishing, 271–288.

Marvin, Simon & Perry, Beth (2005). When Networks Are Destabilized: User Innovation and the UK Fuel Crisis. In Coutard, Olivier; Hanley, Richard & Zimmerman, Rae (eds) *Sustaining Urban Networks: The Social Diffusion of Large Technical Systems.* London: Routledge, 86–100.

Myllyntaus, Timo (1991). *Electrifying Finland: The Transfer of a New Technology into a Late Industrialising Economy.* Helsinki: ETLA.

Nielsen, Kristian (2016). How User Assemblage Matters: Constructing Learning by Using in the Case of Wind Turbine Technology in Denmark, 1973–1990. In Hyysalo, Sampsa; Jensen, Torben Elgaard & Oudshoorn, Nelly (eds) *The New Production of Users: Changing Innovation Collectives and Involvement Strategies.* London: Routledge, 101–122.

Nye, David (2010). *When the Lights Went Out: A History of Blackouts in America.* Cambridge, MA: MIT Press.

Pantzar, Mika (1999). *Tulevaisuuden koti: Arjen tarpeita keksimässä* ("Future Home: Inventing the Needs of Everyday Living"). Keuruu: Otava.

Perry, Ronald (2007). What Is a Disaster? In Rodrígues, Havidan; Quarantelli, Enrico & Dynes, Russell (eds) *Handbook of Disaster Research.* New York: Springer, 1–15.Puolustusministeriö (Finnish Ministry of Defence) (2008). Pahasti poikki: Näin selviät pitkästä sähkökatkosta ("Severely Cut: How to Survive a Long Blackout"). Text written by Jaana Laitinen and Suvi Vainio. Link accessed 26 November 2016: www.defmin.fi/files/1275/Pahasti_poikki_nettiversio.pdf

Revet, Sandrine (2013). 'A Small World': Ethnography of a Natural Disaster Simulation in Lima, Peru. *Social Anthropology* 21 (1): 38–53.

Rinkinen, Jenny (2013). Electricity Blackouts and Hybrid Systems of Provision: Users and the 'Reflective Practice'. *Energy, Sustainability and Society* 3 (1): 25.

Shove, Elizabeth (2003). Converging Conventions of Comfort, Cleanliness and Convenience. *Journal of Consumer Policy* 26 (4): 395–418.

Silvast, Antti; Lehtonen, Matti; Heine, Pirjo; Kivikko, Kimmo; Mäkinen, Antti & Järventausta, Pertti (2006). *Keskeytyksestä aiheutuva haitta* ("The Harm Caused by an Interruption") Espoo: Teknillinen korkeakoulu (Helsinki University of Technology) and Tampereen teknillinen yliopisto (Tampere University of Technology).

Silvast, Antti & Virtanen, Mikko (2014). Keeping Systems at Work: Electricity Infrastructure from Control Rooms to Household Practices. *Science & Technology Studies* 28 (2): 93–114.

Southerton, Dale; van Vliet, Bas & Chappells, Heather (2004). Introduction: Consumption, Infrastructure, and Environmental Sustainability. In Southerton, Dale; Chappells, Heather & van Vliet, Bas (eds) *Sustainable Consumption: The Implications of Changing Infrastructures of Provision.* Cheltenham, UK – Northampton, MA: Edward Elgar, 1–14.

SSFVS (2006). *The Strategy for Securing the Functions Vital to Society: A Finnish Government Resolution 23 November 2006.* Authored by the Security and Defence Committee of the Finnish Ministry of Defence. Helsinki: Ministry of Defence. Link accessed 25 November 2016: www.defmin.fi/files/858/06_12_12_YETTS__in_english.pdf

SSS (2010). Security Strategy for Society. A Finnish government resolution 16 December 2010. Authored by the Security and Defence Committee of the Finnish Ministry of Defence. Helsinki: Ministry of Defence. Link accessed 24 November 2016: www.yhteiskunnanturvallisuus.fi/en/materials/doc_download/26-security-strategy-for-society

Star, Susan Leigh (1999). The Ethnography of Infrastructure. *American Behavioral Scientist* 43 (3): 377–391.

Tennberg, Monica & Vola, Joonas (2014). Myrskyjä ei voi hallita: Haavoittuvuuden poliittinen talous ("Storms Cannot Be Controlled: The Political Economy of Vulnerability"). *Alue ja Ympäristö* 43 (1): 73–84.

Trentmann, Frank (2009). Disruption is Normal: Blackouts, Breakdowns and the Elasticity of Everyday Life. In Shove, Elizabeth; Trentmann, Frank & Wilk, Richard (eds) *Time, Consumption, and Everyday Life*. Oxford, UK: Berg, 67–84.

Ullberg, Susann (2005). *The Buenos Aires Blackout: Argentine Crisis Management across the Public-Private Divide*. Stockholm: CM Europe Volume Series. Link accessed 26 November 2016: www.fhs.se/Documents/Externwebben/forskning/centrumbildningar/Crismart/Publikationer/Publikationsserier/VOLUME_28.PDF

van der Vleuten, Erik (2004). Infrastructures and Societal Change: A View from the Large Technical Systems Field. *Technology Analysis & Strategic Management* 16 (3): 395–414.

Verbong, Geert & Geels, Frank (2007). The Ongoing Energy Transition: Lessons from a Socio-Technical, Multi-Level Analysis of the Dutch Electricity System (1960–2004). *Energy Policy* 35 (2): 1025–1037.

Part V

Conclusions

8 Understanding infrastructure through risk and resilience

Pursuing risk and resilience in the energy supply chain – a summary

In Finland, the European Union, United States, UK, and many other advanced and developing states, from Canada to New Zealand to India, electric power interruptions have once again become a central concern for contemporary security issues. Recently, the growing share of renewable energy in electricity supplies and their known variability or "intermittency" issues have brought the risk of possible power interruptions to the fore. This book was inspired by these debates, but sought to produce greater insight into the large power infrastructure itself, its history and context, and the real work that makes it come alive on a day-to-day basis, with a particular interest in the anticipation and mitigation of electricity interruptions and their effects. The overarching research question asked how interruptions to the electricity infrastructure are anticipated, how they are managed as risks, and how people and organizations bounce back from these interruptions. To consider this question, the book analysed different sites in electricity supplies and their risk and resilience management, pursuing the multiple scales of the supply chain in energy infrastructure (e.g. Hughes 1983; Edwards 2003, 2010; also Karasti et al 2016). Working across national critical infrastructures and their protection and moving to a Finnish city's electricity network company and finally end users, I examined how security experts mitigate electricity outages as national risks and enhance infrastructure resilience, the management of electricity reliability in the liberalized electricity markets and in urban utilities, and the ways in which lay people reconstruct electricity blackouts and their effects as risks in households and bounce back from such disruptions.

I would now like to highlight four main results that arose from my multi-sited inquiry. Risk and resilience are rather inseparable from infrastructures, as they provide vital services for collective life (Graham & Marvin 2001; Collier & Lakoff 2008). But for the purpose of this discussion I will initially assess risk and resilience in separate sections and then synthesize my findings toward the end. Therefore, the first key result concentrates on risk, the ways in which it has been analysed in previous social science research, and how my research can take this research into new directions.

Risk is a popular concept in discussions about protection of national and European critical infrastructures (e.g. Dunn 2006; European Council 2008; US Department of Homeland Security 2013). For example, the US Department of Homeland Security's (2013) report *Partnering for Critical Infrastructure Security and Resilience* has an entire chapter on "collaborating to manage risk" and defines risk as "determined by its likelihood and the associated consequences" (US Department of Homeland Security's 2013, 33). The essence of this collaboration is hence calculating risk-informed decisions. Many social scientists have, however, turned away from such calculative and under-socialized understandings about activities surrounding risk. According to the argument, risks are considerably more situated and interpreted social constructions: in most cases, decisions on risks are influenced by many other things than individuals' calculations of probabilities and impacts (e.g. Douglas & Wildavsky 1982; Summerton & Berner 2003; Burgess 2016). More broadly, to other scholars, official risk discourse also exposes a significant meta-change in the whole society. They claim that we are witnessing a new "epoch" in modern society regarding how it causes, embraces, fears, or avoids risks in distinct and novel ways (e.g. Beck 1992; Furedi 2006).

All of these arguments pave the way for social science research agendas and stress risks as something more extensive than mere calculations, which greatly vary according to situated contexts, as my fieldwork also confirms. However, their potentially unintended bias is assuming that technical risk management can be treated as one entity, which – according to the findings of this book – it clearly is not.

To highlight this issue, the first result of my inquiry tries to apply some popular social science understandings to my fieldwork findings. Using cultural risk theory and situated "actant analysis" in science and technology studies (STS), it argues that while the said viewpoints are insightful, they do not give enough attention to the diversity of calculations, economic and technical data, styles of reasoning, methods, and terminology that constitute risk management in the power infrastructures. The requirements for representative data of the popular social science approaches are also easily beyond the scope of doing a multi-sited field study. The multi-sited research design is, however, key for unpacking risk as a multiple knowledge practice among specialists and lay persons.

My second result then theorizes the multiplicity of risk management further and introduces concepts to scrutinize it in my findings. In particular, I suggest that risk should be analysed through those *techniques* that render it visible to actors, used to represent security, in particular, often narrow yet distinct manners in different sites of the infrastructure. Examples of such techniques include national security catalogues, crisis typologies, market regulatory formulas, power trading software on computer screens, and systems for reporting infrastructure faults. The households' situated reductions of complexity – for example, assigning blame for power failures – can also be theorized as risk rationalizations or techniques. In addition to their use, the historical emergence of risk techniques is a key research object as techniques can both contain traces of their origins and tend to fix what kind of security matters for collective life. Under this result, I also discuss how to analyse risk in occasions where the concept itself is not always well defined or even understood in a similar way by different people and organizations, if it gets used at all. In doing so, the second result highlights that the holistic understanding of risk that some social science research suggests is difficult to accomplish in practice; rather, there are many benefits from deploying more nuanced analytical tools that research in risk governance has advanced.

My third result then subjects *resilience* to the similar kind of questioning as risk and highlights the similarities and the differences between the two concepts. Like risk, resilience also means increasing security in particular ways in different sites of the infrastructure, set against specific historical contexts. In the large power infrastructure, relevant scales of resilience span from national vital systems and their cohesion to highly situated skills in electricity control centres and the resourcefulness of lay people after the power fails. Critical social scientists have rightly pointed out that there is no single definition for resilience, but it would be mistaken to assume that this makes the concept of infrastructure resilience wholly questionable. Rather, because the notion of risk focuses on ex-ante preparedness, resilience adds substantially to risk research by highlighting what happens after a disruption has already occurred (Berglund 2009).

With the power infrastructure whose interruptions are almost impossible to avoid altogether – especially in Finland, with its relatively large number of blackouts compared to many other European countries – understanding resilience becomes particularly important for examining how interruptions are managed in electricity supplies in those situations where they manifest for people and organizations. Furthermore, resilience concerns both threats with a calculable probability and consequence – such as risk analysis – and threats whose likelihoods and effects cannot be calculated with any great exactitude. Hence, the term also opens up the debate on managing climate change and its long-term impacts in important ways, as I show (see Stirling 2014).

The fourth and final result ties the book together by asking what new knowledge the topics of risk and resilience bring for inquiries into expanding power systems, the different layers of infrastructures, and the transitions that energy systems have faced. While a considerable number of social scientists, especially within science and technology studies (STS), have explored such complex, socio-technical energy issues recently, risk and resilience tend to receive rather little attention in these topical discussions. Therefore, I round up this book by suggesting that both risk and resilience open up the discussion on the energy system and infrastructure in a substantial way, which should receive increasing attention in coming studies.

Researching risk in a multi-sited study

In a multi-sited field study, the ethnographic research site is not a given – for example, a single organization or one region. Rather, the researcher has to actively construct what the field study was all about and how findings from different sites cumulate. This cannot be mere naive addition of different findings to an allegedly truer picture (see Gobo 2008). Rather, the way in which the results from different sites are combined depends upon the analyst's theoretical and conceptual choices: the site has to be theorized (Marcus 1995; Pollock & Williams 2010; Collier 2011), which my study did with the concepts of risk, resilience, and infrastructure.

Earlier risk studies in the cultural vein offer one possibility to generalize over the different field sites. The argument there is that all risks everywhere are social constructions and articulated in various ways by different risk cultures such as groups, organizations, or even entire national governments (e.g. Douglas & Wildavsky 1982; Summerton & Berner 2003; Burgess 2016). In my research, to uncover how risk is socially constructed by different actors, one could have studied the interviews with people and policy documents as narratives or "storylines" that feature interacting both human and non-human protagonists or "actants" (see Bennett 2005; Latour 2005, 53).

In this fashion, one could say that one main expert "storyline" of infrastructure risk stresses the centrality of electricity for citizens, technical components, market actions, regulations, and natural causes that all contribute to the risks of power failures as well as risk mitigation. The lay "story" engaged more concrete "actants" such as enforced breaks, relaxing, tangible forces of nature, mundane household equipment, and the role of the family. Infrastructure security policy texts outline generic and abstract actors when narrating blackouts: the entire society is to be protected from electricity outages, major technological and economic changes are looming, centralized authority has to be the decision maker, and citizens play a smaller active role in this "story". In the same vein, the free energy market "storyline" features other non-human economic "actants" such as traders, producers, and retailers, who are assisted by various markets with distinct temporalities and opposed by real-time risks such as weather phenomena, shutdowns at energy generation plants, and price spikes. These results are revealing, but some consequences of this approach became more apparent as my analysis progressed.

The first of these is treating the technical aspects of risks as merely being one entity. With a few exceptions (such as Boholm 2003), the starting point in many cultural risk studies has involved separating a "technical" and "cultural" side of risk and concentrating on how the latter influences the former. This premise has also been productive in many ways: risk analysis in general prefers calculations over more qualitative considerations, *uncertainties* (O'Malley 2004), and this has also been the case in a number of power failure risk assessments (Doorman et al 2004; Kjølle, Utne & Gjerde 2012). Nevertheless, by separating an "objective" risk from its socially or culturally constructed side, the starting point perhaps pays less attention to a number of things. These include how differently even seemingly objective risks can be conceptualized technically by experts, the different tools and techniques that operationalize the aspirations of managing such risks, and the varieties of ways in which these risk techniques and terminology can be used in practice (Helén 2004). Indeed, as discussion about risk governance (O'Malley 2004, 12) has noted, the argument should maybe not be about the existence of either technical risks or risk conceptualizations, but about their combinations: the governance of risk typically is both about intellectual risk rationalities and risk techniques that put these rationalities into action.

To follow similar reasoning by infrastructure scholar Paul N. Edwards (2010, 437), the point is also not to disregard the valuable idea that "social processes are *necessary* to knowledge production"; the point instead is to argue against the more generous notion that "social agreement is *sufficient* for knowledge production". Edwards's point on the co-existence of social processes and knowledge practices is insightful for electricity infrastructure risk, too. Certainly my informants produced different "social constructions" about electricity hazard and negotiated and contested risk interpretations on a routine, if not on a minute-by-minute, basis. But this was not the only relevant aspect. Electricity risk also had its own ex-ante anticipatory actions such as prudence and foresight, and many of these actions, as I found, are shaped intensively by the measuring equipment that is deployed. Techniques such as computer monitors, energy economic formula, and visual diagrams produced their own tangible effects and timescales intrinsically related to people's more intuitive risk interpretations, but often distinct in character.

The real-time sensibilities of the free energy market, for example, were not so much just produced by energy traders' individual risk perceptions. Rather, these sensibilities followed from assembling together working habits, local knowledge, real-time resilient responses, computer monitors, and their effects as the chapter about the energy market control room has discussed. These and other infrastructure risk techniques also emerged from a specific historical background, as I have demonstrated through examples concerning national security practice and energy deregulation in Finland. Based on my study, this history has furthermore stayed relevant for understanding how risks are perceived; many policy documents contained intertextual traces of their origins, which generates specific conditions for what security in these documents can possibly be (Kristensen 2008, 66). To overlook such rich matters of context could in some cases produce a too-partial picture of infrastructure risk and its management. At the same time, the study of risk rationalities and techniques has its own issues that I discuss soon, but I believe that these findings still generate relevant new understanding about power failures, the electricity infrastructure, and its management in more general terms.

I do not wish to understate the major empirical importance of the study of risk cultures in organizations and among different people. Indeed, a more empirical rather than conceptual issue when studying multiple sites and their cultural risk filtering is materials: in technical terms, access to sufficient representative data to find relevant contrasts and contradictions in cultural risk articulations. With this issue in mind, the risk perceptions found in my materials are fairly predictable and do not necessarily generate unanticipated new knowledge about how people conceptualize uncertainties. To a social scientist, it could have been expected that experts perceive both technical and market risks with electricity and that most lay people are fairly relaxed about blackouts if no immediate difficulties are apparent. However, different, more interesting results could have emerged with larger samples of more representative data. Empirical research has already shown that electricity consumption patterns vary visibly among different households (Adato Energia 2008); and the survey in this study and another (Energiateollisuus 2012) indicate that perceptions about power failures also vary according to gender, age, and region. Such variance could be both considered and explained in more depth by future studies. Within this study, however, I decided to concentrate on the technicalities of risk to reveal contrasts in how electricity risk is both managed and enacted in practice by different experts, as well as lay people.

To this end, one could draw on other popular concepts of classic science and technology studies (STS). Certainly, there, analysis of "actants" has not only concerned detailing texts and narratives about technology. Instead, it has been used for uncovering how humans and non-humans relate, interact, and gain characteristics in constantly changing situated contexts or "actor networks" (Latour 2005, 53; MacKenzie 2009, 20). This point on "following the actors" is relevant. It might have been fruitfully used to shed light on the components of infrastructure networks, the rich compositions of their economic actors, and even the emergence of causes that can trigger blackouts (Bennett 2005), but could also pose a potential issue.

Namely, the analysis of mere specific instances of managing electricity and mitigating power failures might prove to be too flat, uncovering only the intricate details of various "ethnographic presents" (Rabinow 2008, 10). Such details from fieldwork are telling, as I have tried to demonstrate, but give perhaps less consideration to many other things that I studied: such as historical contextualization and the different scales and timeframes of electricity risk management that were all considered in the empirical chapters (see also Pollock & Williams 2009, 2010). For example, it is one thing to detail which different actants contribute to the situated making of an energy market bid in practice; it is another to pay attention to the different temporalities of various energy markets, the day-to-day working habits that these markets help initiate, and the historical context behind the existence of a different electricity control room for energy markets and network security. I have sought to acknowledge both concrete situations and the latter kinds of contextual issues in this book.

The issue of extending one's method to many sites is also not exclusive to studying risk perceptions or actor networks. To continue with ethnography, methods such as fieldwork and participant observation underpinned my work. But it was also clear that a substantial effort is required to access field sites and conduct systematic ethnographic analysis, especially when more than one field site is concerned (Pollock & Williams 2009). In the end, I was given permission to interview each electricity control room worker in my study once, rendering my approach merely semi-ethnographic. About 20 hours of observations in highly restricted control rooms is a valuable achievement, as accessing these sites at all is uncommon, but it is still a relatively short amount of time in this research area (cf. Roe & Schulman 2008). Prior to becoming a sociologist, I studied in a technical university and worked in electricity research and energy industries, which likely helped when making sense of my data, and the ethnographic control room materials are still revealing, as I have demonstrated. But they are also restricted in terms of seeing, for example, what happened in these rooms in the months and weeks when I was not present. Similar issues figure in the other field sites: I cannot say what a national security risk would have been like during an infrastructural crisis exercise or a seminar I did not attend, for example, or how risk figured in a home when the power fails.

What is needed to come to a fuller conclusion, I would argue, is a different conceptual reconstruction of what the activities on these sites were all about. I shall now do this by returning to the key concepts of this book. The first is *risk*, then *resilience*, and finally *infrastructures* and *systems*, which unpacks how the study of risk and resilience contributes new knowledge to this area in the social studies of energy.

Risk multiple

Numerous discussions about risk have appeared written by social scientists, experts in safety, policy papers, and others, as outlined in the beginning of this book. In what follows, more attention is given to the ways in which I studied risk empirically. Crucial support to this end was offered by previous studies about risk governance. However, many of these studies have focused on policy fields where the concept of risk is manifest and routinely used. Therefore, in many instances, it has maybe sufficed to formulate only a loose heuristic for the notion of a risk. O'Malley (2004, 1), for instance, charts risk as practices that

> tell us the exact degree of probability there is of us experiencing the relevant harm, although sometimes they only approximate this statistical ideal. [. . .] They [practices of risk governance] seek to make objective, standardised, and exact predictions to replace subjective expectations.

To Ewald (1993, 61), risk management by social insurance can be understood as a schematic "diagram" – that is, a "pure rational representation of this world" or even a "perfectly functioning social machine". These considerations, while interesting and relevant, seem to start with the assumption that rational risk analysis can be easily found in the materials that are studied. As I discovered, however, this was not always the case with the management of Finnish electricity infrastructure risk.

One fundamental initial issue in my analysis was related to the concept of risk. Should the actors themselves draw on the concept of a risk for their practices to be called risk governance? To an ethnographer or a researcher of meaning-making, the answer would probably have to be "yes". However, I decided to loosen this conceptual requirement for two main reasons.

The first reason is related to Finnish. Whether a "technical language of risk management" has now been established as an etiquette in all cultures everywhere (Furedi 2006, 156), risk is still only a recent loan word in Finnish. The first Finnish public policy report about accident risks is from the 1980s (Sisäasiainministeriö

1983). Finnish social scientists started following the theory of the risk society in the late 1980s. At this very early stage, the Finnish journal of sociology, *Sosiologia*, published a theme issue on *Risk Society* in 1989, three years before the English translation of Ulrich Beck's (1992) book. (*Risk Society* itself was never translated to Finnish, but its sequel, *The Counter-Poisons of Risk Society: Organised Irresponsibility* was in 1990; see Beck 1990.) On the other hand, many Finnish words that signify uncertainty and negative outcomes of action are much older. Terms such as *tapaturma* (accident), *vahinko* (damage), *uhka* (threat), and *vaara* (danger) stem from the 16th century from the first systematic attempts to develop written Finnish. This has also shaped fields specialized to risks: for example, until the 1960s Finnish insurance specialists referred to risk with another term *vastuu*, literally, responsibility (Liukko 2013). Even the loan word *kriisi* (crisis) is first mentioned in 1886 and has been in use since the early 20th century (Häkkinen 2004).

A second reason then follows from this and relates to what my informants understood by risk. It is evident from the above that risk is a recent specialist concept in Finnish and when it signified something to my informants, this was typically a relatively narrow meaning, like a financial risk or a life-threatening security risk (which was in turn not seen as an issue of the energy markets). I did not want to restrict my analysis only to those occasions where risk was mentioned explicitly, because either the term was not in use at all – the case for much of the 20th century – or its meaning seemed more restricted than what I found within my field sites and interviews regarding how informants anticipated uncertainties.

To get forward conceptually, Eräsaari (2008, 69) produces a different but related useful summary of risk as a *representation of security*. This is not immediately more concrete than talking about risks; as he notes, the notion of security rarely has a tangible meaning and can even be considered as an "empty concept". Nonetheless, following this line of thought, security is still what many of my informants considered continuously when managing uncertainties. Many of their own concepts mirror this rather directly: the electricity grid control room operators talked about security as their guiding logic and the official name of Finnish infrastructure protection has been either *emergency supply* or *security of supply*. The Finnish name of the latter national practices is *huoltovarmuus*, where *varmuus* means, literally, "certainty".

The energy market control room's representations of security were more ambivalent. Some workers explicitly distanced themselves from all "security" issues, but they also seemingly contradicted this on other occasions: for example, if the purpose of free energy trading is acquiring cheap electricity for the city dwellers, as one of the traders told me, what else would this aim concern but people's financial security? Importantly, these are diverse issues, some of them are more oriented to the markets and others more to public issues, but all seem to be addressing both. My research then supports the argument that risk, as a technique, does not need to be fixed with a particular rationale such as public control or market liberalism, but is a flexible means of maximizing security for various different rational reasons (O'Malley 2004; Liukko 2013).

Even so, the versatility of risk reasoning should not be exaggerated. It is apt to note, as Hacking (2002, 189) does, that a new style of reasoning always introduces innovations and novelties: it pays attention to objects "not previously noticeable among the things that exist". This seems true for a security style of reasoning, too. But in doing so such reasoning may still disregard many other matters. Risk, in the sense of technically representing security, appears to be a measure of deciding about intervening against some harms rather than others. In other words, risk is not merely a danger that happens irrespective of present decisions (Luhmann 1993; Collier, Lakoff & Rabinow 2004; Helén 2004). Hence, to Finnish national security experts in the mid-20th century, for example, problems with the energy infrastructure still represented a danger more than a risk. The risk that needed deciding and mitigating was a military strike. The energy crises of the 1970s helped change this outset: electricity became seen as a vital provision whose risks are a serious issue to be considered and decided upon by national security experts to minimize collective harms. Several similar examples are found in my results: technical energy market quality regulations, actions in control rooms, and even lay risk responses considered some uncertain hazards as risks to be mitigated and others as dangers outside of the scope of reasonable actions and habits.

As risk thus suggests foresight and actions about specific uncertainties, it often seems not only to represent but also fix what matters for collective security in the first place. Hence, as mentioned, the early Finnish national infrastructural crisis planning was all about military threats and the respective risk techniques were not seen as suited to other kinds of problems. Similarly, electricity control rooms are in many ways fixed to make particular kinds of market bids and offers or oversee specific electricity grid inputs and outputs through working routines and technologies such as computer screens (even if this requires considerable experience and skill-based adjustments, as my informants told me). Energy market regulations do change, perhaps more often in consideration of new public issues, but only after regulatory cycles that last several years in Finland, as elsewhere in the world.

A topical illustration of what this could mean in practice is given by environmental issues such as climate change. Even if such issues have become increasingly topical and could motivate broad energy system transitions (Verbong & Geels 2007; Hodson & Marvin 2009), the risk techniques I studied only rarely directly addressed the sustainability of energy systems. In practice, the techniques could only have screened such a risk in special occasions: when extreme storms threatened the functioning of the electricity grid or wind power fluctuations affected the Nordic energy market, for example. Yet, certainly the matters could be more complicated than this: as several scholars and commentators have argued, there are many "complexities, uncertainties, and problems which confront many western societies, in organizing 'sustainably' various aspects of energy, agricultural, water, transport, and health systems" (Hodson & Marvin 2009, 515). On a more positive note, the risk technicalities found ethnographically in this study are what probably needs to be acknowledged, or in some cases even altered, if energy systems are to be transformed on a wider scale.

These observations about the traits of risk techniques and the agency that they try to preconfigure remind us of why more studies of the incumbent system and markets would be warranted in control rooms and elsewhere. At the time of my

study, lay persons had not been offered real-time risk screens similar to the electricity control rooms, but this situation could shift in support of leaner and more
flexible energy infrastructure. Smart electricity metering that is currently rolled
out to households and businesses in many states offers a relevant example. With
earlier household electricity prepayment metering in the United Kingdom, energy
end users were given the possibility to "choose" to use electricity when they can
afford it (Graham & Marvin 2001, 208). The newer smart meters seem to work
by these familiar assumptions and consumerist rhetoric: as energy scholars write,
smart energy technologies' "designers and engineers situate the technology in 'an
ideal' form of consumer behaviour, that is, one that is based on economic rationality" (van der Horst, Staddon & Webb 2014, 1114–1115). At the same time,
the assumptions behind such programmes on more rational behaviour are seldom
discussed in as much depth by designers and have multidimensional effects that
would need further consideration by social scientists and others.

Finally, boundedness was not the entire story about infrastructure risk management when my results are considered. Concerning risk techniques that loosen the
definition of a threat, the question of what this threat is about seems to become less
relevant. Crisis researcher and anthropologist Susann Ullberg (2005, 69) makes
this point clear when she argues that a blackout can emerge as a crisis whether
initiated by a technical failure, a "natural" disaster, human error, or other reasons.
Perhaps this is also why the recent Finnish protections of vital national functions
represent threats as unknown "question marks": if policies cannot for one reason
or the other communicate about what threatens society's vital functions and how
likely that is, why try to determine it? These clearly precautionary forms of thinking (see Ewald 2002; O'Malley 2004) would pose a promising starting point for
further inquiries. Such styles of reasoning, I would argue, were particularly visible
with lay persons, who through their common sense could anticipate imaginative
scenarios concerning what happens when power is out for a long period or during
a cold winter. A representation of certainty about future threats is not always an
indication of the fears that people have when expressing concern about uncertain
failures of everyday infrastructures.

Making infrastructure resilient

In the electricity infrastructure, insecurities are measured and tamed by a number
of related, more-or-less established concepts: such as security of supply, just security, or risk (UKERC 2011). Over the last ten years, however, another security
concept has found increasing attention in energy and infrastructure policy programmes: the term *resilience*. The concept is now deployed in the highest-levels
of discussion over energy security (European Commission 2015), homeland security (US Department of Homeland Security 2013), critical infrastructure protection (US National Infrastructure Advisory Council 2009), and global foreign
and security policy (European Union 2016). At the same time, among social
scientists, it has become almost a fact of life that resilience is not easy to define
but a rather contested, uncertain, and underdeveloped concept (Furedi 2008;

Healey & Mesman 2014; Krieger 2016). Critiques of the concept, discussions of its theoretical base, and discussions of its use as a fashionable term are both relevant and interesting.

Nevertheless, in this book, I took a similar stance on resilience as to risk. The point is that social scientists name practices, patterns of actions, and objects as a result of their inquiries (Rabinow 2008, 26–28); in my case, practices employed for taming uncertainty and using knowledge can be named as *resilient*. I have hence contributed to the research of resilience, and consider it a key term like risk and infrastructure, because it opens up the social science debate and sheds new light on the problem of interruptions in electricity infrastructures.

Just like risk, however, resilience does not translate to Finnish in a straightforward manner. Terms such as flexibility, elasticity, robustness, sustainability, and tolerance are related, but resilience is still often directly used as a loan word, *resilienssi*. The Union Catalogue of Finnish Libraries that spans decades of research only first mentions the concept in 2010 – in a social science volume concerning socio-ecological issues (Kotilainen & Eikko 2010), which also suggests the term *uusiutumiskyky* (renewability) to mean resilience. Articles have a few earlier mentions of *resilienssi* under business journalism (Välikangas & Hamel 2003) and pedagogics (Lahtinen 2008).

As this book discovered, the Finnish programmes on vital systems protection adopted the concept of resilience, also in 2010. But they mainly used it to refer to *psychological resilience to crisis* and never defined the term in so doing. The same area was earlier named as *psychological crisis tolerance*, but both meant the Finnish nation state's cultural, educational, religious, communications, and other cohesive capacities to endure stress and recover from crises. This perhaps expands the scope to the national scale from the earlier psychological research of resilience (Krieger 2016), but is not the only meaning linked to infrastructure resilience (cf. US National Infrastructure Council 2009; US Department of Homeland Security 2013; European Commission 2015).

Infrastructure security strategies in Finland's neighbour Sweden have pursued systematic understanding of society's energy supplies considering issues about anticipation of threats and resilience. The Swedish government's Swedish Energy Agency (Energimyndigheten 2007) defines by *secure energy supply* the Swedish energy system's capacity, flexibility, and robustness to supply energy, but also includes the crisis management capabilities of the market, the public sector, and users in this definition (Energimyndigheten 2007, 10). Infrastructure researcher Björn Wallsten (Berglund 2009, 7–8) interprets this as a two-tier aim: what is at stake is the energy suppliers', energy market's, users', and the public sector's abilities to prevent disruption, but also to handle disturbances after they have occurred. He names the first strategy as *robustness*, the second as *resilience* – similarly to risk assessment and risk perception literatures that have separated the *anticipation* of known threats from *resilience* to recover from known or unknown threats for a long while (e.g. Douglas & Wildavsky 1982; Hood et al 1992).

In sum, resilience suggests a different temporality from the prior anticipation that shaped risk and hence enriches the understanding of what makes infrastructures protected. In the sites studied in this book, building prior robustness against power failures receives much scrutiny – whether through stockpiling, risk management frameworks, or the preparedness activities expected in households. Yet, energy suppliers, people, and organizations seem also highly capable of handling disturbances after they have occurred and often must circumvent prior plans in so doing. Especially when catastrophic or near-catastrophic events are at stake, problems will emerge that challenge existing plans and procedures. The sites in this book address this problem in their own distinct manners – on the national scale, by imaginative precautionary thinking; in network companies, by staying alert to systems and their volatile environments through situational skills; and in energy-using households and communities, by overall resourcefulness (see also Tierney 2003). These discoveries show why the concept of resilience adds to risk research – it highlights objects, patterns of actions, and practices that would be more difficult to interpret as mere risk management. The layered trait of resilience – which can refer to the resilience of systems, personal resilience, or the meso-level resilience of institutions (Healey & Mesman 2014), or divided between technical, organizational, social, and economic dimensions in disaster scholarship (Tierney 2003) – makes it particularly useful in this regards to analyse the similarly layered electricity infrastructure.

A final, more general relevance of resilience is its relation with climate change and issues around sustainable energy transition (Verbong & Geels 2007). Science and technology policy scholar Andrew Stirling (2014, 318) argues that resilience is one of four cornerstones of sustainability in energy systems – others being their stability, durability, and robustness. However, it is important to add that resilience concerns several different time spans when the uncertain future is concerned. Building the resilience of energy systems against short-term shocks such as power outages – through maintenance, contingency planning, and training, for example – typically differs from building resilience against long-term stresses such as climate change (Smith & Stirling 2010). In Finnish programmes on vital infrastructures, for example, the attention on catastrophic power failures is certainly different and not always related with catastrophic climate change. Where these temporalities become each other's alternatives for example in infrastructure investments, short-term often outdoes long-term resilience among energy suppliers (UKERC 2011, 9).

In this sense, the problematic of resilience bounces back to public policy issues and resembles the long-term issues with building infrastructures more generally (Graham & Marvin 2001). Similarly to the national security threats that I studied in the security policy chapters, resilience concerns both calculable threats and disturbances and even disasters that can have an extremely low probability, but high consequences if they occur (Krieger 2016). Among companies in the free markets, investments in resilience to such rare events could be likened to taking insurance, yet difficult to justify in the energy markets that stress short-term, more-or-less real-time competition. That is why UKERC (2011, 51) suggests mitigation of such rare incidents and attaining resilience "in the public interest for strategic reasons". This much is clear. But the extent to which markets provide resilience against shocks and are able to anticipate threats, and the extent to which public interventions in these areas are necessary, is a problematic question that electricity authorities, planners, market designers, and practitioners will have to keep debating over the coming years. Scholars pursuing social studies of energy could become one key participant and share their evidence in these topical discussions.

Energy systems and infrastructures in society

There is no longer a shortage of social studies of energy systems and infrastructures (e.g. Hughes 1983, 1989; Nye 1998; Graham & Marvin 2001; Shove 2003; van der Vleuten 2004; Verbong & Geels 2007; see Silvast, Hänninen & Hyysalo 2013). Nevertheless, with a few notable exceptions (e.g. Collier & Lakoff 2008), issues concerning risk and resilience in the energy infrastructure have not emerged in these discussions and are mainly assessed in their own distinct social science contexts: such as organizational studies (Roe & Schulman 2008) or urban scholarship (Graham 2009). To conclude and bridge between different literatures, I consider how social science studies of energy could be taken into new directions by accounting for the timely problematics of risk and resilience that this book's discoveries have foregrounded.

In this energy research area, the early scholarship built a fundamental point that underlies many of the other works that have followed: electricity supply is something systemic, a large socio-technical system that encloses technical components as well as organizations, laws, raw resources, and scientific works within a single interrelated structure or a network (Hughes 1983). Those elements not enclosed and controlled by the system are merely in its environment. The point on layered energy systems remains central, for example, in understanding how energy systems change when they face transitions to greater sustainability. In practice, multiple levels from political cultures and economic trends to energy sector actors, technologies, institutions, and regulations need to change for a successful transition (Verbong & Geels 2007; Hodson & Marvin 2009). Research into the social and cultural experiences of energy – while distancing itself from the study of systems only – also assumes energy systems simply to be out there and to be shaped by their cultural symbolic meanings (Nye 1998, 2010; see Larkin 2013). Even consumers can be seen as one part of a large system (van der Vleuten 2004) – for instance, when systemic problems exert new pressures on them to use electricity more rationally. All of these system components can participate in how risk management and resilience work in systemic terms. However, if actors are not included in the system and have no visible influence on it, they can be difficult to identify in these same terms, which is where this research enters a problematic area.

Over the past ten years, certain social science studies have raised increasing problems with the concept of an energy system. Their worry is that contemporary energy supply is perhaps less closed from outside contexts than the early research on large technological systems foresaw (cf. Hughes 1989, 53). Rather than closed and centrally controlled supply-based networks, in the past decade, energy provisions have been rather open to political, cultural, and economic aspirations to increase their sustainability (Coutard, Hanley & Zimmerman 2005). Systems theory could explain this, too: system environments do interact with systems (Hughes 1989), but the notion of a single power system that merely encloses what it controls is still problematic. Several others stress that large systems or what they call *infrastructures* rather combine multiple systems and practices: including nation states and economies, institutions and organizations, design, ongoing maintenance, and the heuristics of their users (Edwards 2003; Ribes & Finholt 2009; Pollock & Williams 2010). Originally a 1950s NATO term, but widespread in public and political discussions recently, infrastructures are not merely closed, coherent, and centrally controlled systems. They are rather like "webs" (Edwards 2010, 12) or "open reconfigurable" networks whose coordination is at least partly distributed among different actors (Edwards et al 2007, 12) from international producers even to local users.

All of these ideas, while the said two concepts of *system* and *infrastructure* are relatively similar in many respects, lead us to ask whether infrastructure poses a different analogy from system when considering risk and resilience in energy supplies. I should stress that the concepts are not each other's alternatives, as arguably infrastructures compile several numbers of technical systems and are a type of virtual, second-order "system of systems" (van der Vleuten 2004; Edwards et al 2007; Edwards 2010). I do not hence want to claim that the research of energy systems should be replaced with the research of energy infrastructures – or vice versa. Rather, the two concepts pave the way for different understandings of energy supplies using risk management and resilience terminology, outlined in this conclusion.

In the case of *systems*, the concern is with more-or-less bounded and closed provisions that serve customers regionally, contain heterogeneous components and subsystems, and whose definitions are typically reinforced by electricity legislations, such as those stipulating electricity system operation, licences, or system responsibilities (Edwards et al 2007). Managing the risk of these systems and building up their resilience focuses on power lines, substations, and other electric devices while anticipating threats against their reliable functioning and produces crisis management practices for disruptions that occur. The electricity network control room is one pinnacle of such practices (Roe & Schulman 2008), but in the spirit of socio-technicality, they also happen through other system parts such as laws or regulations based on research work, as my findings showed. However, the shared assumption is that risks can be contained and resilience enhanced through more-or-less centralized control, whether by the control room, national law, or integrated safety studies. While users need to adjust to the energy systems and their risks – and even participate in calculating risks – the actual management practice lies with system builders of various sorts from network companies to engineers, scientists, and energy legislators.

Where regional local electric grids are a case of systems, one might consider internationally connected electricity networks and their deregulated power markets as bona fide energy *infrastructures* (Edwards et al 2007; Edwards 2010). These large structures, such as the common Scandinavian wholesale electricity market, compile different regional and national electricity transmission and distribution systems, such as electricity supplies in cities in Sweden, Finland, Norway, and Denmark, and the national electricity grids in these countries. The goal of such an infrastructure is not central control of a single international system – difficult to establish in any one country, not least politically – but rather a coordination of widely dispersed energy systems. In this case, the coordination is supposed to happen through the mechanisms of the free electric power market in the Nordic energy stock exchange – a kind of a gateway that bridges between energy systems at various scales. Here, ideally, the market mechanism mitigates risk and ensures resilience. This view is shared not only by power stock exchanges, but also the authorities that regulate energy markets and networks, in the cases of this book from the late 2000s.

The competition on such markets and these kinds of highly interconnected networks are also problematic, as social scientists have pointed out. Intense competition may compromise infrastructure resilience (Graham 2009). Additionally the interdependencies of current global infrastructure networks may trigger new risks that have received due scrutiny from risk researchers (Centeno et al 2015). These uncertainties notwithstanding, however, infrastructure building is trying to attain its own distinct goals. The key is that through their wide distribution, infrastructures could become relatively open and reconfigurable and allow for participation of governments, companies, standards bodies, and also users in a more sustained manner than with more-or-less closed technological systems and their risk management. As my book showed, much work remains to be done in these interfaces between designers and users: energy infrastructure design still tends to treat various user groups in a highly idealized fashion, mainly as economic actors to be integrated through bids, offers, price signals, and other simplistic interfaces. Yet, further potential exists: compare, for example, how different it is to become an energy system licence holder in legal terms to using energy services that are linked to international power markets already today in many places. As energy transitions continue and energy becomes not only a problem of technical systems, but also of politics, culture, and economics, these new conceptualizations of energy supply should receive increasing scrutiny by researchers, policy makers, and all others who depend on vital energy infrastructures.

References

Adato Energia (2008). Kotitalouksien sähkönkäyttö 2006 ("The Electricity Use of Households 2006"). Research Report. Link accessed 26 November 2016: www.motiva.fi/files/1353/Kotitalouksien_sahkonkaytto_2006_-raportti.pdf

Beck, Ulrich (1990). *Riskiyhteiskunnan vastamyrkyt: organisoitu vastuuttomuus* ("The Counter-Poisons of Risk Society: Organised Irresponsibility"). Tampere: Vastapaino (German original 1988).

Beck, Ulrich (1992). *Risk Society: Towards a New Modernity*. London: Sage (German original 1986).

Bennett, Jane (2005). The Agency of Assemblages and the North American Blackout. *Public Culture* 17 (3): 445–465.

Berglund, Björn (2009). *Svarta svanar och högspänningsledningar – om försörjningstryggheten i det svenska elsystemet ur ett teknikhistoriskt perspektiv* ("Black Swans in the Power Grid – How Critical Events Has Affected the Security of Electricity Supply"). Dissertation, Uppsala University, Disciplinary Domain of Science and Technology. Link accessed 10 October 2016: www.utn.uu.se/sts/cms/filarea/0901_Berglund.pdf

Boholm, Åsa (2003). The Cultural Nature of Risk: Can There Be an Anthropology of Uncertainty? *Ethnos* 68 (2): 159–178.

Burgess, Adam (2016). Introduction. In Burgess, Adam; Alemanno, Alberto & Zinn, Jens (eds) *Routledge Handbook of Risk Studies*. London: Routledge, 1–14.

Centeno, Miguel; Nag, Manish; Patterson, Thayer; Shaver, Andrew & Windawi, Jason (2015). The Emergence of Global Systemic Risk. *Annual Review of Sociology* 41: 65–85.

Collier, Stephen (2011). *Post-Soviet Social: Neoliberalism, Social Modernity, Biopolitics*. Princeton, NJ: Princeton University Press.

Collier, Stephen & Lakoff, Andrew (2008). The Vulnerability of Vital Systems: How Critical Infrastructures Became a Security Problem. In Dunn Cavelty, Myriam & Kristensen, Kristian Søby (eds) *Securing 'the Homeland': Critical Infrastructure, Risk and (In)security*. London: Routledge, 17–39.

Collier, Stephen; Lakoff, Andrew & Rabinow, Paul (2004). Biosecurity: Proposal for an Anthropology of the Contemporary. *Anthropology Today* 20 (5): 3–7.

Coutard, Olivier; Hanley, Richard & Zimmerman, Rae (2005). Network Systems Revisited: The Confounding Nature of Universal Systems. In Coutard, Olivier; Hanley, Richard & Zimmerman, Rae (eds) *Sustaining Urban Networks: The Social Diffusion of Large Technical Systems*. London: Routledge, 1–12.

Doorman, Gerard; Kjølle, Gerd; Uhlen, Kjetil; Huse, Einar Ståle & Flatabø, Nils (2004). *Vulnerability of the Nordic Power System: Report to the Nordic Council of Ministers*. Trondheim: SINTEF Energy Research.

Douglas, Mary & Wildavsky, Aaron (1982). *Risk and Culture: An Essay on the Selection of Technological and Environmental Dangers*. Berkeley: University of California Press.

Dunn, Myriam (2006). Understanding Critical Information Infrastructures: An Elusive Quest. In Dunn, Myriam & Mauer, Victor (eds) *International CIIP Handbook 2006 Vol. II: Analyzing Issues, Challenges and Prospects*. Zürich: Center for Security Studies, 27–54. Link accessed 26 November 2016: http://e-collection.library.ethz.ch/eserv/eth:31123/eth-31123-04.pdf

Edwards, Paul (2003). Infrastructure and Modernity: Force, Time and Social Organization in the History of Sociotechnical systems. In Misa, Thomas; Brey, Philip & Feenberg, Andrew (eds) *Modernity and Technology*. Cambridge, MA: MIT Press, 185–225.

Edwards, Paul (2010). *A Vast Machine: Computer Models, Climate Data, and the Politics of Global Warming*. Cambridge, MA: MIT Press.

Edwards, Paul, Jackson, Steven, Bowker, Geoffrey & Knobel, Cory (2007). Understanding Infrastructure: Dynamics, Tensions, and Design. Report of a Workshop on History & Theory of Infrastructure: Lessons for New Scientific Cyberinfrastructures. Link accessed 3 June 2013: http://deepblue.lib.umich.edu/bitstream/handle/2027.42/49353/Understand ingInfrastructure2007.pdf?sequence=3

Energiateollisuus (2012). Kuluttajatutkimus sähkökeskeytyksistä ("A Consumer Survey about Electricity Interruptions"). A survey carried out by YouGov Finland. Link accessed 3 June 2013: www.energia.fi/kalvosarjat/kuluttajatutkimus-sahkokeskeytyksis taenergia teollisuus-ry

Energimyndighet (Swedish Energy Agency) (2007). *Hur trygg är vår energiförsörjning? En översiktlig analys av hot, risker och sårbarheter inom energisektorn år 2006* ("How Security Is Our Energy Supply? An Overview Analysis of Threats, Risks, and Vulnerabilities in the Energy Sector in 2006"). Stockholm: Statens energimyndighet. Link accessed 2 November 2016: https://energimyndigheten.a-w2m.se/FolderContents.mvc/Download?ResourceId=2281

Eräsaari, Risto (2008). Representation of Welfare and the Challenge of Complexity. In Kohl, Johanna (ed.) *Dialogues on Sustainable Paths for the Future: Ethics, Welfare and Responsibility*. Turku: Finland Futures Research Centre, 65–71.

European Commission (2015). A Framework Strategy for a Resilient Energy Union with a Forward-Looking Climate Change Policy. COM/2015/080 final. Link accessed 10 October 2016: http://eur-lex.europa.eu/legal-content/EN/TXT/?uri=COM:2015:80:FIN

European Council (2008). On the Identification and Designation of European Critical Infrastructures and the Assessment of the Need to Improve Their Protection. Directive 2008/114/EC. Link accessed 26 November 2016: http://eur-lex.europa.eu/LexUriServ/LexUriServ.do?uri=CELEX:32008L0114:EN:NOT

European Union (2016). Shared Vision, Common Action: A Stronger Europe: A Global Strategy for the European Union's Foreign and Security Policy. Link accessed 10 October 2016: https://eeas.europa.eu/top_stories/pdf/eugs_review_web.pdf

Ewald, François (1993). *Der Vorsorgestaat*. Berlin: Suhrkamp (French original 1986).

Ewald, François (2002). The Return of Descartes' Malicious Demon: An Outline of a Philosophy of Precaution. In Baker, Tom & Simon, Jonathan (eds) *Embracing Risk: The Changing Culture of Insurance and Responsibility*. Chicago: University of Chicago Press, 273–301.

Furedi, Frank (2006). *Culture of Fear Revisited*. London – New York: Continuum.

Furedi, Frank (2008). Fear and Security: A Vulnerability-Led Policy Response. *Social Policy & Administration* 42 (6): 645–661.

Gobo, Giampietro (2008). *Doing Ethnography*. London – Thousand Oaks – New Delhi – Singapore: Sage.

Graham, Stephen (2009). When Infrastructures Fail. In Graham, Stephen (ed.) *Disrupted Cities: When Infrastructure Fails*. London: Routledge, 1–26.

Graham, Stephen & Marvin, Simon (2001). *Splintering Urbanism: Networked Infrastructures, Technological Mobilities and the Urban Condition*. London: Routledge.

Hacking, Ian (2002). *Historical Ontology*. Cambridge, MA – London: Harvard University Press.

Häkkinen, Kaisa (2004). *Nykysuomen etymologinen sanakirja* ("An Etymological Dictionary of Contemporary Finnish"). Helsinki: WSOY.

Healey, Stephen & Mesman, Jessica (2014). Resilience: Contingency, Complexity, and Practice. In Hommels, Anique; Mesman, Jessica & Bijker, Wiebe (eds) *Vulnerability in Technological Cultures: New Directions in Research and Governance*. Cambridge, MA: MIT Press, 155–178.

Helén, Ilpo (2004). Technics Over Life: Risk, Ethics and the Existential Condition in High-Tech Antenatal Care. *Economy and Society* 33 (1): 28–51.

Hodson, Mike & Marvin, Simon (2009). Cities Mediating Technological Transitions: Understanding Visions, Intermediation and Consequence. *Technology Analysis & Strategic Management* 21 (4): 515–534.

Hood, C. C.; Jones, D. K. C.; Pidgeon, N. F.; Turner, B. A. & Gibson, R. (1992). Risk Management. In Royal Society Study Group (eds) *Risk: Analysis, Perception and Management*. London: The Royal Society, 135–191.

Hughes, Thomas (1983). *Networks of Power: Electrification in Western Society, 1880–1930*. Baltimore, MD: Johns Hopkins University Press.

Hughes, Thomas (1989). The Evolution of Large Scale Technological Systems. In Bijker, Wiebe; Hughes, Thomas & Pinch, Trevor (eds) *The Social Construction of Technological Systems: New Directions in the Sociology History of Technology*. Cambridge, MA: MIT Press, 51–82.

Karasti, Helena; Millerand, Florence; Hine, Christine & Bowker, Geoffrey (2016). Knowledge Infrastructures: Part I. *Science & Technology Studies* 29 (1): 2–12.

Kjølle, Gerd; Utne, Ingrid & Gjerde, Oddbjørn (2012). Risk Analysis of Critical Infrastructures Emphasizing Electricity Supply and Interdependencies. *Reliability Engineering and System Safety* 105: 80–89.

Kotilainen, Juha & Eisto, Ilkka (2010, eds). *Luonnonvarayhdyskunnat ja muuttuva ympäristö – resilienssitutkimuksen näkökulmia Itä-Suomeen* ("Ecological Communities and the Changing Environment – Resilience Research Perspectives on Eastern Finland"). Joensuu: Publications of the University of Eastern Finland.

Krieger, Kristian (2016). Resilience and Risk Studies. In Burgess, Adam; Alemanno, Alberto & Zinn, Jens (eds) *Routledge Handbook of Risk Studies*. London: Routledge, 335–343.

Kristensen, Kristian Søby (2008). 'The Absolute Protection of our Citizens': Critical Infrastructure Protection and the Practice of Security. In Dunn Cavelty, Myriam & Kristensen, Kristian Søby (eds) *Securing 'the Homeland': Critical Infrastructure, Risk and (In)security*. London: Routledge, 63–83.

Lahtinen, Aino-Maija (2008). Kirjallisuus psyykkisenä voimavarana – resilience-käsitteen soveltaminen kirjallisuuden lukemiseen ("Literature as a Psychological Resource: Resilience and Literature Reading"). *Kasvatus* ("Education") 39 (3): 262–270.

Larkin, Brian (2013). The Politics and Poetics of Infrastructure. *Annual Review of Anthropology* 42: 327–343.

Latour, Bruno (2005). *Reassembling the Social: An Introduction to Actor-Network-Theory*. Oxford, UK: Oxford University Press.

Liukko, Jyri (2013). *Solidaarisuuskone: Elämän vakuuttaminen ja vastuuajattelun muutos* ("Solidarity Machine: Life Insurance and Transformations of Responsibility"). Doctoral thesis, University of Helsinki, Department of Social Research. Helsinki: Gaudeamus.

Luhmann, Niklas (1993). *Risk: A Sociological Theory*. Berlin – New York: Walter de Gruyter (German original 1991).

MacKenzie, Donald (2009). Ten Precepts for the Social Studies of Finance. In MacKenzie, Donald (ed.) *Material Markets: How Economic Agents are Constructed*. Oxford, UK: Oxford University Press, 8–36.

Manyena, Siambabala Bernard (2006). The Concept of Resilience Revisited. *Disasters* 30 (4): 434–450.

Marcus, George (1995). Ethnography in/of the World System: The Emergence of Multi-Sited Ethnography. *Annual Review of Anthropology* 24: 95–117.

Nye, David (1998). *Consuming Power: A Social History of American Energies*. Cambridge, MA: MIT Press.

Nye, David (2010). *When the Lights Went Out: A History of Blackouts in America*. Cambridge, MA: MIT Press.

O'Malley, Pat (2004). *Risk, Uncertainty and Government*. London – Sydney – Portland: Glasshouse Press.

Pollock, Neil & Williams, Robin (2009). *Software and Organisations: The Biography of the Enterprise-Wide System or How SAP Conquered the World*. London: Routledge.

Pollock, Neil & Williams, Robin (2010). E-Infrastructures: How Do We Know and Understand Them? Strategic Ethnography and the Biography of Artefacts. *Computer Supported Cooperative Work* 19 (6): 521–556.

Rabinow, Paul (2008). *Marking Time: On the Anthropology of the Contemporary*. Princeton, NJ: Princeton University Press.

Ribes, David & Finholt, Thomas (2009). The Long Now of Technology Infrastructure: Articulating Tensions in Development. *Journal of the Association for Information Systems* 10 (5): 375–398.

Roe, Emery & Schulman, Paul (2008). *High Reliability Management: Operating on the Edge*. Stanford, CA: Stanford Business Books.

Shove, Elizabeth (2003). Converging Conventions of Comfort, Cleanliness and Convenience. *Journal of Consumer Policy* 26 (4): 395–418.

Silvast, Antti; Hänninen, Hannu & Hyysalo, Sampsa (2013). Energy in Society: Energy Systems and Infrastructures in Society. *Science & Technology Studies* 26 (3): 3–13.

Sisäasiainministeriö (Finnish Ministry of the Interior) (1983). *Riski-työryhmän mietintö* ("Report of the Risk Working Group"). Helsinki: Sisäasiainministeriö.Smith, Adrian & Stirling, Andrew (2010). The Politics of Social-Ecological Resilience and Sustainable Socio-Technical Transitions. *Ecology and Society* 15 (1): 11.

Stirling, Andrew (2014). From Sustainability to Transformation: Dynamics and Diversity in Reflexive Governance of Vulnerability. In Hommels, Anique; Mesman, Jessica & Bijker, Wiebe (eds) *Vulnerability in Technological Cultures: New Directions in Research and Governance*. Cambridge, MA: MIT Press, 305–332.

Summerton, Jane & Berner, Boel (2003). Constructing Risk and Safety in Technological Practice: An Introduction. In Summerton, Jane & Berner, Boel (eds) *Constructing Risk and Safety in Technological Practice*. London: Routledge, 1–24.

Tierney, Kathleen (2003). *Conceptualizing and Measuring Organizational and Community Resilience: Lessons from the Emergency Response Following the September 11, 2001 Attack on the World Trade Center*. Preliminary paper. Newark, DE: University of Delaware Disaster Research Center. Link accessed 24 November 2016: http://udspace.udel.edu/bit stream/handle/19716/735/PP329.pdf

UKERC (UK Energy Research Centre) (2011). Building a Resilient UK Energy System. Written by Modassar Chaudry, Paul Ekins, Kannan Ramachandran, Anser Shakoor, Jim Skea, Goran Strbac, Xinxin Wang, and Jeanette Whitaker. London: UKERC. Link accessed 10 October 2016: http://nora.nerc.ac.uk/16648/1/UKERC_energy_2050_resil ience_Res_Report_2011.pdf

Ullberg, Susann (2005). *The Buenos Aires Blackout: Argentine Crisis Management across the Public-Private Divide*. Stockholm: CM Europe Volume Series. Link accessed 26 November 2016: www.fhs.se/Documents/Externwebben/forskning/centrumbildningar/ Crismart/Publikationer/Publikationsserier/VOLUME_28.PDF

US Department of Homeland Security (2013). *National Infrastructure Protection Plan 2013: Partnering for Critical Infrastructure Security and Resilience*. Washington: Department of Homeland Security. Link accessed 10 October 2016: www.dhs.gov/sites/default/ files/publications/National-Infrastructure-Protection-Plan-2013-508.pdf

US National Infrastructure Council (2009). *Critical Infrastructure Resilience Final Report and Recommendations*. Washington: Department of Homeland Security. Link accessed 10 October 2016: www.dhs.gov/xlibrary/assets/niac/niac_critical_infrastructure_resilience.pdf

Välikangas, Liisa & Hamel, Gary (2003). Dynaaminen uudistumiskyky eli resilienssi ("Dynamic Renewability i.e. Resilience"). *Fakta: talous ja tekniikka tänään* ("Fact: Economy and Technology Today") 10: 30–42.

van der Horst, Dan; Staddon, Samantha & Webb, Janette (2014). Smart Energy, and Society? *Technology Analysis & Strategic Management* 26 (10): 1111–1117.

van der Vleuten, Erik (2004). Infrastructures and Societal Change: A View from the Large Technical Systems Field. *Technology Analysis & Strategic Management* 16 (3): 395–414.

Verbong, Geert & Geels, Frank (2007). The Ongoing Energy Transition: Lessons from a Socio-Technical, Multi-Level Analysis of the Dutch Electricity System (1960–2004). *Energy Policy* 35 (2): 1025–1037.

Appendix
Empirical materials

Interviews

The work draws on the following interviews, gathered between 2004 and 2008.

Electricity experts

The experts interviewed in the study worked in six different electricity companies and a Finnish authority. All of the respective institutions were located in larger Finnish cities. Most experts were in their 50s or 60s, with the exception of two women, who were in their late 20s and early 30s, respectively. The year in the end designates the time of the interview.

1 Manager, man, electricity transmission company, 2005
2 Manager, man, electricity transmission company, 2008
3 Manager, man, electricity transmission company, 2008
4 CEO, man, electricity utility, 2005
5 CEO, man, electricity utility, 2007
6 Operating Manager, man, electricity utility, 2005
7 Operating Engineer, man, electricity utility, 2005
8 End User Expert, woman, electricity utility, 2005
9 Communication Manager, man, energy consulting company, 2004
10 Communication Manager, man, electricity production company, 2005
11 Energy Market Technician, woman, electricity utility, 2008
12 Energy Market Technician, man, electricity utility, 2007
13 Energy Market Technician, man, electricity utility, 2008
14 Energy Market Technician, man, electricity utility, 2008
15 Energy Market Technician, man, electricity utility, 2008
16 Energy Market Technician, man, electricity utility, 2008
17 Energy Market and Electricity Grid Technician, man, electricity utility, 2008
18 Electricity Grid Technician, man, electricity utility, 2008
19 Electricity Grid Technician, man, electricity utility, 2008
20 Electricity Grid Technician, man, electricity utility, 2008
21 Electricity Grid Technician, man, electricity utility, 2008

22   Electricity Grid Technician, man, electricity utility, 2008
23   Researcher, man, technological authority, 2008
24   Preparedness Manager, man, technological authority, 2008

Lay persons

The lay electricity users were from the Greater Helsinki region and their ages varied from early 20s to mid-60s. Types of housing are included below, as they affect electricity use.

1   Pensioner, woman, detached house, 2005
2   Department Manager, woman, detached house, 2005
3   Teacher, woman, detached house, 2005
4   IT Expert, woman, detached house, 2005
5   Researcher, man, apartment house, 2004
6   Student 1, woman, apartment house, 2004
7   Student 2, woman, apartment house, 2005
8   Student 3, woman, apartment house, 2005
9   Programmer, man, rowhouse, 2005

Participant observation

My presence in two Finnish electricity control rooms comprised around 20 hours of participant observation alongside the control room everyday work, carried out mostly during one week in the autumn of 2008 with a pilot visit in 2007. I used a notebook for observations about these control room working practices – writing down who did what, with which other persons, by utilizing which artefacts, and what they said to me or other persons.

Between 2007 and 2008, I also sat in five specifically themed electricity infrastructure security seminars in Finland, with 25 presentations in totality, participated in by a variety of actors: researchers and authorities as well as other experts and electricity utility managers. This fieldwork was used for collecting relevant policy documents about the seminar topics, including emergency planning, preparedness, crisis communication, critical infrastructure protection, and major electricity supply disturbances.

End user survey

A survey was sent to Finnish lay users from two regions, a city and a rural area, in 2005. The characteristics of this data are as follows:

Response rate	*Rural*	*City*	*All*
Posting (N)	300	256	556
Responses (N)	69	46	115
Response rate (%)	23	18	21

Age and gender	%
Under 40	7
40–49	17
50–59	27
60–69	26
Over 70	21
Women	28
Men	72

Occupation	%
Pensioner	17
Technician or mounter	15
Engineer	7
Economist	7
Construction	6
Manager	6
Teacher or researcher	5
Social security and health	4
Kitchen worker	3
Officer	3
Driver	3
Other	23

Dwelling and heating	%
Detached house	70
Rowhouse	18
Apartment house	6
Other house	6
Electric heating	46
Electric and wood heating	18
District heating	16
Oil heating	14
Wood heating	2
Electric and oil heating	2
Other heating	3
Average N of residents	2.4

Experienced blackouts, %	Rural	City	All
No blackout during that year	25	36	29
Had a blackout during that year	75	64	71
Duration less than 1 hour	60	31	49
Duration 1–3 hours	27	28	27
Duration over 3 hours	10	14	11
Does not remember duration	4	28	12

Index

For Product Safety Concerns and Information please contact our EU
representative GPSR@taylorandfrancis.com
Taylor & Francis Verlag GmbH, Kaufingerstraße 24, 80331 München, Germany

www.ingramcontent.com/pod-product-compliance
Ingram Content Group UK Ltd.
Pitfield, Milton Keynes, MK11 3LW, UK
UKHW021610240425
457818UK00018B/489